Praise for
Unspeakable

"This remarkable story told by a more remarkable survivor, artist, daughter and wife is a must read. It will inspire and challenge you to look deeper than the surface of seemingly fairy tale stories to find the true hero. In these times as we recognize with compassion all the trauma girls endure, let's also celebrate the wonder of the women they have become."

—Rev. Dr. Becca Stevens
Founder of Thistle Farms

"Jessica Willis Fisher has many identities in the world of entertainment. Her incredible gifts have touched millions of people over a career that started when she was very young. Having had the honor of meeting her on many occasions, I feel it's important to add to her list of qualities. Jessica is a survivor. Her life and the unspeakable events she endured will be a source of great hope for those, like her, who have endured too much."

—Scott Hamilton
Cancer Activist, Olympic Gold Medalist

"*Unspeakable* is simultaneously devastating and inspiring. Jessica Willis Fisher's story shines the spotlight on the cruelty and abuse that lies hidden in unimaginable places. The courage she found to reach beyond the stranglehold of everything that she knew to save herself is a miracle. The truth she found set her family free."

—Amy Grant
Singer/Songwriter, Philanthropist

"Jessica's gifting as a storyteller is on full display in *Unspeakable*. Her inspiring journey drives home the innate power in sharing our stories while opening the door for more survivors to do the same. She boldly reminds us that pursuing emotional wellness is not about fixing what's wrong with us but about rediscovering and living into all that is right with us. Her courageous decision to reclaim her voice and advocate for herself and others is beyond inspiring."

—MILES ADCOX
CHAIRMAN AND OWNER OF ONSITE WELLNESS GROUP,
FOUNDER OF MILESTONES TRAUMA RECOVERY CENTER,
AND CO-FOUNDER OF THE OAKS

unspeakable

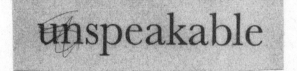

unspeakable

SURVIVING MY CHILDHOOD
AND FINDING MY VOICE

Jessica Willis Fisher

W PUBLISHING GROUP

AN IMPRINT OF THOMAS NELSON

Published in Nashville, Tennessee, by W Publishing, an imprint of Thomas Nelson.

Thomas Nelson titles may be purchased in bulk for educational, business, fundraising, or sales promotional use. For information, please email SpecialMarkets@ThomasNelson.com.

Unless otherwise noted, Scripture quotations are taken from the ESV® Bible (The Holy Bible, English Standard Version®). Copyright © 2001 by Crossway, a publishing ministry of Good News Publishers. Used by permission. All rights reserved.

Scripture quotations marked KJV are taken from the King James Version. Public domain.

Scripture quotations marked NIV are taken from The Holy Bible, New International Version®, NIV®. Copyright © 1973, 1978, 1984, 2011 by Biblica, Inc.® Used by permission of Zondervan. All rights reserved worldwide. www.Zondervan.com. The "NIV" and "New International Version" are trademarks registered in the United States Patent and Trademark Office by Biblica, Inc.®

Scripture quotations marked NLT are taken from the Holy Bible, New Living Translation. Copyright © 1996, 2004, 2015 by Tyndale House Foundation. Used by permission of Tyndale House Ministries, Carol Stream, Illinois 60188. All rights reserved.

Any internet addresses, phone numbers, or company or product information printed in this book are offered as a resource and are not intended in any way to be or to imply an endorsement by Thomas Nelson, nor does Thomas Nelson vouch for the existence, content, or services of these sites, phone numbers, companies, or products beyond the life of this book.

This is a work of nonfiction. The events and experiences detailed herein are all true and have been faithfully rendered as the author has remembered them, to the best of her ability. Some names, identities, and circumstances have been changed in order to protect the integrity and/or anonymity of the various individuals involved.

Though conversations come from the author's keen recollection of them, they are not written to represent word-for-word documentation; rather, she has retold them in a way that evokes the real feeling and meaning of what was said, in keeping with the true essence of the mood and spirit of the event.

Lyrics for "Gone" are used by permission of Jessica Willis Fisher and Bard Craft Publishing.
Lyrics for "My History" are used by permission of Jessica Willis Fisher and Bard Craft Publishing.

ISBN 978-1-4003-3290-8 (HC)
ISBN 978-1-4003-3294-6 (TP)
ISBN 978-1-4003-3295-3 (eBook)
ISBN 978-1-4003-3296-0 (audiobook)

Library of Congress Control Number: 2022930215

Printed in the United States of America
22 23 24 25 26 LSC 10 9 8 7 6 5 4 3 2 1

For all the other invisible girls and boys

Contents

CONTENTS

PART 2

PART 3

Author's Note

I HAD MANY PERSONAL REASONS I WROTE THIS BOOK. THERE ARE equally as many reasons I decided to publish it, but here are a few:

1. To clear the record so I can live honestly and move forward with authenticity, integrity, and courage in my life.
2. To stop the curse and break the spell, bringing an end to the power of shame and silence that allowed abuse to continue unchecked for so long.
3. To change the world—to do my part in helping us better understand how abuse happens so we can work together to stop it, prevent it, and more effectively support survivors.

This book is not fictionalized, and great care has been taken to be as accurate as possible in all areas. No details or events have been disguised except a few names that have been omitted or changed for privacy, including Peyton, Mark, Donal, Maria, Jonathan, the Martins, Christian, and Audrey.

Trigger Warning

THIS STORY CONTAINS NUMEROUS INSTANCES OF EMOTIONAL, physical, and sexual abuse. I didn't get the chance to choose a different life experience. You get the choice of whether to read about it. Reading about these topics may be overwhelming and distressing, especially for fellow survivors with unprocessed trauma. Thank you to those who do not look away, but please be kind and careful with yourself. Following is a list of the most intense and detailed passages and their page numbers, though many other graphic references appear throughout.

Pages 37-38: intense sexual abuse of a child
Pages 87-88: intense sexual abuse of a teen
Pages 206–207: intense physical violence toward an adult

A list of resources and support communities is available at www. rainn.org and ncadv.org among many others. Please reach out for professional help if you or someone you know is struggling or is in a life-threatening situation.

PROLOGUE

July 11, 2017

We drive in silence with the AC on blast, fighting the inevitable heat of a black car under the strength of a rising summer sun. As we near our destination, my husband, Sean, presses my sweating hand into his larger one. Only sixty days before, we'd fed each other cake while I wore white.

"Are you doing okay?" he asks. I can barely nod.

My phone vibrates in my lap, and I swipe to read the latest message.

"They'll be on the right side of the road," I say, "just another mile up."

Gravel grinds under our tires as we cross over the rumble strip and onto the shoulder. My younger brother Jedi hops out of a waiting Honda and into our back seat.

"Thanks, guys," he says, as we continue on our way.

The Cheatham County courthouse is a red brick building with floor-to-ceiling windows and a portico supported by a pair of large Doric columns. Deep-green awnings and matching railings mark the side entrance and the sheriff's office in the back. As we pass slowly, we scan the parking spaces and sidewalks for any news vans or cameramen and see nothing out of the ordinary for a small Tennessee town on a Monday morning in mid-July.

"So far, so good," Sean says, parking on the quiet side street.

The district attorney's (DA) office stands a few yards away, looking for all the world like a miniature courthouse, complete with red brick, green accents, and a pair of columns. I glance at the clock for the millionth time. We don't want to be too early or too late. The schedule has already been moved up, and this last-minute change seems to have succeeded in throwing the press off the trail.

After a few more minutes, Sean squeezes my hand in signal. As we walk toward the entrance, we see a towering figure coming our way, a family friend who happens to be a lawyer. He isn't officially representing anyone but is here to provide moral support. His handsome face is grim and slightly haunted as he shakes our hands inside the lobby, asking how we are. Again, I can't seem to find any words.

The DA emerges with ferocity burning in her outrageously blue eyes. Though she is the shortest of our group, there is no doubt she is ready for battle, clad in a power pantsuit with her hair cut aggressively short. Together, we exit in a tight pod and cross the street toward the back of the courthouse. As a guard ushers us through security, my dress boots ring conspicuously loud to my ears, and I try walking toe-heel to mitigate their clacking racket. "No phones," declare the signs posted on the doors. Sean and Jedi have to stop and tuck in their shirts to meet the dress code.

Once it's confirmed we are in the right location, we try to determine the best place to sit. If possible, I want to be able to see but not be seen. I am here to witness the proceedings, yet I worry my presence may create a scene. The courtroom has three sections of church-like pew seating, with two aisles leading down to diminutive brown picket gates. The folksy quaintness of the swinging gates commands my disembodied curiosity for a moment. Why aren't they intimidating blockades? What is their purpose if not to prevent an impassioned criminal from lunging toward the spectators in a last-minute bid for revenge?

We slide into the front row of the rightmost section, Jedi taking the first space, Sean next, and then me, farthest from the door through which the accused will be led. Light pours in through the windows along the left wall, transforming figures into hazy silhouettes whenever they pass the panes. Each of my labored heartbeats thumps in my ears as the murmuring crowd waits for the judge to appear and begin the day's proceedings. I see the faces of relatives, drawn and somber, and recognize a few dear neighbors. The rest of the audience is strange to me, each person present for reasons unknown to the small contingent representing my community.

How did we get here?

I had been cautioned against attending, warned that whatever closure I hoped to gain would not be found here. Nevertheless, I felt the need to bear witness to the surreal events, no matter their outcome. Other than my lone sibling, the rest of my immediate family chose not to be here. I look at the smooth, newly chiseled jaw of my younger brother, whose gaze stays focused on the corner door. He impresses me with his transition toward adulthood, so much more mature than I was at his age. Gone are the rounded cheeks of the mischievous toddler I once knew, his initially platinum hair cooled to a dusty ash. He is sixteen; I am twenty-five.

I keep a tight hold on Sean's hand, watching the light glint off the diamond set in white gold on my ring finger. Here is a tiny anchor to my new life, shining proof, hard evidence that a better chapter is beginning even as the pages turn to end this old one.

There is rustling in the front of the room, then the bailiff's voice rings out, "All rise."

For a moment I feel as if the assembly might burst into song, like a harmonious congregation risen to our feet in praise of God; but it is a robed judge, not a pastor, who assumes his place before us. A vibrant American flag drapes the wall behind his head.

We don't know when our case will be called. Though my restless feet long to move in their usual subconscious motion, my boots are too boisterous on the hardwood floor, so I knead my thumbs compulsively instead. The attorneys' dialogue is unexcited, their voices easily heard without amplification, working in a rhythm honed by routine and practice. The judge presides, and the defendants speak when spoken to. A part of me continues trying to reach mental preparedness, as if I will somehow be able to think my way through the unthinkable with just a little more time.

The word *murder* brings me to maximum attention. Here, in the speed-trap town of my girlhood, a man attacked his elderly employer and left him to slowly die from his wounds. Shocked by the violence, we listen as details of the crime unfold. The perpetrator, a skinny, long-haired man with facial piercings, pleads guilty and is sentenced to life in prison without the possibility of parole. The weight of permanent consequences hangs heavy in the air. Before he is led away, the daughters of the victim are allowed to speak. One tries to find forgiveness in her heart. The other casts white-hot condemnation into the face of the killer as tears flow down her trembling cheeks. She says it will never make sense to her that he can go on living, even as a prisoner, while her father cannot. I am stunned by the sheer force of her raw feeling.

Just a few weeks before, I had learned this was called a "victim impact statement." The DA took the time to walk me through what I could expect from the final steps of my own justice process. When she gave me a chance to comment on the level of punishment she was pursuing, I admitted I wanted as strong a sentence as possible. As awful as the words felt in my mouth, nothing less would let me feel safe. I wanted to know for certain my perpetrator was no longer at large. She assured me the plea included forty years with no chance of early parole.

"And we will avoid trial," she had added.

A victim impact statement was a chance to say my piece before the sentencing court if I so wished. It seemed only right to me that a victim would be able to face her abuser and declare her truth for the record. On the other hand, I could not fully shake the worry that our hopes for resolution would fall apart at the last moment, sending us to trial after all.

As I listen to the bereaved daughter speak freely, I suddenly wish I'd said yes. I wish I had prepared my own statement, my own letter. I imagine myself up there in her place.

But what would I say?

The impact of everything I've seen and experienced cannot be condensed into a single speech shared with strangers under the gaze of the offender. The weight of it, the whole of it, the complicated details still feel indescribable. Besides, I must stay quiet to protect my mother and younger siblings. I must make myself and my part in our family's history as small as possible so no one will ask further questions, and this will all be over. I cannot say or do anything that might make the accused angry—angry enough to not accept the plea deal at the last moment.

The skinny murderer is led away, and the judge sorts his papers. The bailiff calls for "the State of Tennessee versus Toby Willis."

Unguarded gasps escape behind me. My eyes snap to the corner door, tracking the cluster of darkened bodies shuffling along the backdrop of light, searching for a familiar profile. The clink of metal chains cuts through the electric hush. When the procession rounds the corner, I see my father, handcuffed and shackled. He is dressed in an orange uniform, his shaggy beard grayer than

I've seen before. Though he steps gingerly, as if his bones could shatter at any moment, my stomach roils, and I fear what will happen if our eyes connect. He looks so different, so aged, like a discarded shell of a man. Even his almost eighty-year-old defense attorney looks robust in comparison. I realized later it has been just shy of a year since we'd last spoken to each other, my father and me.

How did we get here?

Together, criminal and lawyer face the dais, making spectators of us in the pews. We, the voiceless, have no lines in this drama. Whatever our diverse emotional investments in the outcome of the scene, we must follow one line at a time, waiting for the moment of resolution.

I cannot see my father's face, so I stare at the right side of his graying head.

The judge is already speaking. "It is my understanding that Mr. Willis is going to be entering a plea of guilty to four counts of rape of a child."

I watch the words enter my father's ear, praying they will not jar him to anger.

"Twenty-five years on count one, twenty-five years on count two," the judge says, checking his information. "Forty years on count three, forty years on count four." Was that correct, he asks.

Yes, says the district attorney.

My father raises a frail right hand and is put under oath.

I wish I had asked if and when the original arrest warrant would be read aloud. Then I could tighten my gut at just the right moment and offset the drop, like on a roller coaster. The date and initials that accompany my father's alleged offenses will mean something to certain individuals in this room. There will be no hiding for me. I admire the steely carriage of the DA and take heart.

The judge asks if my father understands the charges brought against him.

The mumbled response is inaudible in the pews.

The judge asks again. "Do you feel like you understand what is going on in this case?"

I hear the answer this time: "Yes."

Quick, now, I think. *While that word is still in his mouth. Do it now.*

"Do you understand that you have the right to enter a plea of not guilty, and if you plead not guilty you have the right to a speedy and public trial by jury?"

My heartbeat spikes. *Don't talk him out of it,* I beg silently.

"I understand," my father says.

No, please go back to yes. Stay with yes.

The judge plunges on through his script. "Do you understand that if you went to trial you would be presumed to be innocent until such time, if ever, the State proves your guilt beyond a reasonable doubt to the satisfaction of all twelve jurors and their verdict would have to be unanimous before you could be convicted of any crime?"

"I understand."

Is that a tinge of bitterness I hear? Am I imagining a strain of resistance?

"Do you understand that if you went to trial, you and your lawyer could confront and cross-examine all witnesses the State might call to testify against you?"

Memories flood unbidden into my mind and body. I recall what it is like to be caught under my father's microscope, to be interrogated, accused, questioned. Will he get the chance to do it all again, in front of a judge and jury? *Please, no.*

"Do you understand that if you went to trial and you were found guilty of a crime and sentenced for that crime, you would have the right to appeal that judgment and the sentence to the court of criminal appeals?"

"Yes, sir" comes the reply.

I struggle to keep breathing as I imagine a version of this day where the end is never reached, where my father keeps fighting, dragging out the fear and pain. I don't want him to have that chance. Where would be the justice in that?

I know everything is proceeding according to the rule of law, but it feels wrong. Here is a moment of dramatic climax decades in the making. How can any bystander know if the ending is proper and just? Maybe that's why I was given the option to speak. Maybe I am the missing character. I wish I had said yes. But my voice has been gone for so long. Where did I lose it? How will I ever get it back?

There is no script for my role, no archetype, no example to guide me. My proof and its burden are housed in a trembling body and imprinted memories, largely inaccessible by speech.

How did we get here? And what would I have said?

Part 1

1

EARLY CHILDHOOD

WHEN I GO BACK TO EXAMINE THE EARLIEST MEMORIES OF MY life, I can distinguish three short scenes. They are slight and delicate, like tiny glass sculptures, best not to squeeze too tight lest they shatter and disappear altogether. They spring forth without preamble and then dissipate without much in the way of context, unmoored from the gravity of time. Strange what survives the weight of years; strange what falls away.

First, I can remember being potty trained. Or, more specifically, I can remember the last time I purposefully avoided going to the toilet, instead defying my mother and peeing in my panties. I am hiding under the knobby legs of the old upright piano and must have just relieved my miniature bladder because I can feel the carpet damp and slightly warm underneath me. The memory is almost just that single instant. It fades away at the faint promise of the peanut butter and jelly sandwich that will finally coax me out of my hiding place.

Next, I can remember crouching in the dark with expectant glee, each of my limbs spring-loaded as I wait with stifled breath underneath a draped table in a loud and crowded event space. There is a stiff bow in my hair and my socks are trimmed with white lace, folded down to touch the buckled strap of my squeaky patent leather shoes. At any moment, a pair of my young relatives will lift away the tablecloth and find me in our boisterous game of hide-and-seek, and I will shriek in shock and delight before scurrying away at their triumphant shouts.

And finally, I can remember my tiny body lying atop my parents' bed. I am wearing a loose old adult-sized T-shirt in lieu of a nightgown. I can hear the white noise of a shower running somewhere out of sight. My father is there, leaning over me, touching a part of my body I don't have a name for with his large warm hand, talking about things I do not understand. "Daddies like it when mommies do this . . ." His voice is not a whisper, just quiet. There is a flash, a blank of time, and then comes a sequel to this tiny scene, clearly still the same setting, likely only moments later. My father is out of view now and my mother is emerging breezily from the bathroom, as young as I can picture her. Her long, wet hair is twisted up in a striped towel, her body wrapped in a pink shin-length plush robe with matching sash. Her lightly freckled skin is freshly moisturized, and she is bright and happy with little creases at the corners of her eyes. I feel as if I should speak. But I am only three or maybe four and I don't have the necessary words. In many ways, I will stay frozen in the power of this moment for the next twenty years.

Two days after my fourth birthday, my second sister was born. April 15, 1996, is the first anchor placing me firmly in time, the first instance of knowing exactly where and when I was in vibrant detail. These memories are everything the previous ones are not: sharp, exact, full of bold sounds and hurried commotion.

I remember being lifted by my wee armpits toward the textured ceiling and perching unevenly on my grandmother's bony shoulders to reach a board game kept on the top shelf in the hall closet. Behind my parents' bedroom door, only a few feet away, a balding doctor was helping my mother through an intense home delivery. I had just grabbed hold of the soft and tattered *Chutes and Ladders* box from the closet when the bedroom door suddenly swung open wide. For a brief moment I was given a bird's-eye view of the events taking place inside. I saw my mother straining and sweaty, knees propped up with her heels digging down deep into the mattress, the doctor working at the foot of the bed, and numerous bunches of darkly spotted rags and towels, used and pushed aside in haste. The door closed swiftly, and my grandmother whisked me away to the living room.

Later, I would hear that my sister Jet was born blue and floppy, weighing in at a whopping twelve pounds and six ounces. But that was only after I had seen her for myself and knew she was okay, that extra-chunky, velvet-soft little human wrapped up tight and snuggly. It took a while for Mommy to recover, and I can still picture her being carried across the living room by Daddy and his friends in a giant unzipped sleeping bag after she fainted a few hours later.

Mommy consistently maintained she didn't know what she was getting herself into when she married my father. She would usually deliver this line to her audience with dry humor, slightly widened blue eyes, and a small shake of the head.

She grew up "in the henhouse," as she described it—with just her mom, Joann; her grandmother; and younger sister in a little brick house on the South Side of Chicago. Her father, Johnny, was a hell-raiser who'd left his young wife so early on that my mother had no relationship with him until she was an adult and went to college in Florida. Joann rarely said a bad word about Johnny, moved back in with her parents, and put herself through night school to become a nurse. Though they divorced, she would never remarry. My mother, Brenda, framed her childhood as sheltered but loving. "Sometimes it felt like I was in a cage," she told me when I was young, "but my friends were allowed in the cage with me." Unwilling to let bitterness toward her absent father define her, young Brenda was a bright and high-achieving student, popular with both peers and teachers at her conservative Christian high school. There, the students adhered to strict modesty codes in their uniforms and had to sign a statement swearing off movies, rock music, drugs, and alcohol. She said her goal was to be the best Christian wife and mother ever, and she prayed for God to bring her a brave man, like Moses or King David, whom she could help as he worked to fulfill some great mission. By the time she left for Pensacola Christian College to study teaching, she had met my father, Toby.

MOM AND DAD ALWAYS KEPT THE NEWEST BABY IN THEIR BED FOR a while to make for easy nursing during the night. Dad told Mom to do so from the beginning, saying he wasn't getting up to help warm up milk in the middle of the night; she should get over her nervousness about smothering the baby and do the natural thing—breastfeed. He was the son of a pastor, the second oldest of nine children. After the first three oldest kids in his family had been born, there was a gap of nine years before another six younger kids followed. My parents taught me that the Bible said children were a "heritage from the Lord" and that using birth control was a dangerous decision that kept one from enjoying God's blessings and fulfilling man's responsibility to "be fruitful, and multiply."[1] Homeschooling, attending church, and having lots of kids were all things we believed were important and right in our home. Six kids would be born in Chicago in less than ten years: Jess (me), Jair, Jen, Jet, Jack, and Jedi.

I WAS A VORACIOUSLY VOCAL AND BOSSY CHILD. IN PHOTOS AND fragments of grainy home-video clips, I see an overconfident little bundle of sass and curiosity, whose idea of a smile was to grin so wide and intensely that my neck flexed and teeth locked in what could only be described as a grimace. My eyes were green, my hair blonde. I loved grown-ups and their attention, reigning over the younger subjects of the home with a know-it-all air. Though my recollections of these early times admittedly blend together, I remember the days as always being full of stuffed animals, wooden blocks, picture books, and animated playmaking with my siblings.

Picturing my mother in this time, I can see her with a soft and ready smile on her warm face, eyes lit with a lovely spark, her hair a dark chocolate color with bangs frothing above her nose. She is holding up large, colorful phonics charts, patiently sounding out consonants with rhyming vowel accompaniments listed vertically on a ladder. I endeavored to make her proud with my growing ability to enter the world. I still hear her voice, expressive and inviting, reading to us constantly, explaining stories from the Bible and beloved picture books as we listened, sprawling across the carpet and fidgeting in our growing bodies. She was our constant companion, the one who shaped our daily lives and told us of the greater world beyond.

Dad, on the other hand, left early on the weekday mornings—even the extra-cold ones when the dirty gray snow buried and crusted everything—and took the train to work where he did important things on computers for a big company. Our time with him, together as a family, happened during the after-dinner hours and weekends.

I have hazy recollections from the edge of my consciousness of times when he would sit down at the piano I had once peed under in some other older home. As we were drifting off to sleep at night, or sometimes waking slowly on Saturdays, I would hear him playing his favorite classical pieces. He wrote a few songs of his own too. They were simple melodies, but I knew which one he had written for me, and I loved falling asleep listening to "Jessie's Song." If he ever played when we were awake and about, I loved to sit on his lap and lay my hands on top of his, pretending I was playing the notes. Even stretching as wide as I could reach, the tips of my fingers barely reached to where his first knuckle bent down toward the keys.

There was one particular piece we knew only as "The Tickle Song." Whenever Dad began to play it after dinner, an instantaneous frenzy descended upon us kids, and we dropped everything to go squealing around the house, racing to find a hiding spot before the suspenseful melody ended. He started with a slow tempo, exaggerating the minor intervals and speeding up each time the song repeated. We knew from previous experience that Dad would come hunting for us when he reached his lightning-fast conclusion and whomever he found would be pinned down in vigorous tickle attacks until we couldn't breathe for the laughter. I remember his fingers locking my skinny wrists against the ground, pulled straight up above my head, and though I bucked and writhed from side to side, I knew what I was about to feel. As I pleaded for mercy, his grinning face would loom above mine. Dad's bottom teeth were slightly crooked, his stiff dark hair cropped in an extra-close buzz cut that made people assume he was in the military. He frequently wore glasses, and his thick caterpillar eyebrows—which I would eventually inherit—spanned wide above the rims. His eyes were a hazel green and slightly on the small side, like mine. He would fake right, then left, then right and left, weaving like a cobra until he finally plunged his square chin down into one of my open armpits to elicit a shrieking giggle that went breathlessly silent before it came to an end. I loved him.

MY CHILDHOOD NICKNAME WAS KANGAROO, AND I CAME BY IT honestly. One day, Dad brought home a pair of tiny purple boxing gloves, and I quickly claimed them as mine. He had a big black-and-white pair for himself, squishy and easy to shake off when he kept his blows light. I bounced and bobbed with enthusiasm, zinging with the energy I felt after each pop of impact. He would kneel and put up his gloves as I feigned little strikes and lunged to connect with his face or ribs. I remember him being roundly pleased I would engage with such a feisty spirit; he had to be the one to say the skirmish was over. I often would not heed the conclusion, wildly swinging and air-pummeling, turning onto one of my younger siblings, darting around behind my purple-padded fists until the gloves were taken away for a time. I was never in much trouble, confident in the knowledge I was winning Dad's affection. Though the boxing-in-the-living-room phase didn't last long, the nickname stuck for years.

Dad had been a collegiate wrestler at Northwestern with a

full-ride scholarship and dreams of being an elite Olympic athlete until he sustained an injury that paralyzed his body during a match. The doctor had no explanation other than a miracle when Dad later made an almost full recovery, though he would always have a bad neck and back despite multiple surgeries and spinal fusions. He shifted his college courses to specialize in computer programming and dabbled with the budding integration between sound and technology epitomized by the synthesizer.

From my childhood, I had always heard Dad had assumed he would have a team full of wrestling sons whom he would train and lead to athletic success. Three of his first four children were girls, though, and as soon as his toddler son Jair could walk, Jair preferred donning my white tights and dancing along to our worn-out VHS of *The Nutcracker* ballet instead of scrapping around on the floor with his father. I was determined to be whatever my father wanted.

Jair and I were born less than a year apart, making it impossible for me to remember my short eleven-month stint as the only child in the family. After Jair, there was a longer space before Jen arrived, rosy-cheeked and smiling, followed by the extremely shy Jet, who would end up having a surgery a few years later to help mitigate the damage caused to her right arm due to her unusually large size at birth.

MY EARLIEST RECOLLECTION OF CRYING WITHOUT PHYSICAL provocation was during one of the many times Dad tried wrestling Jair. Sometimes these episodes would start as general rowdy play with all the kids, then transition to something else when our father focused his attention on his son. Toddler-Jair tried escaping Dad's just-tight-enough holds, the shadow versions of moves he was trained to employ on adult opponents. Jair would stop resisting, realizing the goal was unattainable, signaling the play was over for him. This was clearly not the result Dad had hoped for. Jair's cries would grow despondent as he was turned and positioned with progressively rougher movements. Even the onlooker began to feel the fatigue. Mom once tried to intervene; Dad snapped at her to "stay out of the way when a father is teaching his son." I would wander around the house, vision blurred, trying not to look or listen, as the witnessing of these sessions brought a heavy sadness I couldn't explain.

ONE EVENING, BETWEEN MY FIFTH AND SEVENTH YEARS, I WAS playing some silly make-believe game, absorbed in my usual childish pursuits, when a sentence my mother said caught my attention. It was getting close to dinnertime and Dad would be arriving home soon. Mom had been speaking to the unorganized lot of us, and we hadn't heeded her until I heard her say with clear agitation, "I get in trouble when you guys don't clean up your stuff!"

I was confused and rather intrigued by this idea that Mom was capable of getting in trouble. How could this be? We got in trouble when we didn't obey what Dad or Mom said, or when our squabbling left visible marks on each other. Most of the time, our disobedience resulted in scolding or a few spanks of the spoon from Mom; and only if needed would there be more serious spankings or the pronouncement of no dinner from Dad after he got home. What did it look like when an adult got in trouble? I noticed she was rushing around the house and her face was twisting up weirdly.

"What's wrong, Mommy?" I asked in concern, finally stopping my play.

In a strained voice, so different from the one she used when she read stories to us, she said that Dad would be home soon. She straightened chairs and tried to wrangle the vacuum away from the cord and plug it in. She said he got mad at her when we didn't do what we were supposed to, when we made messes and didn't listen to her. She began to vacuum, raising her voice to cut above the noise, cycling and stuttering through our names in an urgent effort to mobilize us.

I made a halfhearted effort to pick up some scattered toys, mostly bossing Jair and Jen to join me. Mom eventually broke into pitiful sobs and then I was fully alarmed. I tried not to stare, yet I couldn't look away. I had a groundbreaking thought: When I cried, Mom soothed me. When I needed help, she assisted me. When I pictured the structure of my little family, I saw Mom took care of me, my siblings, and Dad too.

But who takes care of Mommy?

Though I'd never noticed it before, I saw my mother was alone in some elusive way I couldn't comprehend. Prior to this moment, everything in the world had seemed to fit. I assumed everyone was loved like I was, and everything was as it should be. Now the responsibility of awareness tunneled deep into my psyche, and I felt separated from my younger siblings by the weight of knowing, worried that something was deeply wrong.

2

CHICAGO

CHURCH WAS THE MAIN SOCIALIZATION OF MY EARLY CHILDHOOD.
Multiple times per week we attended the small Baptist church with
a wooden steeple on the South Side of Chicago where Dad's father
was pastor. Cousins visited for special holiday services, and the
celebrations would turn into family reunions with sing-alongs and
board games. Dad taught a class for kids during the main sermon,
played piano by sight-reading selections from the hymnal, and occasionally arranged the special music. When everyone rose to sing,
I stood on the pew seat so I could follow along with the adults in
the hymnal. We sang "Come, Christians, Join to Sing" and "Come
Thou Fount of Every Blessing" so often that I had them memorized
down to a word.

When I was two and a half years old, my father's six younger
siblings all died in a sudden and tragic vehicle accident. (The three

adult children, including my father, were not in the car.) My grand-parents survived, but they were badly burned on their faces and hands. They made national news when they held firm to their belief in God's sovereignty and shared Bible verses at both the accident scene and subsequent press conferences. I learned that it was important to share one's testimony to help bring others to our faith.

At six years old, I proclaimed to my mother that I wanted to accept Jesus as my Lord and Savior and be baptized in the little green pool behind the pulpit, where converts were solemnly dunked and received blessings about being raised in the newness of life. I had realized that one never knew when their life could end, even as a child. I was told that, in order to be considered saved, I had to be able to prove I knew who Jesus was—how he had died on the cross and rose from the dead—and I did. I accepted Jesus' offer of salvation by praying and asking God to forgive me for my sins and take me to heaven when I died. Great celebration followed, my baptism was planned, and Dad bought me the most extravagant dress I'd ever set eyes on. It was navy-blue velvet with puffed sleeves, big white ruffles, a white rose at the neck, and edges of snowy lace. I felt like a true princess of God's kingdom walking into church the next baptism Sunday. After the short ceremony, I was told I had two families: one here on earth and another spiritual family of everyone who had ever believed like us, and one day we would all be together in paradise—even my dad's siblings who had passed away.

HEAVEN AND HELL WEREN'T THE ONLY THINGS I WAS LEARNING about. During this time, my father was furtively reaching his hand below my blanket on most nights, whispering quietly to me about how I should be touching myself and learning to make myself feel good, like he had demonstrated on me. He had explained the concept of "coming," although it was something I had not yet experienced. Wanting to please him, I nevertheless claimed I was doing what he asked me, and once answered his routine nightly question of "How many times did you come?" with "Nine." He laughed and called me a liar but made sure to emphasize that the more often I could do it, the better I would be able to satisfy my future husband. He said my mother wasn't well trained in this area and that made their relationship difficult. I took this as the reason Mom wasn't involved in this area of my education.

My anatomical vocabulary was limited, as with most six-year-olds, so Dad taught me to refer to my most sensitive part as my "pussy," which was more specific than the all-encompassing terms our family used when referring to private parts such as *bottom* and *crotch*. The first time I saw what Dad called his "cock" seemed unintentional. He hadn't included it in what he was teaching me so far. He wasn't wearing underwear beneath his gray shorts and, sitting with his legs spread in front of me, I caught clear sight of a mass off to the side of one yawning leg opening.

Dad would sometimes run around yelling "panty raid" and capture us girls jokingly only to tickle us and quickly let us go. More than once, Dad had requested me to remove my panties or refrain from wearing undergarments altogether. I figured it was something he must have asked of Mom, too, because multiple times I caught flashes of something pink underneath the hems of her miniskirts. My own little mound was different from what Mom had flitting under the edge of pleated floral fabric. I found the difference confusing and wondered if that was what mine would look like one day when I was grown up.

I can't remember learning the word *sex*, but I knew it. Likewise, I gathered that the action it involved took place secretly between a mom and a dad with their "pussy" and "cock." Other nuances got filled in whenever I overheard rhythmic noises on the other side of the bedroom wall in the middle of the night. Or when dinner was being prepared and Dad would initiate a flirting game of messenger with Mom. He would summon one of us kids and tell us to deliver some such message in her ear: "What's on the menu for later?" We would giggle and run back and forth between them, carrying double entendres that eventually revealed their hidden meanings to me through repetition, pattern, and context.

Once, all of us kids were in the kitchen when my ear caught an unfamiliar melody coming from the room we shared together. When I bent to look in the keyhole, I was shocked to see my parents' bare bodies moving together, headless torsos slapping and sliding. I stepped back, my face flushing, trying not to make any odd movements that might alert the other kids to what I had just seen. The keyhole seemed to grow wider and wider in my mind, the sounds building louder, until I turned my back to the door and stood guard so no one else would see.

Another Saturday afternoon, I had to herd the younger kids away when I looked up and saw the telltale skin of two stacked bodies on the bed in my parents' room. We were now living on the first floor of a little two-bedroom flat where the living room and the master bedroom were square with each other and separated only by twin glass French doors layered with lace curtains, which proved to be not quite dense enough on that day. The level of physical embarrassment in my body told me this was inappropriate viewing. It made me wonder how my own education figured in to all this. Did I know too much or too little?

GRANDMA JOANN AND GREAT-GRANDMA BOTH STILL LIVED IN the same brick house in Chicago where Mom grew up. It smelled of cozy old upholstery and had lumpy carpeting in the living room and a small grass-and-dandelion backyard. Grandma Joann worked as a nurse and nearly always greeted me with the enthusiastic declaration of "There's my firstborn grandchild!" She had shocks of gray in the front of her cropped dark hair and the kind, steady hands of a professional caregiver. Though there was a twinkle in her eye when she smiled, she was the disciplinarian of the house, and we would systematically test her boundaries to see what we could get away with. Great-Grandma could usually be found in her easy chair, asleep in front of the large box television in the opposite corner of the room, with the reflection of the news flickering across her glasses. She was fat and squishy like the Pillsbury Doughboy, with the softest skin on the pads of her fingers, and had short white hair, which she curled in fuzzy pink curlers. When she was awake, she would regale us with the most sensational stories she could remember—or invent—about her wild youth. They doted on us, kept us safe, and stuffed us full of diagonally cut toast and countless little cups of applesauce.

On occasion, we got to play with Grandma Joann's stethoscopes and would run around checking everyone's heartbeats for good measure. Back at home, Mommy had to make it clear we were not ever allowed to play doctor after she once found us kids in various stages of undress in a makeshift fort in our room. She emphasized there would be no removing clothes, no examinations of bodies with any instruments, real or imaginary, and no more co-ed baths.

OVER THE HOLIDAY SEASON OF 1996, WE'D SPENT A TYPICAL evening with the Grandmas while Mom and Dad went on a date to see *Riverdance*, the Irish step dance and music spectacular, which had crossed from Ireland into the US and was enthralling audiences across the world with high-flying leaps, blazing footwork, and a delightfully appealing meld of all things Celtic and folk. Although we kids didn't attend the show for ourselves, our parents got us the VHS tape of the London premiere as a Christmas present. Imitating the fancy step dancers became our favorite pastime virtually overnight.

After weeks of diligent attempts, we knew the precise rhythms and musical cues for whole sections of the show and would put on dramatic performances in the living room when Dad got home from work. We provided our parents with hand-cut tickets, then re-collected the stubs a few steps later when they sat down on the couch. Out of sight, Jair triggered the soundtrack on the stereo as Jen and I stood with our heads hanging down, our backs facing our audience of two. We took turns doing the dramatic head roll when the fiddle shuffles came in and put our arms up on our hips and stomped in place. Once the complicated footwork was supposed to kick in, we would freestyle it with all the gusto we could muster, trying our best to keep our arms at our sides like we'd seen on the video. At the proper time, we wheeled around to the sound of drums and exited the room just as Jair made his grand entrance as the dashing lead. His small face was set with concentration, arms held loosely parallel to the floor, blond bowl bangs vibrating on his forehead as he danced. He was better than us girls; we looked like human pogo sticks while he glided and spun like a professional.

When the enthusiasm for this continued well into the new year, Mom began looking for a local Irish dance school that would welcome hands-on parents with beginner students. We found out Great-Grandma's deceased husband had been born in America to two Irish parents—straight off the boat from County Mayo, as they say. Although it was only one step back in our genealogy, our Irish ancestry didn't get much emphasis until after we saw *Riverdance*. I was six and Jair was five when we started attending weekly classes with an intensely bubbly dance teacher. Later, Jen would join at four, and Jet at three.

Our teacher urged us to visit the annual Chicago Irish Fest so we could see for ourselves how the rest of Irish culture was interwoven with the rhythms of the dance steps. We went armed with snacks and strollers, wearing T-shirts emblazoned with the name of our new school. More than anything else, I was blown away by the music we saw performed there, driving and celebratory one moment, mournful and passionate the next. Fingers flew on the necks of fiddles and blurred on the metal cylinders of penny whistles and strange pipes. Accordions pumped in and out, and tight, intricate melodies raced over the top of churning guitar patterns that made my heart pound in my chest and my feet move sympathetically.

We brought home a sizable stack of CDs and one cheap plastic-topped penny whistle. Jair picked it up and began figuring out how to play increasingly intricate tunes by listening to the CDs on repeat. Next, Dad purchased a fiddle, and I promptly claimed it as my own. We had a few generic lessons with long-suffering teachers on piano, fiddle, and guitar, but we loved the energetic Irish music the best, and that's where our interest stuck.

CHICAGO DIDN'T HAVE THE BEST POLITICAL TRACK RECORD. FOR decades, corruption had been deeply embedded in the local powers. The tragedy of the death of my father's younger siblings turned out to be tied to a larger plot that eventually came into the public's view. It was determined the vehicle accident was caused by a driver who had obtained his license illegally. A federal criminal investigation built over a decade and eventually uncovered a scandal: local officials had taken bribes and sold illegal licenses to raise campaign funds for a politician, who by then had become the governor of Illinois.

In 1999, almost six years after the accident, my grandparents were awarded a stunning one hundred million dollars in a wrongful-death civil suit that was settled out of court. My father was given a portion of the settlement and decided to retire, which, I learned, meant he wouldn't have to go to work anymore. However, it wasn't long before Dad began working on an idea for a business of his own, a professional sports league for his beloved sport of wrestling that could stand among the likes of the NBA and NFL.

Our parents also began looking for a house to buy. Much to Jair's considerable relief, brothers Jack and Jedi had joined our growing family, so the gender count was even: three girls and three boys, with all the kids—minus the baby—maxing out one room. We soon learned that having a suddenly larger budget made our father a very picky buyer. He developed a habit of walking into the most amazing, sprawling houses we had ever seen and proclaiming loudly, "If I lived here, I would be divorced in a month," because he believed poorly designed houses could cause relationship problems. All told, we searched for a house in the Chicagoland area for almost two years to no avail.

Dad spent longer periods of his newfound time at home at my bedside, and I realized he was now visiting the beds of my sisters as well. We didn't speak to each other about it, and I would turn away and pretend I was sleeping if I ever noticed him lingering or talking to one of them under his breath.

Dad also began a new evening tradition with Jair. At least once a week, Dad would solemnly declare, "It is time!" This was Jair's cue to go get *Stratego*, a strategy board game where two players race to either find their opponent's hidden flag or outmaneuver them by capturing enough enemy pieces to prevent any further moves. Dad pushed Jair to play over and over, turning the game into a repetitive test of the minds. I noticed hot, frustrated tears in Jair's eyes as he continued to see his troops dwindle and his flag captured. It only got worse when Jair began to win.

Mom began spending hours talking with Jair, sometimes while nursing one of the baby boys. Though I don't think I was jealous, I noticed her giving him more attention. I frequently tried to hear what they were talking about but was confused by his philosophical, almost existential questions. "I have to dig Jair out of a pit," Mom would say, sending me to go play. When I asked what was wrong with him, she emphasized how important it was for us all to keep our thoughts positive and our spirits strong. With Dad, Jair seemed either emotionless or angry; with Mom, he seemed either dramatic or despairing. It was clear that Jair struggled more than the rest of us and needed extra help when he was down in the super-deep dumps.

OUR CHURCH WAS GOING TO HAVE A NEW PASTOR WHO HAD SEVEN children. Theirs was the first family I remember being larger than ours. The men of the congregation had a lot of meetings, and I eventually heard that Dad and the new pastor were arguing about how to raise kids and run the church, the patriarchs of the largest broods in the community sparring over their clashing worldviews.

After multiple offers on local houses had fallen through and the situation had soured at church, my parents broadened their real estate search. They said they were tired of the grueling Chicago winters lasting half the year, so they considered Arizona and Florida. At some point, Nashville, Tennessee, entered into their consideration. Dad took a solo trip to the Nashville area with the goal of checking out multiple places. He called Mom from the driveway of the first home and told her, "This is the one, Bren."

After we heard our new home was waiting for us in Tennessee, I begged to see pictures of it repeatedly. I saw exterior shots of timber gables, stone chimneys, and fireplaces. There was a sprawling structure, rolling, tree-covered hills, and open fields. It seemed too good to be true. They decided we would go see it as a family as soon as could be arranged.

From the moment we arrived, the place was magic. Driving down the winding driveway into a horseshoe-shaped hollow, we entered another world altogether. Tall cliffs and a murmuring creek wrapped around the house, which was centered like a jewel at the end of the tree-lined drive. There was a red-roofed barn, a cluster of matching sheds, and an enormously long six-car garage. A gazebo stood across from the house near a private gun range and a fenced rose garden. Halfway back toward the front gate, a covered bridge crossed the creek and opened into a wide field. Over a hundred acres stretched for miles of woods and shaded trails.

The house itself was over nine thousand square feet, and we quickly got lost in its two levels of spacious rooms, connecting halls, and private balconies. Shaped like an *L*, the shorter side of the home was reconstructed from an authentic hundred-year-old log cabin. The longer side was a modern addition fashioned with southwestern tiles and wallpapers, pink stucco, and vintage mission bells hanging in the master bedroom. Dad loved the original section and already envisioned remodeling the new addition to match the old. I just could not fathom that this place was going to be our actual real-life home. A part of me assumed that, at some point, I would wake up from a dream and find myself once again sharing a room with my five siblings in a little two-bedroom flat with a gravel alley and chain-link-fenced backyard.

The morning after seeing the house, we visited a small independent Bible church, then headed back to Chicago at the end of the service. It seemed the next thing I knew, we had moved. Six whirlwind weeks transpired between finding the house on the internet and driving the overstuffed U-Haul truck away from the home of my childhood on a gray March day. The only other newsworthy event in this interval was when I overheard Mommy talking to her doctor on the phone about recommendations for care in Tennessee, and I realized she was pregnant with baby number seven.

I'd be lying if I said I was sad to be leaving Chicago. I was about to be nine years old. I would miss the kids from church, my grandparents, my cousins, and my bubbly dance teacher, but nothing could compare to the vision of life I was moving toward. It glowed with fairy dust and tasted like vacation.

3

GOLDEN AGE

THE NEXT FOUR YEARS WERE IMPOSSIBLY FULL AND FAST. FROM ages nine to twelve, everything about my life changed, exploding outward, funded with the millions. Dad quickly hired contractors to remodel the house, sparing no expense. The quiet groundskeeper stayed on, and we had a succession of housekeepers. We joined the church we had visited, and the pastor got us in touch with a cowboy friend of his who helped us buy sweet-dispositioned horses. We learned how to groom, saddle, and mount, and we were soon confident enough to ride the trails around the property and take little jumps in our oval corral.

Where Chicago had been frigid, hidden under a frozen crust of dirty mud well into April, the southern spring was bursting with flowers, smells, and colors that multiplied in the rich earth with each passing week. A large bountiful garden was planted, and the land came alive. Tiny white buds broke out in waves across the hills and bluebells dotted the hollows. Big fuzzy carpenter bees buzzed and bumbled in front of our faces as we walked. Copper-colored snakes sunned themselves on the boulders in the creek, and we learned how to identify and shoot the poisonous ones with a .22-caliber rifle from the deck. Two black Labradors stayed after the previous owner left, and we renamed them Bonnie and Clyde. Deer wandered serenely across the property, and the raccoon who got in our garbage bins turned out to be as tall as I was when he stood up on his hind legs against the back porch door. If we were lucky, on the hottest summer days we would splash in the creek after our horseback rides and glide on our tummies down the miniature slides carved in the soft, waterworn rock.

MOST CHILDREN I CAME INTO CONTACT WITH DURING THESE YEARS would wistfully admit, "I wish I was in your family!" If I asked why, they would say they dreamed of having more brothers and sisters, or say they couldn't believe we didn't have to go to "real" school.

"Do you ever get to do schoolwork in your pajamas?" kids frequently asked.

"I guess so," I admitted, not even realizing how cool this apparently was. When aloof or bored public-schoolers told me they didn't like to read or play board games, I felt bad for them, internally judging their parents for not raising them right.

Mom ran a complicated household and homeschooled us kids across the spectrum of grades without a specific curriculum. Unlike in Illinois, registration was required for homeschoolers in Tennessee, but Dad decided to keep us off the grid. We were instructed on various evasive ways to answer if an adult ever asked us why we weren't in school.

Never once in my schooling did I take a standardized test. We oldest kids each had a school binder with our name and a stack of sheets with categories, empty lines, and the title "Status Report" across the top. The categories were Bible, Academics, Dance, Exercise, Music, and Art. Each week, we coordinated with Mom to fill out this form, making individual goals in each of the categories. We got them either approved or amended by Dad, and then Mom's job was to make sure we accomplished all the work we had been assigned by the end of the week. If we started slipping on our tasks, we faced punishment or loss of privileges come the weekend.

In Chicago, Bible time had always been a reading hour with Mom. Now, Dad gave us oldest kids the goal of creating a summary for each of the sixty-six books of the Bible. Mom could still read aloud as needed. For our academics, we did spelling tests with Mom and checked reading assignments with Dad. We had a collection of old textbooks from Mom's Christian high school and college. Art was a catch-all that involved activities like sewing, leather carving, tracing studies of the human form, and intricate Celtic knotwork.

I loved reading and hated math. I would read any novel—the classics, poetry, Nancy Drew mysteries, *The Lord of the Rings*, whatever Dad assigned me, and anything else I could get my hands on. I would read in the bathroom, in my bed after the lights were turned off, or when I was supposed to be doing other work. Soon, my reading habits birthed an obsession with writing my own stories and poetry and dozens of journals I never completed. Jo March from *Little Women* was a shining beacon of everything I wanted to be.

Dad repeatedly told us we'd never use certain knowledge later in life. I was always relieved when he gave us permission to skip math-related things. He would get going on a monologue about how ineffective other education systems were. According to him, schools and universities were dropping all the wrong subjects, not emphasizing what really mattered in life, like theology, logic, physical discipline, and the arts. He and Mom would have been better off skipping college altogether, and so would we.

Dad led us in group workouts in our professionally outfitted gym lined with mirrors on the walls. I did not like running, especially in the humid summer air, which felt thick enough to drink. My parents discovered there were only two Irish dance schools in the Nashville area, and we attended classes at the larger of the two schools until they found a private teacher who gave us in-house lessons. I practiced myself into a repetitive stress injury while preparing for my first regional championships. My calves became restrictively tight, and my Achilles tendons started flaming with pain at even the lightest stress. There seemed to be growth-plate issues as well, and the intense banging and stomping required by the hard-shoe dances wasn't helping.

At regionals, Jair and Jen won their age groups, and Jet placed under Jen because there wasn't another category young enough for her. I watched on crutches glumly and was kept from horseback riding and further dance progress off and on until my limbs seemed to finally catch up with themselves and stopped aching the following summer.

MUSICALLY SPEAKING, JAIR BECAME ASTOUNDINGLY ACCOMPLISHED on the whistle by listening to CDs and watching instructional tapes. He played for hours, getting his fingers in tight control, learning to bring out rhythm and expression even in the fastest tunes. I found fiddle difficult to pick up on my own, so my parents located a curly-haired, Montana-born fiddler who gave me lessons for a while. Another local teacher was enlisted to help me over the hump of acquiring vibrato. I asked to quit, but my parents explained there was no quitting in our family.

Jair was the first one to qualify for the world championships in both Irish music and Irish dance; as a result he was the first to travel to Ireland with Mom to compete. I was desperate to see the world, and getting left behind motivated me more than anything else, so I committed to putting in whatever work would get me out there to see it. Dad, Jair, and I also became regular instrumentalists on the worship team at church. Dad had us kids practice four-part harmonies for the selected hymns by requiring us to sing while we did our chores.

For a while, I was drawn back to the piano and the idea of musical composition. I'd been told Mozart wrote impressive pieces of music by the time he was seven, and I'd boldly aspired to try composition for myself at that same age. My first efforts were charitably lost in the passage of time, but the expressive sensibility stuck around. I began spending more time composing and writing. I especially loved showing Dad I was now able to write pieces of my own and was happy to oblige when he asked me to play my little ditties for visitors.

At the peak of our busyness, we hosted large church gatherings and monthly parties for military families from the local army base. Dad ran a wrestling club for the neighbor kids, and we once staged a harvest festival treasure hunt. Mom had two baby girls in a row, bringing us to five girls and three boys, the two newest additions both delivered in a Nashville hospital with midwives, since there weren't any doctors willing to come out to the house like they did in Chicago.

Dad continually expanded his efforts to create the professional wrestling league and hired on multiple full-time employees. The business was called Real Pro Wrestling, or RPW. It was picked up for a pilot, then a full season on television. We traveled to California and stayed in a penthouse during the filming. We met muscle-bound Olympians, and Dad told us girls he'd get us some husbands out of the deal one day. I was proud as a peacock when I got the chance to sing the national anthem at the beginning of the ceremonies. Unfortunately, I got nervous and started about five keys too high. I was thoroughly embarrassed when I couldn't hit any of the climactic notes. Clearly, performance singing wasn't going to be my personal forte.

THOUGH OUR LIFE HAD BECOME A BONA FIDE FAIRY TALE, DAD WAS never happy with Mom in those years. No matter how hard she tried to manage everything he expected of her, he was unsatisfied and said so. More than once he even expressed resentment that there was no biblical allowance for spanking wives. He told Mom to make our punishments more severe but often had to carry out the sentences himself, since Mom usually would appeal to our consciences with Bible verses. She would say we were "ruining our testimonies" and admonish us to be good. Dad only enforced harder and younger with us kids, even instructing other parents who were interested in learning how to achieve the same results with their uncooperative offspring. "Just take away their food and they'll obey real quick," he would laugh.

Since, in Dad's opinion, all children were born with a rebellious sin nature, he stressed the importance of what he called "the War" when toddlers first started to rebel. His method was to break the child's spirit in one cataclysmic confrontation so they would always know who the true authority was. My first observation of this was when Jedi, not yet two years old, threw a petulant fit. The family plans were canceled, clearing the schedule to make way for the ensuing clash of wills, which lasted hours. Dad spanked Jedi hard when he refused to obey, then banished him to the closet where the furious child wailed at the top of his lungs. A short while later, Dad brought him back out to test his resolve, and chubby little Jedi amazed us all by falling silent and narrowing his big blue eyes, blazing with defiance. The cycle of beating and banishment continued until Jedi was worn down and whimpered in surrender. Half the day had passed. I noticed over the years that the end was near whenever the child fell asleep from physical exhaustion. My father would press them harder after they woke, and when they realized even sleep was no refuge, they would often break. If the diapers were negating the effect of the spanking, Dad would remove the shield to strike at bare bottoms.

With us older kids, whippings were employed as strategically needed. We had a strong wooden paddle that hung in a central location; its presence was usually enough to inspire peace. Plus, there was always a hefty belt handy when it took my father's fancy to use leather instead. In a few extreme cases, one or more of us were instructed to hold down the protesting offender while Dad brought down a dozen or so jaw-rattling, bruise-blooming hits, an ardent glint in his eye and his jaw clenched tight. It was better not to move or scream because it only hurt worse when he hit a bone, and if we succeeded in running away or made too much noise, he would start over with fresh zeal. Dad never looked distressed or burdened by his duty; he seemed to revel in it, his wrath occasionally spilling over into laughter at our ridiculous flailing.

AFTER WE MOVED, MY FATHER INCREASED HIS REQUESTS FOR uncomfortable things, like, would I look at his penis? Would I touch it? Kiss it? I worried whether the area was dirty. Wasn't that where boys peed from? I did my best to wiggle out of those requests, though it was difficult to do so whenever I got summoned to his room to give him a massage and ended up alone with him. He complimented me, saying my hands were the strongest or my French kisses were the best of all the girls, even Mom. Something seemed very wrong about him telling me that, but he was immensely displeased if I demurred even the smallest request.

I was taught a woman's lot in life is first to be subject to her father, and then, after marriage, to her husband. In the Bible, there were many men of God who had multiple wives. Dad would say modern society didn't allow men to have more than one wife, then ask, "If I could propose, would you marry me?" I would laugh and say I was too young. "Well, girls used to get married a whole lot younger than they do now, even your age," he'd reply. I was nine.

He expounded further on the topic of marital unhappiness, insisting he was preparing me for my future. I was special; he was making me so. Everything I was learning was to make me desirable to men and superior to other women. He explained men were difficult for women to please since women were not aggressive enough to ever equal a man's drive. I asked why and was told it was how God made us. I learned the Bible said, "Man was not made for woman, but woman was made for man."[1] We were the weaker vessel. But I didn't want to be undesirable or weak.

When Mom wasn't around, he railed on her for gaining weight, saying kids had ruined her body. Though she had furrowed stretchmarks deeply scarred across her belly, I thought she was the most beautiful woman in the world. At the same time, I feared getting my own future scars if they would make me ugly in the eyes of men. Dad asked to "take sexy pictures" of me, saying I should build up a library of images that would forever preserve my young and beautiful body before it was ruined by childbirth and age. My husband would be able look at them to pleasure himself when I was pregnant, fat, and old. Men wanted sex all the time and it was a wife's duty to always participate with enthusiasm. This would inevitably lead to babies and lots of them. It all sounded very difficult to me.

Over the years, I would eventually endure many uncomfortable, humiliating photoshoots where Dad would end up yelling me to tears, saying I was fat, ugly, or untalented at posing. He told me to study lingerie catalogs to learn how to position myself and even photoshopped my teenage waist smaller and chest larger. But I never let him take the naked photos, which he so often asked for.

4

THE INVISIBLE GIRL

THE FIRST SECTION UNDERTAKEN DURING THE HOUSE REMODEL was the second-floor area with the two kids' rooms. The plan was to have a boys' room, a girls' room, and a room in between for the live-in housekeeper. The girls' room would be the largest one, styled like a dormitory, with beds lining each long wall and finished with a peaked timber ceiling.

Sometime during that first year in Tennessee, the whole family—pregnant mother, father, and first six kids—moved into the large Southwest-styled master suite for a short period of time while the other bedrooms were redone. The suite was ridiculously big, almost equaling the size of our entire previous home. There was a fireplace in the spacious area designed for the bed, separate his-and-hers sinks, a Jacuzzi tub, and a glass-doored shower covered in peach-colored stucco with art-deco tiles fashioned like a Mexican blanket.

It was all connected by two open halls running along the sides of the rectangular space, each section blending seamlessly into the next. One could walk along from the bed to the sinks, from the sinks to the shower, through to the closets in the back without navigating any doors.

Mom and Dad's waist-high king bed was put underneath the mission bells in the main area, and we kids had our twin-size beds pushed together like one long temporary mattress twenty feet away. I figured my parents would wait to have sex until they were in private again. Nevertheless, I woke up one night and heard them at it. I had a momentary glimpse of my mother's legs in the air, spread on either side of my father's back. I clamped my eyes tightly shut and shoved my face down into my pillow, trying to be silent while I heard Dad prompt Mom to make up a wild story about her and another man.

I also thought Dad might temporarily refrain from touching me while tucking me into bed, since Mom was there and the other kids were lying closer than normal. Instead, he waited until Mom had fallen asleep nursing the baby a few nights later and, sure enough, I felt his weight settle into the bottom corner of my little mattress. He whispered I should keep doing what he'd instructed me to do. He took my hand, put it on my crotch for emphasis, then pulled away and went to another bed. I let my hand slip back to my side.

These incidents hadn't made me feel afraid yet. None of the touching had been painful; if anything, I had learned it could indeed feel good. It sometimes troubled my conscience when I ignored Dad's commands and then lied to him. I'd fallen into the habit of always answering yes when he asked me if I was touching myself, yet trying to come in bed had become too noticeable. I preferred to do it in the bathroom instead, and only when I felt the urge.

A FEW NIGHTS LATER, I WOKE UP TO DAD LIFTING ME UP OUT OF my sheets and carrying me from the main area. It was the middle of the night, and the silence was broken only by the slow breathing of my peacefully dreaming family around me. Though we had to have passed the king-size bed, I can't remember whether I saw Mom sleeping there. Once we were in the narrow hall, Dad turned into the first opening, with the pair of sinks. Though I have tried hard to forget, I can see the physical surroundings, burned with impossible detail into my electric memory. Upon recall, I would experience the scene again:

> There are tiles everywhere. The ones covering the countertop are an inch square, set with thin grouting. They shine and shimmer like a peacock's feather. Larger tiles frame both sides of the mirror, depicting noble-looking Native Americans on the backs of bowing paint horses and prancing buckskins. I'm wearing a big cotton T-shirt, reaching almost to my knees. My father puts me down on the cold counter, facing him. When I look down, I cannot see myself; my little body has been edited out. I can only feel. Under my thigh, the rim of the sink protrudes hard and slightly round before giving way to a tiny crescent of void beginning to slope away under my left butt cheek.
>
> He says nothing before he begins. My brain does what it can to protect me by immediately focusing my eyes on the tiles. I occupy myself by studying them while my body records its own memories, snapshots of my position, orientation in space, and the sensations in my limbs and chest. My arms are down by my side, bracing for balance. My knees are spread and my father's sandpaper hair, buzzed short and rough, scrapes the inside of my legs while he arranges himself. His jaw is smooth in contrast. I jolt, everything inside of me seizing up, when his probing tongue

37

touches an excruciatingly tender spot. My heart rears and races so frantically I wonder whether I am having a heart attack. I am in extreme discomfort beginning to border on pain as something further inside my private area responds without my bidding. It is way too intense, and I don't want this. I want to get out of my body, but I am trapped.

Turning away from the cowboys and Indians, I look down at him and immediately regret it. In slow motion, he switches to using his fingers, kneading between my legs, and looks up to see if I am watching. The eyes that peer up from under his black brows repel me with their darkness, shining with something awful and terrifying. A foaming wave of heat floods throughout my body, and I wish with every ounce of me that my father was dead.

In a strange flash, like a movie suddenly projected against the back of my eyelids, I imagine grabbing his hair and bashing his head against the edge of the counter over and over again until his tongue stops moving, his eyes are broken, and I don't have to see them anymore. The violent images repeat, overlaying what is really happening. Then a black vortex opens in my gut, and I go tumbling into its center. I don't know how long I am there.

Suddenly, a ghost drifts through the far hall and pulls me back to myself, back to Time. It is only a glimpse, a child-size ghost walking by, dressed in a big shirt like me. My father sees it, too, and he stops abruptly. He fumbles, yanking my panties part of the way back up.

I didn't know which of my siblings got up that night. I didn't know what they saw, if anything. I later realized this experience affected me in a way no other previous incident had. It was as if the memories had failed to store correctly in my mind. Fragments of the scene would make me nervous if they ever came to mind, and I would have nightmares if I thought about it before falling asleep. I developed the compulsive habit of continually moving my feet against each other in a repetitive swishing pattern while in bed, perhaps to self-sooth, perhaps to signal that I was awake until the moment I lost consciousness.

Over time, dealing with those recollections began to train my brain how to react to unsafe memories. In the interest of my internal and emotional safety, they had to be insulated and set apart. Up on the counter, I had been unable to see myself, as if I'd been scrubbed out of existence by some giant eraser. Eventually, I convinced myself it had been some other little girl sitting on the counter. It wasn't me anymore. I hadn't even been there. I had been sleeping.

I came to understand this latest act of my father was the escalation of something that reached back before my discernible remembrance. Each of the previous times he'd touched me now bled together to become one long chain throughout my childhood, the older memories transforming due to the contamination of more current upsetting, unmanageable feelings. The next time he touched me, my brain responded automatically. Every time I needed her, the silent, invisible girl from the counter was standing at the ready with a little black box. When the box was filled with whatever I was unable to handle, she would drop it into the gaping hole that had formed in me, and I could go on smiling, being special, and making Dad happy.

BABY NUMBER SEVEN WAS A GIRL, JASMINE, THE FIRST WILLIS TO be born in Tennessee, precisely six months and a week after we had moved from Chicago. At nine years old, I was now deemed old enough to hold the new baby on my own. She was a truly beautiful baby with big blue eyes, just like tiny Jedi. Four days after the birth, mother and baby were in bed, resting and nursing. I was goofing around nearby when Mom told me to turn on the little gray TV in the corner of the large master bedroom.

Confused by the look on her face, I asked, "What's wrong, Mommy?"

The screen buzzed to life, and a grainy news channel displayed a strange sight. Two matching skyscrapers stood square and bright against a sky billowing with dark smoke. Red banners flashed across the bottom of the screen. The other kids gathered around, everyone trying to decipher what it was we were looking at. We asked Mom where this was happening.

Her face was pale. "New York," she whispered, pulling the baby tighter to her chest.

It was a deeply troubling day, the first time the worries and fears of the global world invaded my home. We saw replays of a tiny speck—shaken news anchors said it was a passenger airplane—crashing into the buildings, causing a fiery red mushroom to bloom and turn black. A building called the Pentagon got hit next, and people kept saying the word *terrorism*. The TV droned on throughout the day, showing footage of dazed people covered in a thick layer of dust, stumbling through huge white clouds, and firefighters helping injured people to safety.

Dad talked about war and end-times prophecies. A chill ran down my spine when he listed the biblical signs that would signal the dreadful Armageddon. I'd heard him mention the topic before, only now I paid attention. We saved the newspaper that day, knowing we were living through a historic moment. I thought of Anne Frank and her famous diary and figured I should probably rekindle my sporadic efforts at journal-keeping.

Mom was emotional. Dad was supposed to have traveled to an international wrestling tournament a few days before but had changed his plans at the last minute.

"He was supposed to be there," she nodded at the screen, "only a few blocks away."

I tried to imagine my father walking through those bizarre, dust-covered streets. What would have happened if he had been there? I pushed back against the memory of my one-time wish that my father was dead. While I had never said it aloud, I knew God sees our innermost thoughts. A sinful thought was just as bad as a sinful action. No, it hadn't been me, I was quick to remind myself. That was the wish of the other little girl, the silent, invisible one. In her defense, she had just wanted to do whatever was needed to guarantee she never had to see those eyes again. I was awash in gratefulness that her wish had not come true. I folded my hands in thanks, hoping it wasn't the end of the world just yet, relieved we would have our smart and strong father to guide us through whenever it came.

5

MASKED MONSTERS

THE STAIN WAS STICKY AND STRONG-SMELLING ON THE TIMBER boards of the new girls' dormitory bedroom. I was sitting on my bed—the one closest to the door—and so was Mom. She had a serious look on her face, which I studied carefully.

"Jess, I need to ask you something," she said, her voice soft. She laid her hand on the bed to draw closer to me. "I need to know, has Daddy done anything weird to you?" She gestured just enough to indicate my body. "Has he . . . touched you? In a weird way? You're not in trouble. I just need to know."

I was shocked, overcome with a powerful sense of déjà vu as a pink robe, shiny skin, and towel stripes came barreling into my head. Mom coming out of the shower all those years ago connected to Mom sitting here on my bed. It was as if a wormhole had opened, a tunnel of warped time directly connecting my oldest memories to the current moment. I found myself on repeat, thinking again what I had thought then. *What should I say to her? How can I tell her?*

Years later, Mom would tell me she had caught one of my younger sisters sticking her hand in her panties and when told to stop, my sister had blurted out that Dad told her to do it. This interaction is what had prompted Mom to question me.

Frozen on my bed, her question hanging in the air, I had the sudden impression I hadn't seen her for a long while, as if I had been on a trip or we had been separated. Where had she gone? Maybe it was the rush of the move, the new house, or the constant arrival of new sisters and brothers, more lessons, more busyness. I looked at her growing belly, already stretching out to house another life, number eight. I knew too much about her, things one shouldn't know about their mother. I knew things about my father. I wondered whom should I protect. I was afraid of making the wrong choice. I was convinced I was paralyzed. Somehow, my head nodded anyway.

"Jess? He *has* touched you?"

I nodded again, my cheeks growing hot with embarrassment. It all seemed so gross, and I was ashamed I hadn't gone to her of my own accord. I was both a bad girl and a tattletale. How horrible. Would Dad be mad? I had a flash of fear he might hurt me. Would Mom break down? Dad had been hard on her lately. She probably didn't think I knew, but I did.

Instead, she told me I was right to tell her and assured me everything would be okay. After repeating that I wasn't in trouble, she said she would talk to Dad.

Everything will be okay. I desperately needed to believe her, to believe the grown-ups would handle this. I never should have been caught between them, dealing with subjects I didn't understand. If they could fix it somehow, maybe things could go back to the way they were before, when Dad would play us to sleep on the piano and no one would be afraid for him to come home.

That night, I gazed at the beams on the ceiling and listened in amazement to the two voices downstairs. It was the first time I had ever heard Mom yell at Dad. Though I couldn't tell whether they were discussing what Mom had asked me about, I felt defended and protected when my feet finally stopped moving and I fell asleep.

Two days later, we had unexpected visitors at our door when we came bounding down the stairs for breakfast. They were family friends from Chicago and had been a familiar and important part of our lives there. There were no follow-up conversations with me after my mother's recent questioning, yet my gut said our friends' sudden appearance was related somehow. After breakfast, Mom turned on a movie for us kids to watch. I buzzed with curiosity the rest of the day, wishing I could be a fly on the wall in the room where the grown-ups were talking privately, but there were no raised voices, no discussion I could hear. Later that evening, the two visitors left as abruptly as they had arrived.

It would be over a decade before I would ask my mother what happened that day. She would go on to tell me she had called and asked them to come since they were the only people in our circle she thought Dad would be afraid of. She said she told them about my sister touching herself and saying Dad told her to do so.

The visitors eventually told me a slightly different story. They maintain my mother claimed my father had said he wanted us girls to be taught to masturbate, and this greatly disturbed them, prompting them to immediately book roundtrip flights. Both my mother and the visitors related that my father was uncooperative and confessed nothing during the confrontation. I will never fully know what transpired; I only know that though they remained a part of our lives, the visitors never asked me whether I was being taught to masturbate, and my mother did not confide in them again.

My temporary hope that things had been set right only made it more confusing when I realized nothing had been fixed after all. Being questioned by Mom brought out feelings I hadn't had to deal with before, from the guilt and embarrassment of finally admitting to her—and to myself—that something bad had happened, to my flinching reaction of fear at the thought of Dad's possible retribution for my failing to keep the secret. I was not punished by either parent and was exceedingly grateful I hadn't had to say more. I felt like I would burn to ashes on my bed if I'd been forced to relate out loud the things Dad had been doing and saying, from the insults about Mom's body to the incident on the sink.

I remember Mom telling us girls we weren't ever to be in their bedroom alone with Dad and that she wanted us to keep watch on each other and tell her if Dad did anything weird. This proved to be difficult, given he was still the undisputed authority of the house; I felt I had no real way to excuse myself when he next requested a foot rub or gave me a command that would violate Mom's directive. He had not returned to tucking me in at night, but he would sulk performatively and say I didn't love him or that I was being mean whenever I rebuffed his hugs, kisses, or secret conversations. These were the things I found least invasive, so I normalized them as the bare minimum of what was required of me. I did my best not to think about anything too worrisome, but a fuzzy undercurrent of tension became omnipresent in my tiny body.

After a little while, he began offering the chance for one of us girls to skip out on chores if we were willing to help with a special job or project in the office. We wouldn't have to clean up or put away our dishes if we would help him with filing or folder sorting. He kept saying he needed a secretary. He already had a real secretary, and I saw her job as infinitely cooler than the jobs Mom gave us. I was determined to be his "little secretary" and go to work with the grown-ups in his office on the far end of the house. Dad soon made it clear the new role had a required dress code: miniskirts.

WHEN HE EVENTUALLY STARTED TOUCHING ME AGAIN, HE HAD TO be subtle about it. I was popping into his office between his meetings and appointments with the assigned tasks he'd conveniently invented to save me from boring chore-world. He had me sit on his lap at the computer, not terribly unlike how I had sat on his lap at the piano keys long ago, and he would dictate things for me to type. Eventually, he took advantage of my position by slipping his hand—the one farther away from the door—around my waist and under my skirt.

At first, I skittered away and ran back to Mom, but I didn't tell, and I didn't stop volunteering. I learned to answer phones confidently and warmly with "Hello, RPW. My name is Jessica. How may I help you?" I sometimes got to hear Dad boast when I handed him the phone, "Yes, that was my eldest daughter. Guess how old she is? Ten." Though his praise was usually reward enough, he bestowed increasing gifts upon me—a trendy charm bracelet or an ice cream treat—sometimes telling me to be careful not to make the other kids jealous. We shouldn't let them know that I was his favorite. If I showed unwillingness, he might withhold a gift or special prize, saying he would save it for "his other girlfriend," then give it to one of my sisters. When a period of resistance continued, he would find some fault in my schoolwork or take issue with my attitude and make a great show of punishing me before the family for my disobedience.

When I found myself worrying what would happen if he ever did something truly horrible again, like putting his head between my legs, I realized I needed a more effective way of internalizing it. I began the crucial work of weaving a special mental mask I would hold in front of my father's face forever. It had to look like him and sound like him so completely that I could convince myself it was real whenever the real thing was too awful to bear. All I would have to do is look at the mask and I would be safe from what was on the other side. I would never have to see those eyes again no matter what he did to me.

One day, I marched out of the kitchen with my nose practically in the air, flaunting the exception of freedom. Dad had chosen me to help. But when I got to the office, it didn't have its usual hustle and bustle, and soon I was bored. I started in on a file reorganization project, spreading vertical stacks of red and blue folders across the floor in neatly spaced lines. Dad was concentrating on something on his computer for once, but I wondered if he was secretly watching me.

I sat with my legs tucked to the side, and when I reached to move a folder, a friction hinted in my crotch. I kept repeating the act and the tickle became more pronounced. I rose to my knees, bent on all fours, and felt the denim skirt stretch tight across my butt. Sure enough, Dad had been watching. I heard him leave his chair and a second later felt his hand on me. With the good feeling came a blinding, world-tilting shame. A flood not unlike the one I had felt up on the counter came rushing through me, only this time the rage and disgust were directed at myself. I wanted to claw out my guts and shove them as far away as I could. I was rotten and sick, and I didn't know why I had done it.

Because you wanted it, came the creepiest, most awful voice echoing in my head, a monster emerging from the pit in my bottomless core. There were no black boxes big enough to shove the beast into. Now I wished *I* were the dead one. I wished I could take it back and be the invisible girl, the silent child no one could see. But I was huge and ugly and once again there was nowhere to go to get outside my body. I could feel wickedness pouring out of my eyes. I needed my own mask now, a decent version of me I could pretend was real.

DESPITE THE ENCOURAGEMENT OF CHRISTIANS AROUND ME, THE Bible turned out to be less inviting than I'd first thought. For all the Sunday school stories I'd heard, my own reading of Scripture revealed less popular tales. I had become a strong and ravenous reader. The more grown-up the book, the better. But the Genesis story of Lot and his daughters truly shocked me.

Lot was the nephew of Abraham who fled the wicked cities of Sodom and Gomorrah after being warned by a pair of angels. His wife lacked faith and disobeyed their instructions, turning into a pillar of salt. I was familiar with this part of the narrative, but now noticed more sordid details. When the wicked city-dwellers had asked Lot to send out the visiting angels so they could have sex with them, Lot offered to send out his two virgin daughters instead. Luckily for the girls, the wicked men declined.

My surprise doubled when Lot again appeared in a later story. He and his two daughters were living in a cave after their escape. The oldest daughter realized they would never have children and persuaded the younger sister to get their father so drunk they could each have sex with him without his awareness. Successful in their scheme, they both bore children whose future descendants became enemies of the twelve tribes of Israel. When I nervously referenced this in a school discussion with Dad, he only raised his eyebrows and said, "I know. Pretty wild, right?"

My bewilderment continued. The kid version of the great flood glossed over the part where every living thing not safely on the ark died in the worldwide catastrophe. The Lord commanded Abraham to bind and sacrifice his son on an altar, only rescinding the order at the last possible moment when the father's total willingness to obey was proven. Another biblical daughter faced a less fortunate ending when her triumphant warrior father, Jephthah, vowed to burn as an offering to the Lord whatever first came to greet him upon his arrival home. His daughter raced out, dancing in celebration, and was subsequently sacrificed. David, of Goliath-killing fame, known as "a man after [God's] own heart,"[1] became a king who summoned a married woman to his palace for sex. After she fell pregnant, he arranged her husband's murder. Despite David's later contrition, God killed the newborn child as punishment.

Once again, I wondered, did I know too much or too little?

Lot is referenced in the New Testament as being righteous and "greatly distressed by the sensual conduct of the wicked," with no mention of his offering his then still-virgin daughters to a violent mob.[2] The book of Hebrews lists David and daughter-sacrificing Jephthah in what is commonly referred to as the Bible's "Faith Hall of Fame" along with Noah and Abraham, saying, "All these people were still living by faith when they died."[3] I kept waiting for someone in my family or my religion to say something about these stories.

Eventually I got the message: these are the things that happen to women and girls—things we never, ever speak about.

SOON, I WAS WORRYING DAILY ABOUT THE STATE OF MY IMMORTAL soul. It seemed certain my original prayer and baptism no longer had me covered. All the killing, rape, and incest made me feel uneasy reading the Bible, and then I felt guilty for being reluctant. I was told God saw no difference between the sins of murder and disobeying a parent. I feared the beginnings of doubt: doubt of my salvation, doubt of God's goodness, doubt of the Bible's truth. I knew good Christians were supposed to be sure of their salvation. I knew we were to let Scripture instruct us whether or not we liked what it said, always submitting to the Word as our final authority, even when it clashed with our human ideas or wayward feelings. But I desperately needed a break and sought out lighter, encouraging stories of more modern Christians.

I read about missionaries and champions of the Christian faith who lived pure and dedicated lives of compassion and service. Some accounts described radical, life-changing conversions followed by a life of inner peace, clarity of purpose, and radiant joy. I had never felt anything close to these feelings they described. Clearly, I needed a do-over. True Christians were *changed* after their spiritual rebirth.

There was only one rather intimidating roadblock. In a recent sermon, I had learned of a teaching that declared God would not hear the prayers of people who knowingly continued living in a pattern of sin. Though they might plead and beg, their cries would fall on deaf ears. The thought burned like a coal through my brain. It wasn't enough to know about Jesus dying on the cross, or to ask him to take me to heaven. One needed to confess their sins and submit to his complete lordship by obeying his commands. I knew it was wrong when Dad touched me, but was the sin mine, or his, or both?

My monster gleefully screamed, *Yours! Yours! Yours!*

No, countered the pretty mask that looked like me. *I don't know anything about that.*

If I knelt to pray, would God hear me? Would he see me as forgivable, or would I continue being both hideous and invisible? It was my most fervent wish that a loving God would not find me unsavable.

6

SUCKER PUNCH

Dad left for a business trip that required him to be away for the due date of baby number eight. Mom was ready to pop, her belly looming large as if trying to swallow her petite frame whole. By now she firmly believed that staying active until the last moments before delivery made for the easiest births. She nested and stuffed the freezer full of easy-prep casseroles and Crock-Pot meals and kept our social calendar going at high speed to distract herself from the endless waiting for her water to break.

She heard a popular Irish band was coming to play a gig in Nashville and was adamant we were going to attend, despite her imminent due date. Corralling her seven rowdy kids, Mom took us to the show, which started past our bedtime. The pub was packed to the rafters when we arrived, already stifling with the heat of sweaty bodies. We, the oldest kids, wormed our way to the front to sit on the sticky strip of floor space at the foot of the stage. Mom squeezed into a corner, setting up camp with the babies who would fall asleep in their strollers.

When the fiddle player started ripping through a set of blazing reels, we kids got up and danced in our spots. The audience roared in delight, and the band egged us on as the energy cranked higher. The pub seemed to shrink smaller and tighter until there was barely any room for dancing at all. So we got lifted onto the bar and continued flashing our best steps. It was soon discovered we were all siblings, and the smiley pregnant woman in the corner was our beaming mother.

At some point during the night, a ruddy, clean-shaven young man with narrow eyes approached my mother and gave her his business card. He leaned close with a grin and shouted above the ruckus, telling her he was building his own Irish pub downtown on Music Row in Nashville and wanted us to come and dance at his grand opening the following year. She took his card and figured he wouldn't remember talking to her the next morning.

Less than twenty-four hours later, Mom went into labor. When Dad called from the airport, about to board his flight home, we were still sleepily recovering from the night before. By the time he landed, Mom had concluded her shortest delivery yet—Julie was born with a single push. Mom was told, "You didn't even break a sweat!"

MY ERA OF BEING DADDY'S "LITTLE SECRETARY" CAME TO AN END as his wrestling venture picked up steam. The number of employees increased, and he went on more frequent trips. This easing of his attentions provided me a season of increased personal privacy. In the lull, puberty hit me like a sucker punch. A day of mysterious gut pain led to the discovery of bright-red blood in my pee. I went with concern to my mother, and she calmly informed me there was no need for alarm; from now on, I would be bleeding and cramping for a quarter of each month like every other woman in the world. How could such news *not* be cause for alarm?

After my initial skepticism, I moved on to a phase of indignation. Didn't I get a chance to opt out of such a painful experience? Wait, did boys have to go through anything secretly horrible like this? No, this was part of the baby-bearing role and therefore specific only to women. Each month there was a window of opportunity where a woman could get pregnant, and if she didn't, this "period" would follow to prepare her for the next chance, three weeks later. I saw the Bible verses that talked about the womanly duty in a new light: "It was the woman who was deceived and became a sinner. But women will be saved through childbearing—if they continue in faith, love and holiness with propriety."[1] The punishment of humanity's original curse not only manifested in the graphic moments I'd witnessed in delivery and birth itself but also in this monthly cycle, forever reminding women of their duty and punishment.

I wished I'd felt safer from my father's wandering hand; however, when I imagined him next trying to touch me and coming away with bloody fingers, I feared I would be relegated back to the laundry and the dishes. My period made it clear I could not win a war against my own biology. No matter my efforts or desires, I was becoming a woman.

MOM BEGAN TO CLASH WITH DAD ABOUT WHAT WE GIRLS WERE allowed to wear. The first appearance of flare pants was a scandal, though why they were more controversial than short skirts was puzzling. We were not allowed to cut our hair, and mine had grown long, reaching past my waist. The length was not for modesty; Dad told us short hair was ugly, and likewise any hairdos that pulled our locks flat or too far back from our faces were outlawed for not being pretty enough. Buying clothes at the mall was a Herculean undertaking, requiring a complex organization of strollers, buddy pairings, and the constant counting of children. As Dad led us girls through store after store, dismissing nearly everything as terrible fashion, I watched keenly for glimpses of what other kids my age were wearing, doing, or listening to. We usually left empty-handed and went to the thrift shop. Then Dad relied on Mom's sewing skills to transform items to his specifications.

Despite Mom's protests, a new rule was established: no girls were allowed to leave the house without getting Dad's "approval" on their outfits and hairdos. A few sharp spanking sessions ensured we knew he meant business. He would have us girls try on any new clothes in hours-long "fashion shows," where he would critique our pubescent bodies, demand that we strike attractive poses, and give instructions for any garment alterations. This tradition progressed through our teen and young adult years until I was awkwardly modeling swimsuits for him in public dressing rooms.

I first heard the angsty harmonies of boy bands and blond-highlighted pop stars in the tween mall stores full of purple glitter fabric and huge heart-shaped cutouts. Dad and Mom both warned us that much of teenage love was dumb and idiotic. Crushes, idols, dating, and the dramatic popularity scene were discounted as a phase of secular adolescence, and it would be wise to omit and avoid it as a whole. It was better for us not to be sidetracked or confused by the messages juvenile society would have pushed into our impressionable heads at school. Homeschooling was also sparing us from the cruelty of other kids, bullies, and mean girls.

I DID GENUINELY WANT TO BE A GOOD GIRL, MY MASKED-MONSTER-part notwithstanding, but I struggled to choose between the differing paths toward womanhood laid before me. I saw figurative halos glowing around the bowed heads of meek, long-suffering ladies who supposedly felt genuine fulfillment in being selfless, caring for children, and keeping a peaceful home. Did they struggle to please their husbands, or had their martyr-like spirits achieved a superior level: ascension into a fellowship of females in direct submission to God instead of man?

Dad regularly insisted all men were like him. I desperately wanted to believe it wasn't true, though I had no firsthand evidence to the contrary. How could one tell what was really going on inside a human soul or a home? Were other families identical to ours, projecting different images on their surface but corroded with the same sickness and struggle within? For years, I'd felt as if the word *dirty* was blazing bright as blood on my forehead, but no one seemed to see it. How could my mother lie next to the man who did such things to me, the knowledge not somehow be exchanged between them as they slept? And what was hiding out of sight in the homes of our friends and neighbors? What was the difference between our "testimonies" and our hidden lives?

SINCE DAD WAS CURRENTLY TOO BUSY TO SINGLE ME OUT, THIS season was my best chance for turning over a new spiritual leaf. If I wasn't currently living in sin, maybe my prayers would get through. I prayed a marathon prayer, confessing and repenting. I hoped to feel that supernatural change of being washed clean by God's miraculous forgiveness. I stayed on my knees in my bedroom and kept at it, eyes squeezed shut, repeating my supplications when I ran out of new words.

I was determined for this second salvation attempt to stick. I recalled Mom's voice reading to us from Genesis, "Why is your face downcast? If you do what is right, will you not be accepted? . . . Sin is crouching at your door; it desires to have you, but you must rule over it."[2] I promised I would dedicate myself to any role or chore with a willing attitude if only God would help me. I would be kind to my siblings, obey my mother without complaint, and never again be involved with my father's secrets. I was twelve, almost a teenager, and I needed to avoid that age category's dreadful reputation. I would cultivate the fruits of the Spirit, which are the identifiers of a true Christian: love, joy, peace, patience, kindness, goodness, faithfulness, gentleness, self-control.[3]

Soon, I did feel something; my body felt lighter and my mind brighter. As I opened my eyes, I was overwhelmed with happiness and gratitude to God for granting me what I so earnestly asked for. I wasted no time in keeping my promises, set on maintaining a momentum of productive righteousness.

For precisely two days, I was able to stay in a state of positivity, having nothing but peaceable thoughts toward all, no matter the task. I avoided Dad and fixated on my new identity: I was a girl remade. God was with me, helping me with his power.

Then, late one evening, the house needed to be cleaned. Dad divided up the rooms, giving us each an assignment. When he came to inspect our progress, he discovered someone had shoved toys and clothes into the upstairs hall closet instead of putting them away properly.

"Who did this?" he demanded, pointing to the space jammed tight with litter.

No one spoke up. He called "attention," and everyone raced to form a line. Again, he demanded a confession, swinging the wooden paddle through the air as he paced before us. Starting at the top, he spanked us in order, down to the youngest not in diapers.

"I'll keep spanking until I get the truth," he warned darkly. "I can do this all night."

The next round of blows was significantly harder, and panic began to rise. We turned to each other, imploring the guilty one to stop the punishment. His fury escalated in reaction to what he took as universal rebellion. Screams followed his strokes, which began falling in places other than our bottoms, a twisting hip, a flailing leg, whatever lay under his descending arm.

Dad announced he was setting a timer for ten minutes. When the time was up, the beatings would continue. Not until after the timer and the paddle made a few rounds did a younger sister confess in sobbing whispers. Since Dad was out of the room, the rest of us were faced with the choice of potentially saving ourselves or protecting our sibling. What would he do to her if we gave her up?

Even all these years later, I cannot recall how the episode ended, whether we turned the horrified culprit over to her fate, if our mother intervened, or whether the danger dissipated with the timer's last countdown. I have asked my siblings who are old enough to remember, and so far, none have been able to recall the resolution. Why can I not picture how I finally left that room or went to sleep that night? What remains is the vivid sight of plum and claret bruising, a kaleidoscope of pain upon our legs that we endeavored to hide from our dance teacher for weeks afterward.

My only other clue about how that night resolved is the memory of the next time I looked into the hall closet where the condemning clutter had been shoved. I stood there during chore time with a limp rag in my hand, staring without sight at the brooms and mops leaning against the back of the wall, enveloped in a dark cloud of terrifying feelings and thoughts. I remember churning with rage, despair, betrayal, and hopelessness, each overpowering internal reaction crashing into the next, struggling to gain dominance. I had just talked back to my mom, the taste of my vehemence still bitter and biting in my mouth. I can't recall why I had argued with her, but I knew I had broken my resolution to be a good daughter. The words racing through my head were unbearable—what I now think was the delayed reaction to however the beatings had ended that night.

Hot tears tumbled down my cheeks as I tried praying, *Dear God . . .* only to falter in shame. I was a liar. The fruits of my spirit were dark and unholy, my face was downcast, sin was crouching at my door, and I was unable to master it.

The masked monster inside me laughed. *See? God won't listen to you. He won't hear your prayers. You are not worth saving.*

Alone and overwhelmed, the fear of my spiritual fate and final destination was overshadowed by the present and overwhelming threat of the now. My soul's fate notwithstanding, I had to do whatever was required to stay on my father's good side—or else I could face obliterating episodes of violent rage at any moment.

7

THE FIRE

THE HOUSE WAS NEARING COMPLETION ACCORDING TO DAD'S grand vision. It had been almost four years of blue painter's tape, the constant whir of machinery operating around the corner, and waves of workmen coming and going. The finish line was finally coming into view.

In the last expansion of his design, Dad had visited prestigious recording studios around Nashville and decided to add one to our home. Music was a significant industry in town, and, over the years, he'd invested enough money into our music lessons and growing collection of instruments to assume that, at some point, someone in the family would pursue a career in music. The young man who gave Mom his card at the concert the night before Julie was born did not end up forgetting their conversation, and he had since followed up to repeat his request for us to dance and play some traditional tunes at the opening of his pub, officially booking us for our very first "gig" that coming spring.

IN 2004, WHEN THE TALL TREES THINNED, SHAKING LOOSE THEIR colorful clothes in the face of winter, we made plans to spend part of the holidays at a neighbor's cottage that was just visible at the top of the cliffs next to our house. My heart was filled with expectations of an extra-special Christmas season. Dad never let us have a Christmas tree in our house, due to its origins as a pagan symbol, but Mom adored decorations and overcompensated by wrapping everything in greenery and lights, including mantels, pillars, railings, and banisters.

Back in Chicago, each winter of my childhood brought multiple deposits of heavy snow, blinding white in the sunlight and substantial enough for tunnel making and fort building. In stark contrast, our first year in Tennessee brought zero snow. We heard about a southern phenomenon called "ice storms," where the temperature would hover just above freezing, keeping rain from turning to snow during the day, then plunge overnight, locking everything in a thick coat of heavy and dangerous ice.

That December, we went to bed one stormy night and woke to a jaw-dropping sight. Every surface, every object, as far as our eyes could see, had been frozen in a layer of brilliant crystal ice. Without stopping to properly bundle up, we tumbled out the front door into the frigid air to further take in our transformed surroundings, impossibly coated in clear, sparkling glass. We took pictures documenting the momentous event and "skated" across the front yard, which was solid as an ice rink. Our power went out, and the ice buildup would certainly frustrate any immediate repair efforts.

We left early to go to the neighbor's little cottage, which still had power, taking the old logging road at the back of the property because the steep front driveway was impossible to climb. We watched *It's a Wonderful Life* on Christmas Eve and slept in rows of cushy sleeping bags under the twinkling lights of an ornament-laden tree. I felt cocooned in a comforting haze of my own nostalgic emotions, the sugar buzz of homemade cookies fading in my belly as I drifted off to the sound of my many siblings breathing beside me. I had one last thought before dreams took me: when I was grown, my house would always have a decorated tree for Christmas.

On the morning of December 26, a Sunday, we returned home via the old logging road. Though our electricity had come back on, the heat wasn't working. Dad took us oldest three to help him clear the driveway of ice, something that needed to be done before any repair trucks could expect to get to the house. We armed ourselves with picks and shovels and banged, scraped, and chipped away at the layer of ice, slowly revealing the pavement beneath. It took us the better part of the day to accomplish our goal. Afterward, we spent the evening at the mall, first enjoying a belt-bursting dinner and then walking over to the adjacent theater to catch a late movie.

On the drive home, almost everyone was asleep except for Mom and Dad. There was a new redbrick fire station at the corner of our turn off the highway, and its floodlights were on when we drove past. A couple of minutes later we found ourselves traveling behind a bristling fire engine with lights on, no siren. We wondered if perhaps they were driving for a nonemergency reason. Then I looked to the sky and saw a faint orange glow radiating above the black lace patterns of the treetops. When the fire truck turned onto our street, we grew solemn. Every bend in the road intensified the ominous hue in the sky, signaling whatever was burning was *big*. It was not until we were less than a mile away from home that I whispered, "Mom, I think it's our property."

The other kids began to wake up. My heart thumped with dread as we watched the fire truck turn through our gate and tilt down the freshly deiced driveway. We gasped in horror as the house came into view. The golden fantasy, the dream home, was blazing from its foundation. Roaring flames ripped and snapped, shooting high into the sky and out of sight. One side was nearly level, only scraps of roof and crumbling stones visible through the billowing smoke. Then I remembered my clothes, shoes, books, and toys were all inside.

Dad leaped out of the van to join the firefighters, pulling out a handful of items before his offices succumbed to the inferno. Mom prayed, grateful that her children were safe. We were numb with shock and crying. But when the flames reached the leftover fireworks stored in a back closet, we burst out laughing hysterically at the sudden boom of ridiculous pink and purple sparkles crackling above the withering structure. Whatever was in the van with us amounted to the sum total of our belongings. Any old junk made us celebrate, a pair of missing shoes, a CD, a single mitten. We were all at a loss for words, flooded with adrenaline and relief. My sister's voice trembled as she joked, "Let's go back and watch *It's a Wonderful Life* again."

WE STAYED AT THE NEIGHBOR'S COTTAGE FOR THE NEXT FEW days. When the ashes were finally cold, we were allowed to go see the wreckage. As Mom drove, she said the fire truck we'd followed down our driveway was called because the engines already at the scene had run out of water, unable to get the thirsty flames under control. There had been a routine investigation by the local authorities, and they were pretty sure a power surge had hit the oldest part of the house and immediately exploded some piece of electrical equipment. If we had been home, we might not have survived.

With this grim thought in the forefront of my mind, I stepped out of the van and into the graveyard of another life. The bones were everywhere, melted bits of metal half-buried in the gray sea of chalky ash, fragments of glass and perilous towers of leaning stone where the chimneys and fireplaces had been. With the building gone, the remaining footprint didn't seem to have the correct proportions, like the space was too small to ever have contained a house of such volume and magnitude. Weaving through the devastation like a demon's reckless roller coaster was the metal roof, shriveled and shrunken into violent twists and loop the loops.

Despite Dad's investment in expensive fireproof file cabinets a few years before, anything and everything stored on disks and tapes ended up melting just enough to be unreadable, a loss of practically all our home videos and photos Dad had made the effort to digitize. I'd printed out and filed a few of my poems, short stories, and even a few portions of my attempts at writing an overly ambitious fantasy trilogy. After the scorched drawers were pried open, the loose pages were brittle and charred deep brown around the edges, the clotted ink abnormally shiny, radiating an unmistakable smell that flooded my nostrils.

Losing the rest of my creations was a crushing blow to my spirit. I was overcome with urgency to recapture what I could before my memories drifted away and were forgotten. I used the mini keyboard at our neighbor's cottage to document all the musical compositions I could remember. I filled dozens of notebooks with scribblings and bits of writing that now existed nowhere other than my head. Dozens of songs and stories slipped away before I could set them down. Not terribly long before, I had longed for a clean slate, a new start, a blank page. This was not what I had meant.

THE INSURANCE COMPANY ASKED MOM AND DAD TO WRITE UP AN exhaustive list of all our belongings destroyed in the fire. It was the first time I heard mention of our insurance company, and I was mighty glad to know they existed. Their first move was to get us into a hotel in downtown Nashville. Mom began hunting for a rental house in our area that would allow a family with eight children. Insurance would foot the bill.

Hotel life lasted around six purgatorial weeks altogether disconnected from time. Though we were given strict orders not to watch TV, it provided instant access to a constant stream of kid-centered content. I swear we played the Disney channel for hours every day, which updated my impressions of what kids considered popular and cool at the time. Little good it did me—all my flare jeans and lip-gloss tubes were gone. Local families gave us cardboard boxes of old clothes their children had outgrown, and Mom bought us underwear and socks from Walmart.

Next, Mom bought a new arsenal of musical instruments. Before Christmas, we had been preparing for our first gig at the Irish pub's grand opening on Saint Patrick's Day. Rather than cancel after the fire, my parents figured it would be better for us to have something to work toward. Dad was gone trying to rescue his business, and every day Mom was either on a phone call or in a meeting about insurance stuff. Dad had picked a policy designed to award him the amount of money needed to rebuild the house, and there was potential difficulty in determining that exact cost since the house had been under construction for four years.

If the plan was to rebuild, we would need to be as close to the property as possible, and this swiftly narrowed Mom's rental search. She eventually called our new neighbor in the house directly next door to our property. It had three tiny bedrooms and one bathroom, and when she called to see if the owner was willing to rent, he told her to drop by and they could talk about it. We moved in the beginning of March. Due to our approaching debut gig, time was finally moving fast again.

WE ENDED UP PLAYING AT THE SAME IRISH PUB IN DOWNTOWN Nashville for eight Saint Patrick's Days in a row, our band growing in confidence and membership each year. I don't remember much about our 2005 debut except I loathed the experience and swore I would never do such a thing again. The pub owner was kind and encouraging despite our obvious lack of experience, and he invited us back to play again the next year if we worked up a full-length set.

Soon, Mom and Dad had to decide whether they should continue prioritizing our intense tutelage in the arts. They figured we had come too far to give up and waste our previous efforts, so they outfitted the garage of our rental house with a wall of mirrors and a sprung plywood dance floor that would cushion our feet. Mom ordered new school textbooks, and we did our best to reboot and maintain our pre-fire schedule. They urged us to keep practicing our steps and master our instruments despite the downgrade in facilities. I sensed the golden age of my childhood was over. I wondered what our family's future would look like and whether we would ever truly get our home back.

8

BETWEEN

WITHOUT FANFARE OR EXPLANATION, MOM STOPPED GOING TO church right before baby number nine, Jamie, was born. She and Dad frequently had closed-door discussions early on Sunday mornings. These left Mom's face mottled and swollen, and Dad's dark and stony. Two weeks past her due date, she was induced at the hospital because the baby was getting dangerously big. Labor was a long and strenuous affair, since her body initially refused to be hurried along by the drugs. Jamie emerged a day later with the thickest dark curls I had ever seen on an infant. Dad once again began meeting with the church elders and pastor. I don't know if what followed was a clash of prophetic interpretation or differing views on leader qualifications. Eventually, our family stopped going to church altogether.

In that same season, the father of another local family we had known awhile came to speak with Dad. They, too, were reconsidering their membership at a local congregation. From their conversation, a home fellowship was born—an unofficial church that met in rotation in the houses of the families involved; no pastor, no tithing, just fathers leading their families in imitating the early church of the New Testament. These Sundays became a full-day hybrid of Bible study and potluck, with eventually anywhere from three to seven families attending at a time. At first, I found it awkward as we took turns preparing music, reading long passages of the Scriptures aloud, and discussing interpretations and applications.

Within this new religious environment, we kids were put on the spot in the middle of open discussion to see if we were paying attention or properly absorbing what was being taught. Where my place in the pews had given me a sense of anonymity during the traditional sermon, here I was vulnerable to the floodlight of public examination, with my father the chief inquisitor. While there was no official leader in the home gatherings, I felt my father dominated. I began to lean into the participation, feeling an intense intellectual engagement I had never experienced in church. I was determined to show Dad I could hold my own in theory and intellect.

We hit a practical difficulty when we came to the book of First Corinthians and encountered this verse: "Women should keep silent in the churches. For they are not permitted to speak, but should be in submission."[1] Due to the group-wide commitment to literal interpretation wherever proper, a general consensus admitted the girls and wives should pull back, allowing the young men to lead in preparation for the day they would be the fathers, responsible for guiding their future households.

In our now-year-round school assignments, Dad began to interrupt us older kids with growing monologues in which he would range through far-reaching subjects and posit personal theories. They reminded me of his Sunday contributions, only longer and wilder. I leaped at the chance to engage in any test where I could excel or prove my diligence. When Dad would reappear after being away on trips for the wrestling business, he would monopolize the rest of our day with an impromptu lecture on his philosophies of religion, fashion, or dance.

When we weren't doing our shrinking schoolwork assignments, Dad continued to push us to find other performance talents. We had previously been exposed to a dance style called West Coast Swing. Now Jen and Jair displayed strong interest and watched hours of championship-level routines on video. They imitated, and Dad critiqued. It was a social dance, where girls and guys danced together to blues, swing, hip-hop, and current pop radio hits. As their skills grew, Dad became certain they could be contenders for a national title. Over Thanksgiving, Dad took them to California for the US Open Swing Dance Championships, where they won their age category.

The floodgates of couples dance were thrown wide, and Dad encouraged us to incorporate ballroom, swing, and Latin styles into our growing repertoire. Six stair-stepped siblings all doing Irish dance was a crowd-pleasing novelty, so we performed *Riverdance*-style in the evening exhibition shows at these dance competitions, enabling us to avoid paying what would have been costly entry fees in the other categories. We became the homeschoolers who wore spandex and sequins, the Christians who didn't go to church, "that family" with a million kids.

UNFORTUNATELY FOR MY CONFIDENCE, MY BODY WAS CHANGING in awkward ways. Right when I began appearing before more judges and audiences, I was trying out training bras. My eyebrows became embarrassingly bushy, creeping toward each other on my forehead. Though my hair was growing darker all the time, Dad said he preferred me artificially blonde, like Mom, so I'd been allowed to start going with her to get our long tresses bleached. I liked being golden. I was distressed by the arrival of other, unmentionable hair, the thickening of my thighs, and the ever-present trio of gaps in my front teeth, which I dreamed of one day fixing with braces. When Dad started requiring me to step on the scale once a week, I was humiliated to see the pounds climbing, even though I knew I was still growing at ages thirteen and fourteen. Though Dad had used the restriction of food as a group punishment off and on for many years, putting me on diets was new.

Dad found opportunities to squeeze my budding breasts, casually commenting on their progress whenever I was summoned to give him massages in his bed. If I was rubbing his back, he would try to push my hands down under the covers, and when I resisted, he banished me with cold insults or accusations that I was cruel and unkind.

Fear bloomed in my belly when it was time to line up outside in the airless heat for our mile-long runs. We ran to the bridge up the road and back, Dad standing in the front yard, his eyes flicking from the stopwatch in his hand to see who came last. Apparently, I had adopted a funky way of running to compensate for my earlier dance injuries and Dad was determined that I break this habit. He had me run back and forth in the yard, ridiculing my motions while the other kids watched. Or he would run behind me to the bridge, shouting menacingly while my heartbeat thundered in my ears, throwing in a few sharp kicks at my heels for good measure. This made me trip and cry, and I heaved hard to keep breathing, even as searing wings of fire spread open in my lungs. The fear transformed into involuntary terror, gripping my body with an automatic frenzy, as if my flesh was convinced my father would gnaw my ankles to the bone if he made the effort to catch me.

As I collapsed onto the carpet of the living room, my vibrating limbs cherry-red and slick with sweat, the panic would fade with the slowing of my pulse until I could rally myself toward the garage for the rest of the group workout. Later, when I was eating dinner or listening to a lecture on the importance of knowing hand-to-hand combat, my body accepted the belief that the creature always running behind me would consume what it wanted, and my cries would not stop him. I could not make myself ugly enough to escape his unwanted attentions, nor could I make myself perfect enough for him to value me as I wished.

DAD BEGAN OVERRULING MOM'S DIRECTIONS; DISPARAGING HER efforts at parenting, teaching, and managing; criticizing our lack of discipline and unsatisfactory results. It was painful to watch him gradually demote her from the rank of parent. To my dismay, I found myself snapping at her, talking back, and causing drama. It was frustrating to see her perpetually give to all while neglecting herself, and it hurt when she rejected affection. I didn't know how to react when she insisted she didn't have time for showers, food, or sleep. The declaration "I love you, Mom" was sometimes met with the response that if I loved her, I'd clean the house.

If any of us cried in front of Dad, whether from emotional or physical pain, he would command us to "make a graceful recovery," demonstrating what he clearly assumed was a demure and winning smile. If any of us offended him, we were instructed to find ways to earn back his favor and get out of "negative territory." When he was pleased and in a good mood, his favorites were given exemptions from work, selective power, and, most importantly, a store of goodwill that could save them from serious punishment after the next failed task or test.

I GREW INCREASINGLY CONCERNED ABOUT MY LACK OF REGULAR access to my would-be peers. Being homeschooled, home-churched, and home-trained in the arts, I sorely missed a larger social community. I was regularly reminded that my upbringing was superior to most and my parents were making good choices for me. Still, I could tell from the poster bins at Walmart that normal teens were allowed to hang tributes to their favorite bands and celebrity crushes on their bedroom walls. During this season of emerging desires, I spent enormous amounts of time escaping into literature, reading late into the night under my covers. I found poetry and classic literature, and they spoke to me of passionate love, loss, and hope, articulated in dramatic, searing words. My heart whispered to me that there was something real in these tales, to last so long and be so widely read. My creative output increased as I began to use imagination as a destination, a place where I could escape and dream about alternate ways of life.

For years, my default manner with any cute male was a dreadful combination of verbal combativeness, desperate attention-seeking, and brazen condescension. Meanwhile, Dad repeated his long-standing rule: anyone who wanted to date his daughters had to wrestle him and win. I was instructed to share this information with any boy who flattered or befriended me, and I had thus been eight years old the first time the curly-haired son of a family friend emphatically threw down a bouquet of flowers and stomped across a field to lunge headlong at my father's legs.

Mom, for her part, seemed to have lost her belief in the existence of romantic love. She became vocal about the futility and disappointments of marriage, telling me on multiple occasions that loving relationships between men and women weren't real, and the sooner I learned to forget the illusion, the better. If she had the chance to do it all again, she never would have married. She wished she could be a computer or a robot, to be rid of all emotion and pain.

"Wanting what you'll never have will only bring you pain," she said. "Try not to need it, don't expect it, and you won't miss it."

9

A GAME OF CHICKEN

FROM 2005 TO 2007, DAD'S WRESTLING BUSINESS RALLIED, THEN folded quietly. Once it was dead, my father turned his gaze fully upon his children. We would be his new business venture. He became intensely involved in every area of our lives, directing us to drop whatever interests or studies did not have a place in his larger vision of what our family would become.

Whenever we let the groundskeeper and the teachers go, or when Mom worried aloud about whether we were going to have the cash for groceries at the end of the month, I wondered where the money had gone. Hadn't we been rich? Mom said we were now in a lawsuit with the insurance company and competitors had sabotaged Dad's noble efforts to help his fellow wrestlers. There was next to nothing left because he'd put almost everything into his dreams. Thankfully, he had invested some of the original millions into something called "an annuity," which would continue to pay him a decent monthly sum for the rest of his life. Mom said this monthly income had been keeping us afloat since the fire but was being strained by our family's ever-growing enormity—little JoyAnna brought the kid count into the double digits on a crisp December day.

BETWEEN THE MUSIC AND DANCE, WE TRANSITIONED FROM PER-forming once a year to performing once a month. Although our second annual Saint Patrick's Day gig at the Nashville pub had been better than the first, we still needed to learn how to talk to an audience and sing. We weren't thinking big enough, and Dad told us we were lucky he was there to push us. As the teachers faded out, our quality of technique took a hit. But Dad was convinced stage presence was more important, and we would capitalize on the fact that we were a self-contained family unit doing it all ourselves, all siblings, all so young and impressive, and under his leadership and philosophies we'd be accomplishing something other people, other families and fathers, could not. Were we a band? A mini dance troupe? We didn't ask; we went where we were pushed, one goal after another appearing on the calendar, giving us something specific to work toward. While audiences might be delighted, my father's voice would be ringing louder in my head, "Sell it! I don't believe you! Convince me!"

He navigated the family toward the identity of the outsider; we knew things other people didn't, and we were going somewhere they couldn't follow. Friendships with neighbors or fellow musicians and dancers had a controlled and strategic place in our life. We let loose during fun times and social gatherings with an almost manic energy of release and relief. Mom repeated such sound bites as: "We are intentional about who we let our kids connect with; we want them to be inspired by the best. Our kids don't waste time with friends; they always spend their time accomplishing something amazing together. Kids get in trouble when they do nothing."

JAIR REMAINED MUSICAL LEAPS AND BOUNDS AHEAD OF THE REST of us. While Dad intensely obsessed over every detail in the life of his daughters and wife, I concluded his only goals for Jair were to make sure he got tough at some point in his life, and to push him in the arts so as not to waste his clearly viable talent. For years, Jair had insisted he hated Dad and wanted to be nothing like him, but these protests seemed to fade after Jair began to compete, and then win, in wrestling.

In late 2007, Mom connected with a Chicago music teacher who was looking to fill out two youth bands he was planning to take to the world championships of Irish music in 2008. Dad decided we needed to compete and win strategic titles that would boost the accreditation of our developing act. He had now taken us three oldest to compete in Ireland, but the lack of official school affiliation seemed to be a major roadblock. This teacher in Chicago sent us a batch of tunes to learn, and we played the recordings over and over to memorize them on our various instruments. Then we packed up and headed to Chicago for a weekend of auditions and rehearsals.

THE BESPECTACLED MUSIC TEACHER GREETED US CHEERILY WHEN we arrived at a large home in a southern suburb of the city. I was intensely excited and nervous to meet other kids my age who shared my love of Irish music. Dad stayed in the corner of the big room to keep an eye on the proceedings. Once it was established that everyone knew the core material, the teacher experimented with having players split off into harmonies, background parts, solo moments, and instrument changes. After we wrapped for the evening, we were told to come back the next day. We were in!

My elation was cut short when I noticed an ominous storm brewing in Dad's face. We zipped our cases and shuffled out in a chaotic herd. He waited until the van door slid shut and then burst upon us in outrage. With averted eyes, we listened to him berate us for our lack of assertiveness, initiative, and leadership. He expected us to be the best, the most dominant, and we'd held back, embarrassing him.

"Jess, you are so passive and mousy," he railed. "You are not *nearly* aggressive enough!"

I mumbled the necessary apologies, placating him, a habit formed after unsatisfactory practices and evaluations at home. He mocked my timid motions from the rehearsal and turned his eyebrows up in an exaggerated expression of worry.

"What's your excuse, guys?" he glared back through the rearview mirror. "Why do I spend all this money, time, and effort trying to help you get good if you're just going to drop the ball when it's time to rise to the occasion? I expect excellence! You should be the best in there."

To my surprise, he called out Jair, demanding, "How come you didn't show them what you could do on the cello?" The cello was the newest instrument in the house, and Jair was the only one who could play anything halfway decent on it. In the chilly hush, Jair's face was unreadable as Dad's insults gathered steam.

When we pulled out of the suburban neighborhood, Dad got on the highway heading south.

Mom looked at him in bewilderment. "Toby? Where are you going?"

He didn't speak, instead letting the meaning of his actions sink in as the van's wheels spun high-speed back toward Tennessee. We didn't deserve to be a part of this band; we didn't deserve to have friends and make music, so we were going home.

Throughout my childhood and teenage years, I felt embarrassed when Dad abandoned plans due to our mistakes or failures. I found myself wondering what others would think when we didn't show up to things, or schedules were changed last minute and without explanation. I didn't want people to know about Dad's anger, or that it was our punishments that frequently overflowed and ruined lovely plans. That night we'd planned to stay with friends we hadn't seen in years, and they were expecting us for dinner. Dad was showing us that pleasing and obeying him was more important than keeping appointments. He didn't care what other people thought; he would take away any reward if he found us unworthy.

Though Mom tried to negotiate a compromise, Dad refused to turn around or slow his course. Each of us took turns begging for forgiveness, except Jair. Soon we were nudging him, motioning and whispering that he needed to say he was sorry. Dad could not let Jair's defiance beat his fatherly wrath. It was a game of chicken—a test to see whose will could hold out longer.

We traveled almost two hours south as the sun slid farther down in the sky. Suddenly, the van lurched sideways, vibrating on the rumble strip as Dad pulled off to the shoulder. When the engine switched off, my sleepy body snapped into high alert, predicting an incoming spanking. I was in the front row, smack-dab in the middle of the whacking zone. But Dad didn't come to the side door. Instead, he stood by the forward corner of the van, hands on his hips, shoulders slumping dejectedly, watched the passing traffic. We renewed our pleading with Jair.

"Jair, can't you just apologize? The rest of us already did."

Mom also reminded Jair that even if Dad was in the wrong, the child was still required to submit to the parent, in deference and respect. She was a dedicated believer in apologizing whether or not one was at fault. When she faced forward again, we realized we couldn't see Dad anymore. This development spread fresh alarm throughout the vehicle: we had been left on the side of the highway. I could hear Dad's implied condemnation: *Look what you've done.* We opened the side door, both to look for Dad and to let in fresh air. It had become stuffy inside the packed van without the air-conditioning, and Dad had taken the keys when he got out.

We began to theorize about where Dad could have gone. Our eyes strained up and down the busy road's edge, hoping we would discern his returning shape. We circled the van to make sure he wasn't hiding. While looking for the keys under the driver's seat, someone realized the black 9-mm Glock handgun that was usually stowed there, locked in a travel case, was missing. Within minutes of this discovery, we were hoping against hope our father hadn't taken it with him into the scraggly Illinois tree line to purposefully end his life. We asked if anyone had seen the gun earlier on the trip; if not, perhaps it had been left at home. While this was obviously much more likely, I was stunned at Jair's sudden reaction. He collapsed on his knees into the stiff grass, his head thrown back to face the sky with an expression of anguish, and his fists balled tight at the end of his extended arms. The game of chicken was over.

DAD WAS STILL MISSING WHEN A PASSING COP PULLED UP TO SEE IF we needed any assistance. We scrambled back into the van and the toddlers shushed at Mom's warnings. Mom told the cop we were on a family road trip and her husband had pulled over while most of us were asleep. She assumed he was checking a tire or something, and we didn't know where he'd gone. The officer took a moment to absorb her story, then peered into the van to ask if everyone was okay. Though Mom said we were fine, I wondered who else had the word *gun* ricocheting around their head as they smiled and nodded. I always felt nervous around police officers. We had long been told if we misbehaved in public and Mom or Dad had to spank us, there was a chance that cops, medical workers, or nosy neighbors might try to take us away from our parents by calling the Department of Children's Services. So I held my breath in the hope we would avoid further questions. The officer drove away and was gone for twenty nail-biting minutes. When he came back, Dad was with him, as impenetrable as a brick wall.

"Found him at the nearest gas station, ma'am," said the cop. "Are you sure you're okay?" he asked one more time. When Mom assured him we were, he dipped his hat with a nod and left.

Jair and Dad had a short conversation out of earshot, then they both climbed back in the van, and we turned back toward Chicago. We arrived at our friends' home at an ungodly hour of night and went straight to bed in sleeping bags on their basement playroom floor. As I faded into dreams, I tried to keep my emotions in control. I didn't want to admit how betrayed the temporary abandonment had made me feel. Dad was making it clear: he could only take so much disappointment.

10

DISCOVERY

THE BEGINNING OF 2008 WAS FILLED WITH PREPARATIONS FOR both the Irish music competition and our annual pub gig. On Saint Patrick's Day, in the middle of the show, Mom broke a guitar string and had to step aside to replace it before we could continue. We had no backup plan for this turn of events, and the empty seconds stretched out like millennia as I froze at my mic in the fringe of the stark stage lights. Dad had been hard after me to learn to sing for this gig. I had a short list of traditional songs whose melodies I could hum. Instead, I was obsessed with a ten-minute-long recording of an epic poem which had been set to music. For some strange and terrifying reason, standing in the vacuum of the silent stage, those poetic verses were the only words coming to mind.

"Tell a joke!" someone in the family hissed from behind me as I stepped closer to the mic.

I announced to the jostling, beer-sloshed crowd that I was going to sing a cappella. Though it took a few lines for the crowd to notice my voice, thin and unpracticed, they grew quieter as I continued. I closed my eyes and disappeared into the story of the song. The words were over a hundred years old, and as I conjured them, I felt connected to the singers and keepers of folklore. Whatever this powerful magic was, I desired to be a part of it, to both lose myself and find myself in something bigger, older, and powerful enough to make a boisterous crowd hold their breath. I felt suspended in a welcoming eternity. As the song ended, I opened my eyes. Mom stood ready with the new string.

I VENTURED FURTHER INTO COMPOSING, SEARCHING FOR MORE OF what I'd tasted under the influence of the old song. Around the same time, a huge wave of creative inspiration came when we met another band of Irish-music-playing kids while performing at a local festival. They were close to our ages and lived in a secluded Christian village, all homeschooled, home-churched, and taught to be different from the world. In some ways, they seemed like our family on steroids—if we kept going in the direction we were headed for another generation or two. We traveled for hours to visit their unique community multiple times. Dad compared philosophical points and expressed to us how he could envision a compound and community superior to theirs. I was given permission to keep in touch with the young men in the band if it produced tangible results. We shared original tunes through carefully monitored emails, which drove my desire to learn more about music recording. Dad had accumulated equipment, and we soon had the solid beginnings of a home studio set up in my parents' room across from their bed.

That summer, I spent many late-night hours watching Dad learn how to use editing tools so I could replicate what I remembered the next morning. He gave me special permission to document my compositions and a free pass on any chore duty if I was writing or recording. When I took one of my piano melodies and layered in pads, beats, and vocal effects, Dad encouraged me to flesh it out in its entirety, saying he liked what I had so far. He kept checking in on my progress after each session and commented on one piece's climactic style. After a few more choicely worded compliments, I realized he was implying he found the piece sensual, even orgasmic, and wanted me to know as much.

ABOUT A WEEK LATER, I WAS LISTENING TO THE PIECE FROM THE beginning, checking to see if I should mix any of the layers differently. I was lying on the bed, my head propped up on my elbows, eyes closed, my bare feet swaying back and forth to the trancelike rhythm. As the track played, I heard it like one sees an X-ray, hearing past the surface to trace the bones and the layers all knitting together. The bedroom door opened and shut, and tension immediately jumped into my body. I wished I wasn't on the bed. Dad walked to the computer as the drums and vocals ended.

"Mind if I start this over?" he asked, his thick finger already pressing the space bar without waiting for my answer.

There was no transition; I went from floating alone in my musical world of calm to my father's heavy form behind and above me, my mind locking me away from my body, which went senseless. My thoughts were spacey and disconnected. He took his penis out of his pants, bent back the waistband of the black shorts he'd bought me, and pinned me to the bed with his weight while sliding back and forth against the top of my butt.

This isn't happening, I tried to tell myself.

The song was almost done when he shifted, and my entire body jolted. From what I knew, he was only a few inches away from my entrance. His weight withdrew from my back, and I could breathe again. I was worried by how agitated he seemed, mortified as he examined my newly fuzzy area.

What happened? What is he looking for? I panicked.

The invisible girl couldn't help me much anymore. I felt like a flapping fish out of water, clumsy and stupid. I was barely sixteen and terrified by what I didn't know about the body I was living in.

THE NEXT TIME I WAS ABLE TO GET ON THE INTERNET WITH NO ONE around, I googled, "How many holes do girls have?" and "How do I know if I'm a virgin?" Both searches delivered a wealth of information. While I sighed with relief to know my father had not vaginally penetrated me, it was chilling to realize how close he had been. I could never feel like a "good girl" again. I stumbled across a forum of people talking about harmful sexual encounters and was stunned to learn other girls suffered under the sexual attentions of their fathers. I closed the internet window hurriedly when I found a post by a girl who'd been impregnated by her father. Because of my period, I knew I could get pregnant, and that was almost on par with death in my mind.

My father and I crossed into a new era. Though he would always continue his suggestive comments and "accidental" brushes, he never again performed another explicit sexual act on me. Over time, he would make increasingly wild remarks, like how he wished he was free to take more than one wife and was jealous of other men who could have me. Leaving no room to doubt his meaning, he once said, "I know it's crass, but I wish I could fuck you." No one had ever said that word to my face before. As much as it should have disturbed me, I found it easy to tune out his words, to block them from my conscious recall, thankful for whatever kept his hands away. He soon made it clear there were other, nonphysical things he wanted from me.

In May, we qualified for the Irish Music Championships with the Chicago-based youth band. We would be going to Tullamore, Ireland, later that summer to take our shot at the world title. To my great relief, Mom would be accompanying us oldest five kids while Dad stayed home with the younger half, since he had gone last time. Traveling with Dad had already resulted in some deeply disturbing memories.

In August, our youth band placed second in the world, three points behind first place. It was a superb result for an American band. Dad swore, however, that we were done going over to Ireland, done trying to play their game. I wondered how much money had been spent on the trip, all for a near miss and no titles.

The lawsuit with the insurance company dragged on into its fourth ugly year. Somehow, they kept paying our rent, allowing us to upgrade to a bigger house. We were a family of ten kids now, seven girls and three boys. The new rental had six bedrooms, so each of us older girls shared a room with a younger girl, spreading us into a sisterly buddy system. My parents moved into the second-biggest bedroom and the rectangular master bedroom became the music studio where I would spend most of my time.

In January 2009, Dad made "write a song" one of my sister's school assignments. My sister protested, pointing out she had never been assigned such a task, so he added me to the project. Though he had long been pushing me to write lyrics, I had so far resisted. I ignored the assignment, and when my sister and I missed the deadline of the week, he marched us to the piano and pulled a love song out of us, line by line. Dad didn't seem perturbed when the lyrics I coughed up dreamed rather pointedly about being set free from chains and calling for someone to find me and help me escape. Instead, he wanted to arrange and record it as soon as possible.

We debuted the song at our next annual Saint Patrick's Day gig. The heavy prerecorded elements made it difficult for me to hear my own voice, and I chickened out on most of the important notes. I shriveled in embarrassment and left the stage, once again swearing to myself I was done with performing. I headed to the bathroom, trying not to cry while navigating the inebriated crowd. Suddenly, a short, red-cheeked man bounced into my view.

"Are you guys signed?" he shouted above the racket, inches from my face. He had a foamy drink in his hand, a twinkle in his eye, and a few flecks of spit at the top of his goatee. "Are you signed?" he repeated. When I shook my head, he asked, "Who's your manager?"

"My mom, I guess," I answered.

He put a hand on my shoulder, and his shiny forehead bobbed forward as he declared with a grin, "This is your big break!"

We'd had people give us cards, make claims, and try to impress us with credentials before, but Mom and Dad had generally steered clear of the music industry and its offerings. This guy chatted animatedly with my mother and kept insisting this was our big moment. He called the next morning saying he was serious about wanting to help us and invited us to play a mini showcase for his boss, who ran a country music label.

There was much hubbub at this opportunity, and Dad decided to overhaul and optimize the band. Mom was out because she was now pregnant with baby number eleven. Jet was told to step up to the plate and learn to play whistle, and Jair switched to guitar, all in a matter of a few short weeks. Dad arranged for the showcase to be professionally filmed so no matter what happened with the label, we could have snazzy footage to use for our own purposes. During practice, Dad told me to stop shutting my eyes when I sang, stop being mousy. I needed to move more, be more expressive and entertaining, stop looking so terrified. We didn't talk about what would happen if the label liked what they heard.

The day of the filming came, and the sight of the stage made my gut clench tight. Fog machines were pumping out billows of smoke and the technicians were testing spotlights and swirling beams of color. The drums drowned out all other noise in my ears during sound check, and the flashing lights turned everything beyond the stage edge into a blinding black sea. I would have to focus on invisible points and smile at imaginary faces while trying to move, entertain, and sing on pitch.

It was all over in a flash. A wave of people moved forward to congratulate us as soon as the lights blinked off, and we beamed bright smiles, shook hands, and recited our names and ages when asked. Dad talked up our future potential and elaborated on plans for domination in music and dance.

After the first label officially passed on signing us, the industry man promised to introduce us to other business associates, his interest in our future unabated. In the meantime, he advised us to consider narrowing our focus to better convey our brand. Dad rejected the idea that we needed to limit ourselves to be understood or fit into a preexisting category inside an industry. We weren't just a band, or a dance troupe, or a family. We were the living test results of his philosophy, which he would share on his terms or not at all.

He had been toying with the idea that maybe television would be a good fit for us. He began staging parts of our everyday life and got a videographer friend to film us. Combined with the showcase footage, they created trailers and mini episodes in case there was an opportunity to share them at the next big meeting. The sooner I got used to seeing my face on-screen, the better.

DAD INSISTED HE HAD GIVEN ME THE PERMISSION AND OPPORTU- nity to create, and now he asserted his right to see the results. He would find me bent over a notebook or journal in the studio, work- ing at the edges of an idea, and would sneak up and snatch the papers away. Though I'd scramble and lunge, he would run out of the room as I yelled in panic, "I'm not ready to show anyone yet!" He ignored my protests, waving my half-written verses triumphantly above his head.

If I pursued, he ran to his room and locked the door. If I caught him or fought, he swatted me away. If I wrestled harder, he pinned me to the ground. When he centered the entirety of his weight over my chest, it was a fight just to breathe, and he laughed when I pinched, dug my nails into his limbs, or tried twisting his dead- locked fingers. Since the days of Jair's toddlerhood, we'd all been conditioned to ignore whoever might be receiving this treatment, so my mother and siblings tuned out the periodic commotion, just as I had when I was younger.

We attended a swing dance competition in Atlanta where I met a young tap dancer with violet eyes. We danced for hours on the last night of the event, then tumbled into a pair of chairs to catch our breath. He pulled my seat closer so we could continue talking over the music without having to shout. "Tell me a secret," he said cheekily, and my heart lurched at the suggestion. I asked him what he meant. "Tell me something about you no one else knows."

Though I never saw him after that weekend, I wrote in a fever of delicious sensations all the way home to Tennessee. Spinning the words "tell me a secret" into lyrics and a melody, I let myself imagine what it would have been like to tell, to ask in return, and what might have followed. I felt like leaping and screaming in exuberance when I finished, emerging from the flow of inspiration with a new sense of identity, tiny and juvenile as the initial taste may have been. Thus, I confirmed, it was the pen, not the stage, that was capable of lighting me up with a blaze of pleasure. Never leaving my seat in a raucous van, I had found another world. I could visit it anytime I wanted; all I had to do was go inward and let the words come out.

When Dad finally heard it, he decided the song was perfect for one of next year's swing dance routines. To me, this confirmed the message that I had the continued favor of my father and his permission to write if I was willing to pay the required tax. I surrendered. If I brought a new song to Dad—and by extension, the newly emerging band—with reasonable frequency, I was given the freedom to stay up past bedtime and express to my heart's content. Boys remained a consistent source of material, along with folklore and our accumulating travels. Sometimes I was still in the studio scribbling or recording when the purple-pink light of morning crept up from the horizon. Then I would sneak into bed next to my sleeping sister with a heady buzz behind my aching eyes.

11

FIRST KISS

For the first time in Tennessee, Mom was going to try a home birth. We were still forty-five minutes from a major hospital, and no doctors would come to the home. I suppose she figured that between the midwives and her, they had more than enough experience to bring a baby into the world. She carried late, and it wasn't until a clear Sunday morning in early October that the signs of imminent labor began.

Although I had hovered at the edge of a handful of births, this one felt different. I was nervous—less about my mother and more about how much closer I figured I was to my own childbearing. I was seventeen. Much emphasis had been put on the goal of being prepared for marriage and having babies by age eighteen. Suddenly, that seemed too close, too fast. I was assured my preparation was superior to most girls'; I knew about nursing, the importance of keeping the baby in the parents' bed, how vaccines and birth control were bad, how delivery should be natural—no drugs or painkillers—and in the home if possible. As I imagined my own body going through what my mother was about to go through, I did not feel ready.

When the two midwives arrived, Mom was already set up in her bed. Events went much the same as what I remembered from previous times, except now we older girls helped in switching out towels and placing warm oil compresses on my mom's swollen vagina. Dad was not a man who waited nervously in a quiet lobby while his wife labored. He was up on the bed bracing Mom during contractions and telling jokes during the breaks. Mom's face went brilliantly red, sucking in great gulps of air to bear down on the task at hand. Her grip on Dad went white-knuckled as the midwives encouraged her. In my childhood, it had been a point of pride that she did not scream. Now I didn't know how she couldn't. The opening began to dilate further and what I knew was a head began to show.

"One more push," the midwife urged, "and this boy will be here."

Dad was sweating and nodding. "Good job, Bren. You're almost done."

But they were wrong. Instead of passing, the contraction seemed to stay, refusing to give up its grip on Mom's distended belly. The concentration wavered in her face, overshadowed by the first appearance of fear. Her next gasp was different, and her eyebrows turned sharply upward. "The pain . . . ," she was saying. "Something's not right."

The midwives glanced at each other nervously.

"It's not supposed to feel like this," Mom cried urgently. The baby was now in a stressed position and things needed to continue progressing or there would be real danger both for the baby and Mom.

In a moment, everything shifted. We were going to have to rush them to the hospital and every second was going to count. Dad shouted for the boys to take the bench seats out of the van, and blankets were thrown hastily in the vacated space. Mom had to be carried from the bed, an ashen-faced Jair helping Dad with the load down the stairs. She was covered as best as possible and moaning quietly. A midwife climbed in alongside them. Dad would drive and Jair would have to do his best to brace Mom during the ride. Jen and Jet would stay and watch the little ones. Someone tossed me the midwife's car keys in a rushed arc, and they landed in the dusty grass at my bare feet. I tore into the house to grab my shoes and my brand-new, barely used driver's license. I hit a hundred miles per hour in a stranger's car, trying to keep the van in sight as it sped down the highway toward the city. By the time I arrived at the hospital, Mom had already been rushed away into surgery.

THE GRAVITY OF THE SITUATION WAS THROWN INTO STARK RELIEF only after the drama had run its course. Mom had almost died, and baby Jaeger with her. She had needed an emergency C-section and two units of blood. The stress of a recent cough had likely weakened her abdominal muscles, and her compromised uterus had shredded under the extreme strain of trying to push the baby out. I heard no discussion or consideration of how much preexisting damage could have come from the ten previous births. Because the baby was already in the birth canal, there were no external signs of the tearing and hemorrhaging back at home, only the sudden and inexplicable pain. When the doctors began operating at the hospital, it was in the last possible moments to prevent death. There was talk of large pools of blood being mopped up from the floor. Though the surgeons worked for hours trying to stitch everything back together, they said it was highly unlikely Mom would be able to have any more children.

WE RARELY MET ANOTHER FAMILY AS LARGE AS OUR OWN, BUT when we did, there was a strong chance we shared similar beliefs. If our parents got along, we might get new homeschooling Christian friends out of the bargain. And if any of the kids happened to wrestle, dance, or play music, our parents would usually make great efforts to get us together. Mom and Dad were transparent about this being an intentional way to filter the people we had the opportunity to be interested in. Dad was determined that we should find people who checked the right boxes for marriage and that any potential relationships would be handled according to his detailed rules.

I felt both anticipation and apprehension for what I'd been prepared for my whole life, eager for the permission to begin a relationship but not ready to experience what I had just seen my mother endure. If I met and liked a boy around my age, I was allowed to exchange approved letters or an email once a week. Despite this rule, I sent frequent volleys of flirty emails, knowing I would eventually be chided. I was disheartened by how unsuitable Dad found each crush. I would argue, prod, and debate until I found something of my own to criticize, and then my interest would fizzle out.

Sometime in my seventeenth year, we met an extra-large Catholic family with many handsome sons. The boys wrestled and joined the army, the girls did Irish step dance, and sing-alongs were common at their family gatherings. Dad surprised me when he indicated he was not deterred by their religious beliefs, saying he could change someone's mind on doctrine as needed, if all other aspects were suitable.

Peyton, the third oldest son, seemed more than suitable to Dad. He was a respected captain in the army, kind, easygoing, and joyous. In his midtwenties, I found him both endlessly dreamy and intimidatingly mature. His hair was close-cropped, and faint freckles dusted his square-jawed face.

My parents thought it was high time to resurrect our old tradition of hosting parties for servicemen and their families. We started a potluck-and-outdoor-fun day on a monthly basis, and Peyton brought the men who served under his command. He was so completely sweet and attentive to everyone, playing with the little kids and conversing politely with Dad, that I seriously doubted whether he was interested in me at all.

When it came time for Peyton to leave town for specialized training, Dad decided I hadn't done enough. "Who's taking him to the airport?" he asked. Peyton had told me his travel plans were already set. Dad was decisive. "You should ask to take him instead."

At my age, I was embarrassed to admit I was still afraid to drive. Despite my misgivings, I didn't think of refusing Dad's suggestion. I asked Peyton if I could be his ride to the airport and he said yes. Dad said I should kiss him goodbye. Mom thought this was too much, but when she wasn't around, Dad later reiterated the idea while I was giving him a foot rub in his room. "You kiss him before he leaves, Jess." I wondered if this was a test. He insisted he was serious.

IT WAS OVERCAST YET WEIRDLY BRIGHT ON THE DAY I WENT TO PICK up Peyton. My hands trembled slightly on the flaking steering wheel. When I parked at the predetermined place, I was seized with the indecision of what to do in the moment. Should I park, turn off the car, and get out? Should I help with the bags, or wave casually from the driver's seat? I was going to feel awkward no matter what; this was the first time I was allowed to be alone with a man who may or may not have had an interest in me.

He said hello, courteous and neutral. I could barely conduct any conversation on the way to the airport. Without looking over at him, I tried to imagine touching his lips with my own. We pulled up to the terminal's curb and got out. He retrieved his bags. I hugged him and said a modest goodbye, accepting the inevitability of my father's disappointment. After he stepped away, there was an interval where his scent hovered on my person and I noticed it perfectly matched his manner: pleasant, polite, and unassuming—something nice to be around.

"One more thing," I stammered and tipped forward, moving my face toward his until our lips made a whisper of contact. He made no move. I instantly knew that I should never again let my father's commands be the reason I do such a thing. Peyton did me the courtesy of not laughing or running, instead folding me into another hug where it was impossible to see his face. It was all I could do not to spew out a torrent of apologies for making it so awkward. I would likely never have to see this man again, but I had to go home and face my father.

When I arrived home from the airport, Dad was waiting expectantly for a report, sitting on the pillows at the top of his bed with his computer open in his lap. I told him it went fine.

"Did you kiss him?" he asked me point-blank.

"Yes," I admitted.

His mouth twisted wryly, and he refused to believe I'd obeyed him. My foolishness saddened me. Didn't I yet know how pointless it was to try to please him?

"Liar," he said. And it stung.

12

TIME BOMB

SOMEHOW, AGAINST ALL ODDS, MOM WAS PREGNANT AGAIN. Number twelve. *How dare he?* I found myself fuming. It had been mere months since his wife had nearly died on an operating table, yet my father couldn't be bothered to think about anything beyond his own pleasure. In the past, Mom had confided in me how Dad tended to get impatient about the resumption of his sex life after she gave birth. She seemed worried, frightened even, but there was nothing she could do about it now. An early C-section would be scheduled, and we prayed her still-unhealed body could hold out until then.

Despite the doctors urging her to take it as easy as possible, Mom continued to be our *de facto* manager and booking agent, learning how to leverage connections and social opportunities to advance the band's growth. That spring, we were offered a slot during Dollywood's upcoming bluegrass festival, only six weeks away.

"Well, we don't play bluegrass," Mom explained to the booker.

Dad, however, seized upon the opportunity as a sign and decided not only would we learn a new style of music within the following six weeks—and buy and learn how to play new instruments—we would also record our first album to sell at the event. Deadlines were good, he assured us; they would push us to accomplish what we thought was impossible.

Although we did not become a bluegrass band by June, we surprised ourselves by indeed producing a CD by the deadline. It had a four-part harmony gospel song, a few Irish-styled originals, and new hastily written songs that referenced either hoedowns or God. We pulled all-nighters printing and labeling them ourselves, marveling at the physical result we could hold in our hands after what felt like a crucible of effort.

ONE ACCOMPLISHED DEADLINE BEGAT ANOTHER. DAD ACQUIRED a new favorite saying: "It's your job to know." It proved versatile and effective, echoing through our home with repetitive intensity, bringing clarity to every situation: No, we could not expect more time to develop a specific skill, nor could we hope for help or support from Dad. Life-changing career opportunities were revealing themselves daily, and somehow, we were dreadfully behind.

Dad elected himself the leadman, the general at the top of the pecking order, to whom we needed to feed information and results in a timely manner. Other parents failed to love their children when they didn't push them hard enough. When we seemed ungrateful for his efforts, he was quick to point out how he was sacrificing many a dream of his own to help us be successful. If, as a boy, he had received the training and support he was giving us, his achievements would surely have outshone us all.

"Do you think Mom and I get to do what we want?" he would question us, answering himself after a purposeful pause. "No, we don't have time for that! We're too busy helping you. A team is judged by its weakest player, a village by its weakest member."

My journal entries oscillated between self-criticism when I lacked productivity and relief when I won my father's praise. I would gush with exuberance after days of songwriting or traveling, then struggle to keep a consistently positive outlook, writing, "I need to keep God's will in focus and be kinder to my siblings." And, "Only Jesus can save me with his daily grace. I am sick and fallen. God, please help me keep my eyes on you. Forgive my bad attitude. Make me kind and pleasant."

OUR BURGEONING CAREER WAS NOT THE ONLY SOURCE OF PRES-sure in our lives. As our family's unique worldview continued to evolve, Dad introduced us oldest kids to the Christian concept of "systematic theology," the comprehensive discipline that sets out to determine what the Bible teaches on fundamental topics such as ecclesiology (the study of the church), soteriology (the study of salvation), and eschatology (the study of prophecy and the end-times). It was another step toward heady intellectual knowledge. A part of me saw it as a theoretical exercise rather than the natural result of sincerely held beliefs. It seemed unlikely that my father could truly believe these endless doctrines. He scoffed at me when, in a moment of vulnerability, I asked him to pray with me.

"Look," he said. "I don't know what you want from me, but if we're going to discuss spiritual things, you need to get your systematical theology done. Then we can talk."

I had long heard terms like *Antichrist* and *the day of the Lord*, but it wasn't until our home church worked its way through the book of Revelation that my father expected us older kids to learn, memorize, and keep watch for the awful signs that would signal God's impending physical return. Dad saw himself at the forefront of the search for prophetic truth, warning there was hardly anyone else in the world interpreting the Scriptures with such accuracy. He came to believe practical preparation would be wise, so we began stockpiling food rations in the old gun range on the property where the house had burned down. He purchased more guns, including a slew of class-three AR-15 rifles fitted with silencers. We were taught about the 1992 tragedy of Ruby Ridge, where a secluded homeschooling, end-times-prepping family had been targeted by government agents with devastating consequences. It served as a chilling example of how we might one day need to be prepared to defend our freedom.

"The government can't take away a kid who's carrying an assault rifle," Dad taught us.

At the time, I was unsure which possibility was more frightening—the idea that the fast-approaching end of the world was going to be so unthinkably horrible, or that we might have to defend ourselves against domestic forces intent on tearing our family apart. On good days, the danger was hardly believable, but I was good at half-believing unbelievable things.

WE WERE SUITING UP FOR OUR GROUP RUN ON A SUNNY MORNING when Dad came down the stairs with his laptop tucked under his arm. I was battling nausea attacks before workouts, especially if I knew Dad was going to be present. Instead of joining us, he launched into an update on the latest end times theories he had been debating online.

"So, here's a wild question," he began with raised eyebrows. "When Satan and the fallen angels are kicked out of heaven and sent to earth, will they be visible or invisible? If they are visible, it's gonna be crazy—a straight-up alien invasion. Think *Independence Day*, and all the other movies."

Everyone within earshot took this outburst in stride.

"And just think," he continued. "Jesus will be showing up with his own alien-like armies soon after. We know *that's* going to be visible. Scripture says the whole world will see it. So, maybe when Satan arrives, he'll say he and his demons are allies coming to help defend against an intergalactic dictator who's coming to conquer the planet and subjugate humanity. Satan could literally convince the world their only hope is to fight back, to rebel against God."

Dad regularly reported to us the relevant news out of the Middle East, highlighting people and events that seemed to be lining up with prophecy. He was more certain than ever that the end was drawing near. I struggled not to be disappointed when he first warned I might not live long enough to be married.

"I wonder, too," said Dad, "when the rapture happens, right before Jesus wages war, what does that look like? The Bible says it's an awful time to be pregnant or old. What if the rapture is more like a rescue mission, where we have to go to an extraction point if we want to make it?"

I stared down at my double-knotted running shoes as he continued.

"The Bible says even some of the elect will be deceived. What if it's a choice? You would have to be willing and able to board the helicopter or know enough to get on the right UFO. If you don't know your eschatology, you could get it wrong. If you don't run fast enough, you might miss your ride."

After Dad wrapped up his remarks, I stepped out on the porch with an extra prick of discomfort in my belly. I began running down the driveway, fighting an all-consuming cocktail of resentment, panic, and doubt building inside me.

If that's who God is, I don't want to be on his side.

The strength and bitter venom of my rebellious thought appalled me. Who was I to judge God? If he wanted, he could strike me down right now. I was teetering on a slippery slope, feeling my belief waver. Did I *really* in my heart of hearts believe God was coming back? Maybe I wasn't scared enough. As my heartrate rose and my breath became labored, the familiar animal terror began to push my feet forward. This time, it wasn't my father snapping at my heels; it was the God who saw fit to put me under my father's authority in the first place.

I thought, *Dad is a raving lunatic.* Then also, *What if he's right?*

I wished so badly I could prove he was wrong on so many things. If he was wrong, I wouldn't have to fight back such fear. I hoped not all men were like him. I hoped I wouldn't die before my adult life began. I hoped God wasn't the sort of God who would leave someone behind because they couldn't run fast enough.

ONE SLOW AFTERNOON LATER THAT SUMMER, I PICKED UP ON AN eerie energy shift in the house. I was drawn down the hall to the boys' bedroom, knowing I would find a storm inside. Mom was sitting on the floor. A few other kids were there, a tense congregation.

"What happened?" I asked Mom, after a stretch of charged silence.

Her face was as grim as I'd ever seen, nostrils flared with force.

"Dad has been doing inappropriate stuff to one of the little girls," she pronounced quietly.

I reeled, my awareness splitting in an instant. At first I assumed my ears had stopped working correctly; my heart was not similarly confused.

In the years since Mom had first asked me if Dad had touched me, there were sporadic clashes about suspicious behavior on his part, where she would confront him or demand to know what was going on, checking with us girls or threatening to do something.

"What do you mean?" I floundered, my pulse pounding. "What . . . like me? When?"

Mom jerked her head in a terse nod. "Worse. She just came to me, crying."

I had never shared any details with Mom. I had protected her from knowing. How could she compare what had happened to me? I wanted to never go back, to never speak of it.

Jair barreled into the room behind me, and I turned away, trying not to look at him. My throat felt like it was constricting, as did the walls of the room, folding in and down upon my head. *Bury me*, I pleaded.

"What's going on?" Jair demanded.

"Dad has been molesting the girls," Mom said eventually.

I was shocked. *Molested.* The word ricocheted with blinding speed around the inside of my skull, numbing everywhere it hit. I clung to the square post of the bunk bed, suddenly queasy. I had thought the word was impossible to speak. Mom had not used it when she questioned me years ago; I assumed we would never let it be said in our home.

Jair whirled to me, to Mom.

"Did he rape them?" he asked hoarsely.

"No!" my lips burst out in unison with my mother.

Stop listening, I begged my brain. *Stop tape. Stop rolling.* And I did. I ceased being actively present in my body and mind, suspending the attention required to produce clear memories. I didn't want to remember.

At some point, Dad, we older girls, Jair, and Mom ended up in the studio, sitting in a semicircle, saying strange things, like "Dad has a problem." Mom considered leaving with us kids. Dad claimed he had no memory of abusing or molesting anyone, then finally gave blanket apologies under pressure and without confession. The younger sister who had come to Mom was brought upstairs and Mom asked if she thought Dad should be made to leave. But no one made him go. I don't remember anyone asking for the details of what had happened.

Dad could be put in jail for what he had done. I don't know what it was that made me inwardly acknowledge this for the first time. Perhaps because it was happening to someone else, I finally saw his actions for what they were—a crime. But him going to jail didn't seem like a solution. It seemed unthinkable. It would only wreck and destroy our family. I still wasn't ready to give up on the hope that he would change and everything could be okay. The unity of our family, therefore, depended on our forever silence and our collective ability to adapt and manage this issue. It would be different this time; it would stop, and it would stay in the past. He said he was sorry.

I wouldn't talk about it; I would bury it. A new sense of vigilance was layered into my psyche. The weight of responsibility, worry, and danger loomed in every potential word I had to be careful never to say. It was as if a bomb was now strapped tight to my chest with the clock counting down just out of my view.

At some later point, I heard a rumor that Jair had pulled a gun on Dad. Apparently, after he had been told about the molestation, Jair confronted Dad on the front porch, demanding to know whether he had raped us. A shot may or may not have been fired into the ground. Dad had denied any wrongdoing, even going so far as to accuse Jair of committing a crime for pointing a gun at and threatening his father. Decades later, after talking with multiple siblings, some people's memories placed me at the scene, but to this day I have no memory of it.

Going forward, we all spoke as little as possible about Dad's problems, trying to believe the good in him would eventually win out. I remember vague conversations with my sister Jen, cautiously asking each other if we would ever risk telling our future husbands what had happened to us.

Mom advised pointedly, "Some things should stay between you and God."

Another time, she held a Bible in her hands, weeping. "It doesn't tell me what to do, Jess," she whispered brokenly, raising the open book like she meant to pass it to me. I wanted to tear it from her hands, throw it to the ground, and stomp madly until every page was ruined.

OUR LAST SISTER, JADA, WAS BORN LATE IN OCTOBER, JUST A FEW weeks after Jaeger's first birthday. The C-section went according to plan, and while the surgeons were in there, they tied Mom's tubes.

Now we were twelve; there would be no baker's dozen. At eight girls and four boys, the clan was complete.

A few weeks later, I found myself alone in the studio, feeling my way on the keys, playing chords and simple melodies that wordlessly reflected my inner heaviness. In the quiet, the tumult raged, fighting to the surface. How could I think I could keep such horrible things hidden forever? I began to cry. I was on the brink, wondering whether using songwriting to tap into these thoughts and sensations would be dangerous. One word came to my lips, and I sang it softly. Over and over, I repeated with the music, "It's unspeakable. It's unspeakable."

Out came an agonized lyric, the song knowing and saying things I'd spent endless energy trying not to know or think. It came all at once, more confession or journal entry than art. Later, I asked both my parents to come up to the music room alone. I played them the song with no explanation. Afterward, they sat silent as stone statues. Their faces were rigid and mute even as they left the room and closed the door. We never spoke about it again and I pretended to unwrite the song in my mind. I had the distinct impression that even though I'd felt the air passing through my throat and knew the words went out into the space, no sound had been heard. My voice was gone.

13

MEGAPHONE

With a final death gasp, the fire insurance lawsuit went into arbitration. Dad said he had to accept a lesser settlement that would never let him rebuild the house that burned. Despite this bitter loss, his plans had grown. He now dreamed of developing the property into a self-sufficient community with a large central building for gatherings and surrounding smaller cabins, residences for his future adult children and their spouses who would figure into the family business and grow the dynasty in various ways. He would soon buy a tour bus and top-shelf professional music gear so we could accept more gigs on the road. The family's performances would need to fund our future.

Dad was confident that if we could reach critical mass, our gravity would begin to pull others in. He fed on comments from his old production connections and exclamations of our growing audiences:

"Wow, you should get your own TV show!" Thanks to the sizzle reels and short teaser videos, a television deal finally did come knocking. A country TV channel, GAC (Great American Country), made an offer to shoot one pilot episode of a reality show about our family. The irony was not lost on us; we were not a country band, and we hadn't had a TV in our home for over a decade.

A whirlwind of production crews took over our daily lives for weeks at a time. Dad sparred with the writers and directors while us kids made friends with the assistants and audio guys who taped tiny mics to the inside of our necklines and waistbands. It was amusing and sometimes annoying to have to enter a room three different times or start over a conversation for the cameras. Nothing made me forget how to speak or walk quite like a cluster of cameras hovering over my shoulder. Our home environment had shifted so far from the experience of my early childhood; between the fear, the secrets, the pressure, and the endless performances, we almost didn't feel like a real family to me anymore. I felt like we were turning into cardboard cutouts, displayed under bright lights for an audience to see. Behind the curtain, I imagined our two-dimensional silhouettes connected by a chaotic tangle of cords and strings just out of view, each pulling and tugging in contradicting directions. I was happy to dance at the end of my string if it kept our secrets safely hidden and Dad in magnanimous spirits.

"THE PRODUCERS ARE LOOKING TO INCORPORATE A LOVE INTEREST for you, Jess," Dad informed me at the dining room table. He said it was a chance to showcase our beliefs on dating and relationships for the cameras. "They think it would make great TV if there was a guy who was willing to wrestle me."

No one had piqued my father's interest since Peyton, our friend from the large Catholic family, so I had no approved love interest to speak of. After I turned eighteen, a young man from our old church who'd joined the Marines came back around for a bit. He was the first man to tell me he'd marry me. Despite having finally gotten braces, I made out with him, feeling a desperate need to right the wrong of kissing someone who hadn't kissed me back. We both knew Dad would never let me date him or anyone else in any normal manner, and it ended abruptly. My braces came off just in time to avoid the television show.

Mom and Dad looked at each other across the table. "What about Mark?" one of them asked.

My face burned hot. Mark was the wrestling, fun-loving cousin of family friends, whom I had only briefly met. There was no denying I had flirted with him.

When Mom called him later on, he said yes—he was willing to be on the reality show.

The day he came rolling up the driveway in his truck, the production crew wired him with a microphone before he came into the house. The plan to shoot several scenes had been made without me and included Mark eating dinner with the family, shooting guns with my brother, and wrestling Dad. I was assured by my parents and the crew that nothing would be made awkward, but it got so bad so quickly, I asked Mark to step outside and turn off his mic. As I began apologizing, I noticed the crew trying to shoot footage of our private conversation. I was left standing in the yard, utterly incensed, as he was whisked away to interact with my brother and father without me.

Mark and I were asked about each other in separate interviews and I squirmed at the pointed questions, each of which was focused on whether I thought Mark was attractive or interested in me, trying to evade having to say something I didn't mean, and failing miserably.

It wasn't until the pilot episode aired that I saw the end result. I was mortified. Mark had jumped through the hoops Dad had set out, including wrestling him on camera. Dad gave us permission to go out for dinner and we met up with my siblings for games afterward. It was exciting to dress up and be allowed to spend a few short hours being someone else before my coach turned back into a pumpkin. I was expected to report back about the evening, and so were my siblings. Dad quizzed me, wanting to know if we talked about "the important stuff" to his satisfaction. We hadn't, of course; I had been trying to enjoy myself.

Mark continued to come to the house, and Dad added pressure with each visit. "When are you going to talk about theology, Jess?" he would ask. "What about creation?"

He challenged me to get results quickly or I would not be allowed to waste time. I needed to inspire Mark to get on board with the family's beliefs and expectations. From what I could tell, Mark's most zealous passions were focused on the next approaching hunting season. He cared about his family and would rather make sure everyone was having a good time instead of talking about books or debating Scripture.

"Don't let your heart get involved," Dad said. "Falling in love is easy. Save feelings and emotions until after you've had all the hard conversations."

I played it out as long as I could, until permission expired and Dad told me Mark was off the list. During the next family trip, I was disturbed by how quickly the attachment and chemistry vanished in the short time apart from Mark. He grew reluctant to communicate, and I eventually sent him a breakup email without ever really having had a chance to be a couple.

I decided that, in the future, I would stay away from official intentions so Dad wouldn't get more involved than he already was and the pressure wouldn't pile up so fast. Once Mark was out of the picture, Dad joked that he could hold a tournament for my hand since I was finally of marrying age.

"Which would be better for TV, wrestling or jousting?" He winked.

WHILE THE TV PILOT WAS DESIGNED TO HIGHLIGHT THE LOVE lives of us young adults, our newest collective undertaking was happening largely offscreen. The album we had made in a rush was not of a quality suited for wider release, so Dad hired his cousin Christian to work more regularly in the studio. We settled on making an album of Irish-inspired original music that could stand as our first official release to the world. We were simultaneously making one more push to win the group division at the world championships of Irish music we missed back in 2008. Dad had recanted his vow about not competing again; he seemed to want the title too badly. We could debut our album in Ireland while we were there, and if we pulled off both the win and the album, it could create a buzz around our name that had eluded us so far.

Jair and I learned to engineer along with Christian, and Dad tasked us with making sure the recording goals were accomplished. I would be confident and proud of what we were working on, only to feel defeated when Dad criticized our progress. We sometimes had to start over on a song after days of tracking. If Dad didn't like something, there was no room to negotiate. My belief in my fiddle-playing ability suffered gravely.

One summer afternoon the band was rehearsing newly arranged songs when Dad took issue with my performance. He yelled until I cowered on my knees, my creative compass whirling. I didn't know how to fix it.

"Play!" he screamed at me.

I fumbled worse the second time, wanting to disappear into the floor, my eyes stinging with tears. "I'm sorry," I cried, as I lowered my hands, intending to plead for a break.

In a sudden, violent movement, he snatched up a nearby drum-stick and hurled it full force at my face. There was no time to think; I saw his eyes flash and go hard, his jaw grind, his arm whip in a blur. Reflex kicked in and I ducked down behind the only thing available. With my eyes shut tight, I felt my fiddle take the blow. The scroll exploded, splintering the fingerboard in my hands as the snapping strings and crunching wood made a terrible, gut-wrenching clamor. I stayed frozen in shock for a few racing heartbeats, trying to process what had happened.

He'd tried to hurt me. Then I bent over the wreckage and sobbed.

I was afraid to keep grieving publicly, uncertain Dad wouldn't punish me for the damage to the instrument. If only I could turn back the moment and take the improvised missile on my chin, or my nose. I turned to the blank page for solace, pouring out a mournful lyric. In the song, my fiddle transformed into a young woman who tragically drowns in an accident. Though I was scared to sing the finished song, I faced no punishment for writing it; Dad was happy to use it for the band in the future, so I practiced singing it until I no longer cried when I got to the chorus.

I couldn't bear to get rid of the fiddle fragments, so we took them to a luthier's shop in a desperate hope that my instrument could be repaired. A few weeks later, the owner called me and said his friend had been able to give the instrument a new head and neck—a miracle. When I played her again, she still had the same sweet voice. I never asked how much Dad ended up having to pay for his outburst.

I WAS NOT THE ONLY PERSON TARGETED DURING MY FATHER'S FITS of violence. During the same season, Jair defied Dad by initially refusing to get up out of the studio chair during an argument. When he finally rose and left the room, it was with obvious annoyance. I became aware of the ensuing altercation a few seconds later when a short series of heavy footfalls crossed the loft floor above my head. A sharp crack followed, and shouts went up around the house. The unmistakable sound of tumbling bodies brought witnesses to the scene in time to see Dad and Jair fall through our parents' bedroom doorway and land heavily on the bedroom carpet. They brawled with a frenzy as the little kids wailed in panic. Mom bent over the fighting figures, screaming for them to stop so harshly her voice went almost immediately hoarse.

Dad commanded Jair to surrender. Jair insisted Dad was trying to kill him. They reached a physical stalemate, each clenching a hold they refused to give up.

"I'm the father," Dad wheezed, looming over his grown son. "He has to obey me."

Jair eventually loosened his arms only for Dad to keep his elbow barred across Jair's throat for another significant moment. As soon as he was free, Jair ran outside and refused to come back until after it was dark.

The rest of us tried to make sense of how the fight began. We learned Dad had chased Jair across the loft and swung the wooden paddle full at Jair's head. Jair ducked and the harsh blow fell instead on his left shoulder and collarbone. Seeming certain Dad was trying to kill him, Jair scrambled to defend himself.

The paddle wound was ugly. Jair's shirt was stained with blood, his shoulder swollen and excruciatingly painful. Despite weeks of prolonged bruising, he played his guitar as best he could, even as the instrument strap cut into the exact spot of injury.

IN AUGUST, WE FINALLY CRACKED THE COMPETITION CODE. WE'D signed up with a different traditional music school and brought in a well-known Irish fiddle player as musical director for our group. Other young musicians and friends were added until we hit the max of twenty band members, including the oldest six kids in our family. In County Cavan, Ireland, we played together under an enormous white tent while rain bombarded the roof above and the panel of distinguished judges listened closely. When our group name was not called for third or second place, we knew it was all or nothing. Then first place was announced, and there was a moment where no one spoke or moved. Each of us was checking whether we'd heard correctly before Jair bellowed a victorious yell. It was us. I will never forget the high, the happiness, the sense of teamwork in that special moment. I will always be proud to have been a part of that company.

We released our CD that week, playing a concert as "the Willis Clan" on the big outdoor stage in the Irish city square, and it felt like this was the real beginning. Up until then, when Mom spoke of us as a band, a professional act, it always felt embarrassing and not entirely true to me. Not to say this particular gig went significantly better. Pitches were still missed; we pushed and pulled outside the beat. Still, we were getting to the point where we could look across the stage at each other and feel a spark of joy when we nailed an ending or locked a harmony tight. I was getting used to the seizing panic of not knowing what to say between songs.

We landed our first festival that year, which went on to be the cornerstone of our touring. I only wished Mom and Dad would not continue to inflate our reputation beyond our skills, credentials, and preparation at nearly every turn. Dad insisted life was war and we needed to be the best and crush the competition, but when our band played slots between my longtime heroes, I pinched myself to test whether it was real.

After waiting to see how the first episode would be received, GAC came back and ordered a full season of the reality show. The cameras followed us to dance competitions and concerts. Dad determined our next album would need to be countrified. When I questioned why we were doing TV, Dad said it was God's will for our family. It widened our audience and the reach of our testimony more than any concert ever could. Both he and Mom liked to say, "If God doesn't want us to do something, he knows how to stop us. Remember us trying to find a house in Chicago? All we have to do is walk through the doors he opens for us, and he will direct our steps."

At the time, I needed to believe we had long been preparing for a purpose, a specific calling, and Dad was the one with a grand vision of what that was. When critics shared concerns about the conflicting elements of our message and brand, Dad instead countered that it was our goal to be "the Navy SEALs of life," an elite team that was the best at anything and everything. Such a message made me feel like my family membership could be revoked at any time; I wasn't anywhere close to being the best at anything I did. Dad nevertheless shared grand ideas of revolutionizing education, society, and art.

At some point, I was told I had concluded my high school education—without ceremony or verification. I suspected there were major holes in my learning and was afraid I would be found wanting by others if I ever took a formal measure of my schooling.

Meanwhile, the cameras gave Dad an audience to witness his genius as he stalked through the house demanding updates and status reports about costumes and chores. "Impress me!" was his new favorite catchphrase. Now he had his megaphone; and with it, he could continue to grow his power.

Part 2

14

STRING THEORY

IT BECAME HARDER THAN EVER TO KEEP TRACK OF MY INNER SELF. Everything was about the family, the band, God's will, preparing for the next opportunity. I was merging with the whole, dancing on my string. It was confusing for those who tried to get to know me and confusing for me. If an original thought or feeling slipped through in a moment of vulnerability, I would negate it with my own lips a second later if doing so would keep me in good standing with my ever-present father. I modeled the teachings and proclaimed the party lines.

For the better part of a year, I was allowed to be pen pals with an idealistic young man from Missouri who was nuts about everything Celtic and Tolkien. I channeled into him my outbursts of angsty energy and ideological sound bites. Instead of going glassy-eyed, he responded in kind. He was eager to become my father's disciple on every subject and would have been first in line if Dad had actually hosted a jousting tournament. As our connection strengthened, Dad became wary and warned me to keep my options open. He now told me I should actively collect and maintain a roster of guys without becoming exclusive with any of them. It would be better to let time tell who was willing to learn and achieve the most. Instead, when the boy from Missouri next came to visit, I fell asleep on his shoulder. Afterward, Dad banished him soundly and I did not outwardly protest.

I was pushed to compile a checklist of requirements for any interested suitors and found myself increasingly discouraged. Our religious beliefs were enough to narrow the pool of potential candidates to almost nothing. I fell into disillusion. I had let my father mold me according to his vision, yet it was never enough, the target was always moving, the punishments were escalating, and I didn't like who I had become.

MY FAMILY COULD DROP PEOPLE WITH BREATHTAKING SPEED, ONE day welcoming an individual or family into our life, dazzling them with energy and aggressive positivity, and then judge them, make them "other," and leave them behind without explanation. Our closed system and hectic schedule left little time to examine or contest who was cast off in our wake. If Dad feared attachment or influence had developed between an outsider and one of us kids, a ruthless banishment would be triggered, accompanied by ridicule or criticism as needed. He didn't bother trying to hide these tactics and articulated them as one of his choice methods for maintaining unity and control. He called it his "string theory."

"It's one of the main problems in society today," he said. "Parents lose influence over their kids when they send them outside the home for education and relationships. Imagine a string between the parent and the child. Then imagine strings between the child and their friends, teachers, and the outside world. The parent's string needs to be strong enough to win the tug-of-war when the child is pulled in another direction."

When he removed people from our lives, he was actively chopping off developing strings, ending potential threats that could lead us away from him and the family's direction. Over time, I wondered if bits and pieces of me were getting amputated along with my would-be bonds.

Mom never pushed me to acquire suitors, but rarely would she go against Dad and make allowances for me to cultivate real connections, even with other girls. More than once, I sat at her feet begging for the freedom to have regular relationships while she continued to disapprove of my spending time with people without agenda. "Why are you guys so obsessed with having friends who don't want to do anything?" she asked, letting her exasperation show. "It's such a waste of time!"

I couldn't articulate what I knew I was missing and so strongly desired to build. Soon, I was twenty-one years old without a car, a phone, or money and time of my own. What I wanted couldn't be built through weekly emails and annual group visits.

EVEN BOOKS BECAME DANGEROUS—POTENTIAL STRING-BUILDERS and sources of dissenting viewpoints. My parents had always done their best to monitor and vet any movies and music inside the home, with books being the least regulated. I talked Mom into buying a popular young adult series called *The Hunger Games*. I passed the series down to my siblings as soon as I was done. We were primed to be enthusiastic for any fandom, already functioning as a built-in club of trivia geeks. Discussing this world created a buzz of conversation Dad couldn't help but notice. He became furious with Mom for not consulting him about the purchase, letting his kids read something he knew nothing about. The books were confiscated, and Dad gathered us oldest kids for a meeting when he had finished reading them for himself.

Although I don't know what I had been expecting, I was thoroughly surprised by his quiz: if I had been the girl in the love triangle, which boy would I have picked? Option A: the traumatized, broken baker boy who had gone through hell with her? Or option B: the handsome yet radicalized military upriser? I knew whom Dad would want me to claim, so I chose the baker boy.

Dad was incensed. For hours, he lectured the group of us angrily, at a loss at how I could be so stupid. Didn't I know the end was coming? We could very soon find ourselves having to protect our stores of food by force or fend off unbelievers who had taken the "mark of the beast." How could the rest of my family count on me to keep the faith if I fell in love with the wrong kind of guy? I needed to make sure my future husband had all the right priorities in life and was fully committed to raising our children accordingly. Mom was prohibited from buying anything without Dad's permission for a while, and she was visibly defeated, humiliated by the new low of her allowances.

∽

IN SUMMER 2013, WE MET THE MARTINS, A BLUEGRASS BAND OF three brothers and a sister from Missouri. Fresh off their victory at an international youth competition, their harmonies were tight, and their groove was perfectly pocketed. They would soon move to Tennessee and start attending our home church gathering. And Jair would take a shine to the sister, Maria, who had just turned seventeen.

JUST AS I REACHED MY PEAK OF RELATIONAL INDOCTRINATION, I was blindsided by someone who turned my internal landscape upside-down. It was high summer, and I was waiting to see a new buzzworthy band from Ireland in a festival crowd that smelled of sweat and beer. When the guitar player stepped onstage, everything else in the world vanished. As his eyes fell on mine, I heard a bell of recognition ring deep within me, saying my soul had always known this person. A knee-jerk reaction of fear gripped me, as if a live wire was dangling out of my body and there was no way to protect against what would come next.

We watched each other throughout the festival weekend, across crowds, across the performers' green room, across the after-hours parties in the hotel hallways, until the event was almost over. Then we stayed up talking until 3:00 A.M. on the final night. His name was Donal, and I wanted to know everything about him. Introductions felt almost superfluous. We talked with easy intimacy about writing songs and the creative process, which books had changed our lives. He asked me if I thought the head ruled the heart. I didn't know how to answer, but I felt as if I was holding my breath whenever he was out of sight.

Our bands ran in the same circles, and I saw him again two weeks later, after which unforeseen circumstances left him with a ten-day gap in his schedule with nothing to do and nowhere to be. Then Mom did a strange thing. She somehow persuaded my father to let Donal come stay with us until his next gig.

There was zero chance this person would satisfy my father's list. I fell deeply in love with him anyway, and I realized it was my first time. We kissed and told each other how we felt before he left.

When my parents found out, they figured he couldn't be much trouble half a world away. I would be allowed to write him letters as long as I behaved myself. I felt betrayed when Mom urged me to find out if he believed in literal interpretations of biblical prophecy, saying, "Jess, feelings aren't going to matter when the end times come."

I was stuck between my head and my heart, neither one able to bring the other into submission. So I wrote letters begging Donal to change into someone I could be with, while his kind dissent showed me another way of being and feeling. Mutually inspired, we sent a torrent of newly written songs back and forth. The parts of me I feared had been permanently lost or chipped away had instead been growing just out of sight. Thanks to Donal's encouragement, I changed in ways that made me unable to ever fit back into my perfectly arranged progression of boxes to be checked.

I believed I would never find someone I loved as much as him. He assured me great love not only awaited me, but he would always be there, a true friend along the way. I was heartbroken, and for a time, rejected his promise that I would ever find another connection as beautiful as ours. But I was wrong, and he was right.

15

BOTS

Our GAC reality show finished airing and was not renewed for a second season. Once again, according to Dad, the problem was everyone else's lack of vision.

Gone were the days of sporadic monthly gigs. Our schedule became tightly packed with back-to-back appearances. As the year 2013 ended, Dad heard about an open casting call to find "the next *Sound of Music* family." Musically inclined kin were encouraged to submit audition videos featuring a song from the classic musical. The winners would be flown to New York City to appear live on the *Today* show. If we claimed the spot, we could secure an even bigger megaphone than our canceled show. We submitted a video and progressed through the ranks until three families remained. The final vote was put to the internet. The results weren't exactly a landslide.

Dad became suspicious. "Look," he said, pointing at one family's number. "Every time we get close, the count jumps. I think they're cheating." We asked how they could possibly be cheating. "Bots," he said. He described programs that were able to repeatedly click on any website button.

A few hours before the deadline, he called us kids to the loft. "I've set up the three desktop computers to keep pace with them," he informed us. "They probably didn't expect me to be able to do what they are doing. But I know my stuff. All you guys have to do is make sure the programs keep voting until the cutoff tonight."

The other family's number did jump funny like Dad said, yet who would care enough about this little competition to cheat their way to the top? It hit me with palpable irony: us. At the last possible second, I saw the two tallest columns shrink by almost a third each and then disappear. An automatic message announced the contest was over. I could have sworn our column had been highest.

We reported to Dad. He seemed pleased. "They didn't even cheat well," he scoffed.

THE DAY WE APPEARED AS THE WINNERS ON THE *TODAY* SHOW, I felt a wave of relief and elation that would develop into a reoccurring pattern over the following years. We would undertake a last-minute task, unprepared, stretched to our limits, Dad at the helm, following a vision only he could see. When the test was over and we survived by the skin of our teeth, I would be grateful we hadn't fallen apart. In those moments, my siblings were like fellow soldiers who had my back in combat; no one else could understand what we'd gone through together.

Not for the first time, *America's Got Talent* (AGT) reached out to us. Back when we had nine, ten, and eleven kids, they seemed to find us in whatever world we appeared. Their scouts now found our *Today* show performance and once again asked us to audition. My parents hadn't liked the possibility of losing control of the band due to AGT's contracts, but Dad now seemed convinced he could play according to his own rules and win. He said yes.

My experience on AGT was a blurry tunnel of fantastic chaos. The contestants and crew were friendly and exuberant, bonding through the surreal process. When disagreement cropped up within the family, Mom urged us to embrace a new interpretation of *The Hunger Games*. "Guys, we are in the arena now. The enemy is out there. We can't be fighting each other." She still chose to see God's will in every open door and continued to pray that our testimonies would bless others.

By the time the live rounds began, we were driving our bus into downtown New York City to film at Radio City Music Hall, then sleeping overnight in our bus bunks on our way to play county fairs in Michigan and Indiana. I felt our audiences shifting. It was wild and a little scary to be recognized by an increasing number of strangers.

We self-released our second official CD and went straight into recording a third. What little time we had at home that summer was spent working in the studio and washing mountains of laundry to repack for the next leg of the tour. If we happened to be free on a rare weekend, we gathered with our home church group who seemed simultaneously happy for our success and wary of fame.

Jair continued to show interest in Maria Martin. Dad gave Jair the green light to spend time getting to know her and her family. Around that same time, I made the mistake of riding in the truck of a young songwriter who'd caught my eye. Dad warned me he would pull out his shotgun if the kid ever came around again, and I dropped him like a hot potato.

AFTER WE WERE ELIMINATED FROM AGT'S QUARTERFINALS, WE received a call from the TV channel TLC. They wanted to make us an offer for a brand-new reality show. There was no time to waste. A new show meant the album we were working on should be our most mainstream one yet. Dad wanted me to sing differently. He would listen back to what I had recorded for the day only to shake his head unhappily.

"It's not even close," his voice came biting through the headphones.

We were working on the lead vocal for a love song I'd written. Again and again, he cut me off midphrase. "I just don't believe you. I don't believe what you're saying," he said. "You're not *going* there." He clenched his fist to his chest. "Sell it to me!"

The printed lyrics turned blurry and began to dance on the page in front of me as I tried again. He yelled and hurled cutting insults. I thought of Mom telling me she wished she could be a robot so she could function without emotions, and work without having the human weaknesses of needing to eat, sleep, or cry. I understood. I wished his words couldn't hurt me, but a hard knot built unbidden in my throat until my voice was choked tight and gave out completely. In disgust, he let me leave the studio, knowing I had passed into a useless state.

I stormed to my room and yanked on my running shoes. Down in the basement, I jumped on the treadmill and began running, the next thing I was supposed to do on the schedule. After a short burst, I slowed to a walk.

I promised myself, *One day, I'll be standing tall and he won't be able to touch me.*

I realized I was rejecting my mother's despair. Not only did I want to keep feeling; I also wanted to fan myself into an inferno of passion. I began singing underneath my shaky breath:

I'll keep walking down this road I'm on,
knowing you'll be gone,
and I'll be fine

I stomped my feet with each step and the treadmill shook.

I'll keep going till there's no more fear,
knowing I'll be here,
and you'll be gone

AT SOME POINT, DAD MUST HAVE REALIZED HIS OVERBEARING methods were hurting his results. I found it difficult to keep performing while worrying whether there was any throwable object within his reach. For years he'd justified the need to push us all, but he was starting to hit an invisible breaking point, which forced him to change tactics. Jair and even the younger boys were now significant physical opponents. No longer could he preach "might equals right" as a way of guaranteeing his rule. He began to complain, "I don't want to have to be the bad guy all the time." He emphasized we were young adults who needed to take responsibility for our own work. The day would come when he wouldn't be around to tell us what to do. Would we give up on everything we had worked on? Would we get lazy like the rest of society and lose all ground gained?

"You should report on your siblings when they don't do their tasks," he said. "It's your job to keep each other on task. Remember, our team is only as strong as its weakest player." While failure continued to provoke punishments, he tried to spread the responsibility of carrying them out, even going so far as occasionally encouraging us to "beat up" whoever was slacking off.

"When your brother or sister is lazy, they are stealing from you," he insisted.

Dad encouraged Jair to take increasing control of the band, saying we sisters would one day have husbands and children taking our allegiance and attention away from the family business. "But if we continue to train them right, we can have the younger girls come in and take the older girls' spots," he said.

Sometimes he let his dreams run unchecked. "If each of you twelve kids have twelve kids of your own, that's a hundred and forty-four grandkids. I could one day conduct an orchestra of all family members!"

COME AUTUMN, THE BAND HAD A FEW DAYS OF DOWNTIME between gigs in Florida, and our parents decided to book a beach house on an island in the Keys. Mom was understandably tense anytime Dad would have her wear revealing swimsuits, a sure opportunity for him to ridicule her body. Meanwhile, she was expected to plan and administrate a leisurely stay while giving no outward sign of effort or stress.

One evening at the beach house, I planned for dinner, hoping to take something off Mom's plate. By the time she made it to the kitchen to communicate her contrasting plan, I dug in and pointed out I'd already begun my prep. After he became aware of our conflict, Dad scolded Mom, not me, saying she was ruining the atmosphere with her grumbling.

Later, my brother Jedi and I got into an argument. Clashing with my mother made me feel helpless and irritable, and it sent me back to my old habit of relentlessly bossing my younger siblings. When Dad again took my side, Mom stepped in to defend Jedi. Dad ordered her to the bedroom and locked the door behind them, repeating the pattern of countless confrontations.

I stepped outside, trying to escape the cloud of drama, ashamed of my petty attitude. Taking a seat on the porch, I watched the sun lengthen on the endless water until the murmur of the waves brought me some measure of calm. I closed my eyes and heard a thin snap followed by an anguished cry. Confused, I looked back at the house and realized the windows of my parents' bedroom were open. There came another series of cracks and disturbing whimpers, continuing until their source was unmistakable: the blows were being dealt by my father; the pain was my mother's. Her sobs built to a wail and then fell muffled by what I imagined was a pillow over her face. Voices shrieked inside my head, *Stop him! Save her! This is all your fault!*

I rushed into the house, first thinking I was going to her rescue, but then I realized I was simply unable to bear the sound of lashes falling on flesh. I turned on the kitchen faucet, grabbed a rag, and set to wiping the island counter furiously. *I heard nothing. I saw nothing.*

When I next saw my mother's face, there was no forgetting. "Please, Jessie," she begged, "you cannot get me in trouble anymore. He's beating me."

She dressed for a run, her face pale and swollen above her sweat-shirt. Four-year-old Jada knew something was wrong and threw herself around Mom's legs in the open doorway, refusing to let her leave. "No, Mommy," she wailed.

Trying to smile, Mom peeled her baby's arms away and passed her to another sibling. "Everything's okay," she said, and fled.

When she didn't come back by dark, Dad became restless, pacing through the living room. She hadn't taken her cell phone. "I'm going to look for her," he said.

Though the island had only one main highway, he couldn't spot her.

She returned hours later, so exhausted she seemed completely empty of everything, mechanical and blank. It looked as if she had finally achieved the robotic programming she had wished for. No one asked where she had gone. We were simply relieved she had come back at all.

16

CATCH

Apparently, I first met Sean Fisher side stage at the Grand Ole Opry on October 10, 2014. The night was full of loud celebratory energy, and it was hard to see in the dark. The red-velvet theater curtains were pulled wide, and clusters of people stood in the wings craning their necks to glimpse the famous acts rotating through the spotlight. It was a particularly momentous night to be there: it was the Opry's eighty-ninth birthday.

Pete Fisher was the general manager of the Opry at the time and could usually be found just out of the audience's line of sight on stage right, greeting the artists coming on and off. Mr. Pete, as we came to call him, was incredibly warm and engaging with everyone, the sort of person who looks you in the eye and genuinely asks after you—whether or not you are famous. Nearly invisible glasses perched on his face, which flushed pink under the lights.

Over the recent months I felt he'd made a point to get to know me as an individual, beyond me being the oldest sister of a dozen faces. He had invited me to come stand beside him so he could introduce me to passing people of note. Tonight, a large wooden multitiered cake decorated with musical notes and stars loomed behind us, awaiting the show's festive finale.

The Willis Clan performed two numbers and ended with the little kids emerging for a dance. The crowd genuinely roared. We pinched ourselves as we got to watch the rest of the performers rock the house.

At some point, I was introduced to Mr. Pete's son. I know I had to have smiled and shaken his outstretched hand, but in truth, I don't remember. I was used to meeting prominent people in the industry, famous songwriters I should get to know or an artist on the top of the charts of whom I knew nothing. I have a vague impression that I must have looked at this handsome, well-dressed man and thought, *Phew, at least I don't feel dumb for not knowing who this is.* Then I promptly forgot meeting him at all.

THE NEXT TIME WE PERFORMED AT THE OPRY, DAD INVITED Mr. Pete to dinner. "Bring your wife if you'd like," he encouraged, and, after a laugh, added something to the effect of "And if you have any sons, bring them too. I have a lot of daughters to marry off." We traveled to gigs, prepared for our new TV series, and appeared at the Opry a few more times before a date was eventually set—a Monday evening in January. Dad wanted to get Mr. Pete's professional advice, and we would likely do a musical show-and-tell after dinner.

Monday evening, I put on a plain black T-shirt, jeans, and a dash of makeup after helping make dinner. The doorbell rang and

Pete and Hope Fisher were welcomed in. They both happily greeted everyone as children grouped by the couch, appeared from around corners, and bounded down the stairs. Miss Hope was as kind and warm as Mr. Pete. They mentioned their son was driving from work and was a few minutes away.

During a new wave of introductions, the front door opened again. I physically jolted, froze, and immediately thought, *I wish I was wearing something better than a black T-shirt.* Perhaps I had a hazy, subconscious recognition from meeting him at the Opry a few months beforehand. Regardless, something about this person caught me in those first few moments of the second time around.

To my embarrassment, Dad shouted, "Attention!" A few of my siblings seemed to catch the shift of potential in the air, throwing me arched eyebrows and teasing glances. We shuffled quickly into line, calling out our names in order. The rapid roll was over in a few seconds and the trio of Fishers blinked, completely unaccustomed to such a greeting. After a pause, Miss Hope motioned to her lone adult son standing behind the couch—"Well, here's Sean!"

Everyone laughed and went into the dining room. Sean was upbeat and open, tall, with dark, wavy hair and golden-brown eyes. As I watched him move, speak, and interact with his parents and my younger siblings, I kept thinking I saw a light around him, coming up through the ground and hovering around his head and shoulders, some sort of compelling visible energy drawing me in. When the meal was over, Dad indicated it was time to transition to the studio upstairs. I was glad Sean followed along to listen. I sat in the chair at the main desk and sampled through our recordings, delighted when he made any observation or sign of appreciation.

As Mr. Pete and Dad began talking, Sean and I chatted to the side. He spoke of the outdoors and adventure trips, describing his unique job at something called an experiential therapy retreat. He managed the hospitality elements, coordinating details such as delivering handwritten notes and placing roses on the pillows of the guests working through the frequently taxing and emotional programs. Passion radiated from his face as he outlined the reasons someone might seek such intense therapy. He admitted that employees were required to participate in a program to help them better understand the experience of the guests, and I wondered if the light I saw was the spark of transformation, a byproduct of his own recent growth and change.

I was leaning in, trying to decode my attraction to him when it occurred to me: *Those programs were made to help people like me.* I shoved the thought away, not wanting to consciously admit the connection.

I laughed lightly, "So, it's your job to be romantic?"

Before he left, Sean found a way to casually make clear he was not in a relationship, and I made sure to mention my email address. I didn't want to say I had no phone at age twenty-two, and certainly didn't mention the one-email-per-week rule. My iPad was set up for instant messaging through my email address, and Sean and I soon began conversing with frequency.

IT SEEMED MY FATHER'S INTEREST IN MR. PETE'S ENDORSEMENT translated into a preliminary approval of Sean. He came to nearly every one of our Opry shows that followed our second meeting, and I took the liberty of inviting him to visit our Sunday gathering where he was drawn in by the chaotic vibrancy of big-family energy. Sometime later, he would remind me we actually had met the previous fall.

In a bold move, Sean bought a leather journal for us to exchange periodically. He didn't inquire as to the details of my communication restrictions, but, in my mind, the journal played perfectly into an undefined gray area. We each wrote to the other at length about our days and thoughts. His parents had used the same method to keep in touch during long-distance seasons at the beginning of their relationship. He discovered my taste in music and sent songs that paved the way for the confession of attraction. There seemed no hope of keeping this man out of my parents' view. His intentions were obvious.

Within a few weeks, Dad sat me down to reiterate the terms of any outside connections. He listed things he liked in Sean, seeing possible synergy between his personality and the band's future networking needs. But I had to be careful not to jeopardize our industry connection with Mr. Pete. I would do well to keep feelings out of the matter until Sean's qualifications in important areas could be examined.

I didn't mention the journals, the love songs, or the increasing frequency of our instant messaging.

"Keep me informed," Dad said, reiterating what had become his constant mandate.

BEFORE I WAS FULLY AWAKE, I COULD HEAR RUSTLING IN THE kitchen and giggling in the hall. It was early on Valentine's Day morning. I opened my eyes to see my thirteen-year-old sister already up and dressed. She was the current "buddy" with whom I shared a room and bed.

"Why are you up before me?" I asked, disoriented. She was

bouncing with excitement and pointing out our window. I froze. "What is it?"

"Just look!" she burst out.

I rubbed a hand across my face and crawled across the covers to see outside. Two miniature wooden-framed chalkboards lay on the porch floor. *Good morning*, they read in yellow handwritten letters with an arrow pointing to the left. I bolted out of bed, then hesitated in the middle of the room.

"Do I need to be dressed?"

My sister nodded.

I threw on a flannel shirt and jeans, gave my hair a quick toss, and ran to the porch. A trail of messages descended the hill around our rental home with arrows leading up the back-porch stairs and in through the kitchen door. On the counter was a bouquet of flowers and a note asking, *Will you be my valentine?* Best of all, Sean Fisher stood beaming by the breakfast table.

Without hesitation, I threw my arms around his neck, delighted and shocked he had pulled off such an operation. Mom was looking on with conspiratorial warmth, leading me to believe she had smoothed the way.

Sean stayed for our traditional Valentine's breakfast of fresh cinnamon rolls, then joined me at the dining room table to cut hearts out of construction paper with the little kids. When Dad came downstairs, he wore a slightly territorial air, acting surprised to see a visitor in his home, which made me question whether Mom had checked with him. Sensing it was time to go, Sean said goodbye to all as I waved from the kitchen.

Since there was enough festive commotion going on, I made a split-second decision to follow him out. I called his name as loud as I dared. He whirled around at his car door to see me running barefoot

over the yard. I hesitated not at all and kissed him full on his aston-
ished mouth. I felt a knowing flood from my head to my toes.

"I had a plan," he laughed. "I was going to kiss you at a water-
fall, silly."

"Please do," I said.

OUR PLANS NEEDED TO BE REVISED. SEAN'S INITIATIVE (AND MINE)
meant I would have to lay out the terms of my father and see whether
they scared him away. When I told Sean we would need to conduct
certain heavy conversations early on, he was largely unfazed. He
did point out the unconventionality of having such polarizing discussions so quickly, but he was game to jump in, fully expecting
his willingness to be rewarded at some later point. High on gusto,
low on predetermined positions, he went with the flow because the
current was strong. So many things in my life happened because of
a force that was useless to challenge.

Sean came to local performances, we wrote letters when I was
out of town, and his visits to our home were scheduled when cameras were least likely to be there.

I was surprised to find an ally in Jair. I'm not sure we had ever
been particularly close; for so long, our interactions had been nearer
to those of stressed coworkers than affectionate siblings. Now he
was overflowing with feelings, and I was the only other person who
was resonating at the same frequency, experiencing a similar daily
rush of emotions.

When Mom and Dad upgraded to the newest iPhones, an old cell
phone became available for Jair to use in his progressing courtship.
He tucked away in his bus bunk with the curtain drawn, talking
with Maria Martin. He began sharing the phone with me, passing

it over when Maria was busy or when Sean was planning to call. I took my turn in my bunk when I could, using my pillow to shield my voice from the rest of the family.

The Grand Ole Opry became synonymous with Sean for me. It was a place where he had every right to appear without needing an invite or permission. For us, Valentine's Day marked our attachment to each other, though my parents had yet to recognize it. Sean was not accustomed to pursuing someone who was so restricted. Although I could tell he didn't think my family's involvement was entirely warranted, he made the effort to see it as endearing and agreed to speak to my father about me.

Soon after, Dad sat me down to say that while Sean seemed like a nice guy, I could do much better. Though we were both disappointed as I shared this report with Sean, he kept his good-natured chin up and continued to come around whenever he could.

OUR CHURCH WAS STILL MADE UP OF LARGE FAMILIES WITH STRONG fathers who led the discussions in turns, with short presentations based on weekly Scripture studies. It was not often that we had outside visitors, so Sean's persistent attendance didn't fit into the normal pattern of things. He leaned into the awkwardness by volunteering to make a presentation of his own. I was nervous he would be shot down, but the fathers decided to let him speak. Though I was dying to know what he was planning, he declined to give away his plan.

The following Sunday, my heart was in my throat as Sean stood in the center of the chairs circled around the Martins' living room, a large ball of rainbow yarn in his hands. He invited everyone to join him in a visualization of community and connection.

"One of the ways I believe God speaks to us is through the people he puts in our lives," he said. He thanked the group for welcoming him and inspiring him in his spiritual walk, passing the yarn to a specific elder who'd encouraged him recently. With each passing, the yarn-holder had to share something meaningful with someone else, and soon the crisscrossing thread showed the many ways we were linked together in shared empathy and fellowship until the ball was gone and everyone was woven inside a multicolored tapestry. I was relieved and proud.

After a shared meal, children ran about, the women continued to visit, and the men analyzed people's contributions late into the afternoon. In a natural lull, Dad cocked his head at Sean and smiled. "You might not know," he said, "but I have a string theory of my own, and mine's quite a bit different from yours."

I watched Sean listen politely as Dad briefly explained his philosophy of protecting the ties of family loyalty. In that moment, I failed to realize how truly opposed the two concepts were: one man was building relationships through vulnerability and shared experience, the other was bent on defeating any outside threat to his power and control.

17

TICKTOCK

"MARIA KNOWS," JAIR SAID CALMLY, AND ALL THE OXYGEN LEFT the room.

He had gathered the oldest three girls, Mom, and Dad for a special meeting in the studio. The little kids were sent away and the door was shut. Weeks after Maria's eighteenth birthday, Jair proposed. He'd secured her father's permission with the TV cameras following the highlights of their courtship process, making me wonder why Jair was allowed to pursue a relationship so easily.

"What does that mean, Jair?" someone finally asked.

"Maria knows Dad did stuff to the girls."

The room erupted with incredulous exclamations.

"What did you tell her?" I demanded. This was my waking nightmare. Even though I knew he had heard accusations over the years, I had never directly told Jair anything that had happened to me. I thought he couldn't possibly have any correct information.

He raised his hands in a gesture of defense. "I didn't say anything. She said she could tell." He shrugged. "She has a radar for that sort of thing."

Was this how it went? I wondered. *Would the bomb finally explode after all this time?* I needed Jair to recount every word, every expression, any minute reference exchanged so I could know the extent of the damage, the length of the fuse.

"There's nothing to *know*," Dad said assertively, speaking over the stir, "because there is nothing going on."

I desperately wanted to go along with the statement. There *was* something to know, of course—a great terrible knowing housed in my body and fractured memories.

Dad turned to me and my sisters. "Ask the girls," he said, mostly to Jair. "Ask them how I've been doing."

I eventually felt forced to speak and settled on what felt closest to the truth: "This is the best things have ever been between Dad and me." Over the previous six years, I had learned to suppress my reactions to crass comments, lewd jokes, minor grazes, and convenient brushes. At this point, I felt any confrontation or dramatics were my fault. Problems occurred when I let myself be caught off guard or my emotions flared out of control.

No one else offered a contrary viewpoint and instead confirmed, yes, as far as they knew, Dad had been on his best behavior. He kept repeating himself, doubling, tripling down on what he'd said before—that nothing was going on—willing us to understand that he meant nothing had ever happened at all.

"Look, if anyone ever asks you about it, just say, 'nothing is happening,' okay?" he instructed us. "Nobody has proof of anything."

But what if Maria did have some sort of proof? What had she

seen? Was the word *dirty* finally visible on my forehead after all? We girls decided we should have a careful talk with Maria as soon as the opportunity presented itself. The family meeting ended without anyone asking our five other younger sisters for their account of Dad's latest behavior.

OUR GIGS KEPT US MERCIFULLY BUSY. THERE WAS NO DOWNTIME anymore. Between concerts, we filmed scenes for our reality series showcasing the local attractions of wherever we were traveling. In Indiana, we drove go-karts and rode behind racehorses around a casino track, making sure the producers got shots of smiling siblings. Back at home, our pop album was ready for its finishing touches.

Sean Fisher reached out to Dad, asking permission to invite me to see a museum exhibit with his parents later that month. He thought the four of us could go out to dinner. I don't know if it was due to the presence of chaperones or the opportunity for me to get more face time with Mr. Pete, but Dad said yes. I was thrilled, hoping this meant we would be able to conduct an official relationship. Sean was likewise elated.

Impulsively, he messaged to see if I was free to meet him on his way home from work at the end of our driveway. There was something he wanted to give me, and he would rather not wait until our date. I told him I would try to slip away.

When he sent his ETA, I ducked outside "for a quick run." Happy butterflies careened through my stomach as I jogged down the gravel lane, catching sight of Sean's car as I rounded the second curve well away from the house. His face was shining as he swept me into an embrace.

"I want you to have this," he said. It was a guitar pick charm on a dainty chain with the word *hope* emblazoned in the middle.

He clasped both his hands tight around mine. "I love you," he said in person for the first time. "I know it will be hard to make things work with your family, but I'm in this for the long haul." He told me the necklace represented his future hope of marrying me.

I marked the date in our leather journal, which was currently in my possession:

March 24, 2015. Today you told me you would marry me.

ON THE NIGHT OF OUR DATE, I CURLED MY HAIR AND DONNED A black dress and heels. Sean arrived early and found me ready to go. We slipped out amid teasing jibes from my siblings.

Being alone for the full drive was almost too much. It was a quiet moment after so much nonstop activity; I didn't know what to feel first. Sean took my hand, and I began to cry. In some sense, I barely knew this person, yet I felt dangerously close to exposing myself in a way that could not be undone. Our mandatory conversations about God, family, and future plans had punted Dad's objections down the field. Mutual confessions of past attractions only brought us closer, and Sean had let himself be far more vulnerable than I had. Everything I'd pushed down for close to twenty years was suddenly floating just below the surface, and withholding felt like betrayal in the face of sincerity and accumulating intimacy.

"What's wrong?" Sean asked gently, letting me lay my head on his shoulder.

"I don't know," I lied. The ticking of my time bomb was now obvious in my internal stillness. I realized anyone I wanted to love put themselves at risk just by being with me. If I really cared for Sean, I would send him away, keeping him and his family far from the blast zone.

Mr. Pete and Miss Hope stood to greet me at the restaurant. Our January visit felt like a lifetime ago. Hope told me to drop the "miss," and I tried, though Pete's "mister" stuck around longer due to force of habit.

Hope's manner and appearance struck me as both endearing and unique. She was tall with strawberry-red hair, light green eyes, and freckled skin tanned to a warm bronze. As we gathered around a plate of fresh hummus and pita, she waved away any expectation of formality or reserve. "We're just so glad to get some time with you!" she confessed, remarking on how often Sean talked of me.

Before long, she jumped right to the point. "Jess, what exactly *are* your family's rules for dating?"

"That's a good question." I laughed awkwardly, feeling embarrassed I couldn't explain.

At the museum, I was introduced to Fisher family friends for the first time. We wandered through the massive exhibit at our own pace, learning about Johnny Cash, Bob Dylan, and the group of musicians known affectionately as "the Nashville Cats."

On the way home, Sean drove me to a wooded park. Massive trees loomed in the headlights as we wound our way up to the top of a hill. The summit was an overlook, with the distant lights of downtown glowing on the horizon. I was shivering when he parked facing the view, and not from cold. I didn't think of blast zones or guilt. Our lips and hands explored until it was painful to stop, then we retreated to the safety of our seatbelts and headed toward my home.

I watched his taillights recede down the driveway before entering the dark, quiet house. I climbed the stairs and felt a wave of unmistakable déjà vu. My parents' bedroom door was intentionally open, and Dad sat waiting at the back of the bed, laptop resting on his legs. His face was lit by the machine, questioning, judging. I waited for him to speak, knowing he would.

"Did you behave yourself?" he asked, finally.

"Yes," I answered.

Arms crossed, he smirked bitterly. "Liar." This time, the accusation didn't hurt.

Forty-eight hours later, I was on a plane to New York with Mom and Jair. We were sent, cameras in tow, to represent the band at key meetings important to the release of our new album. I messaged Sean between each filming. We were undeniably attached, vaulted far over the line my parents were trying to hold.

Long distance loomed just around the corner. I would be gone most of the summer, touring in locations as far as California and Ireland. Although we hoped Sean could come see me on the road, I would be largely unavailable and hard to reach. He offered to buy me my own phone. I declined. He bought a second leather journal instead so we could each always have one. I promised to send snail mail every chance I got. He gave me a quilt he'd slept with for a week. There was no way around it; we were going to miss each other terribly.

FOR JAIR'S TWENTY-SECOND BIRTHDAY, THE TV PRODUCERS FLEW Maria out to meet us in Minnesota. We were kicking off our tour with a short residency at a corporate convention in Duluth. We girls hadn't yet found the right moment to have our delicate conversation with Maria, and the film crew planned to keep her busy with sit-down interviews until she left.

On the night of April 12, I was tired and preoccupied when I walked back toward my hotel room after an evening workout in the gym downstairs. We were driving to South Dakota basically overnight, planning to leave in the bus sometime around 2:00 A.M. the next morning. It was the day before I would turn twenty-three, ending the tiny yearly period when Jair and I were the same age. A hot shower on my mind, I swiped my key card and entered the room. Mom and one of my younger sisters sat on the end of the bed, their faces distorted with distress, puffy from tears. My gut fell. No words were needed for me to intuit what had been discovered. More inappropriate behavior from my father.

If I went back out into the hall, could I undo the moment? If I shut my eyes tight, could I unsee? I'd accidentally unlocked the past, finding another girl crying on her bed. Perhaps I was intruding upon my younger self, looping back in a different body, causing multiple timelines to collide. This was the first time I had been present at the excruciating initial moment of a sister's tearful confession.

"When?" I asked them.

While Jair, Mom, and I were in New York, I was told.

I could barely look at my little sister. *How much? How long?* I could not ask her; I had no right. Less than a month ago, I had supported and defended Dad to the rest of the family. He had made a fool out of me, lying to our faces. I had listened to him claim nothing had ever happened, knowing full well it was a lie, choosing to neither protest nor dissent. I felt guilty, complicit.

My mind was lava. "I'm going over to your room," I told Mom. She came with me.

The sight of my father made me wonder whom I hated more, him or myself. My voice vibrating tightly, I told him I wasn't going to give him any more chances. I wanted this audible venom to bore into his ears and his face. I wanted to break him with words. My heated anger teetered on the edge of total fear.

The combination brought a flash of momentary clarity; this ship was going down, and I didn't want to drown. This nightmare was on repeat, but I wanted to wake up.

I jabbed my finger, pointing at him. "As soon as I can figure out how to do it, I'm getting out of here."

Mom confirmed this was the last straw. Something was going to have to be done this time. As soon as we had a spare moment, Dad was going to have to get help. After a while, he shrank and became dejected.

"I have a problem, guys," he lamented. "I should leave so the band can carry on."

Mom was furious. "Toby, we can't do this without you! Why can't you just stop?"

At some point, another sister joined us. We asked him if he was even a Christian.

Dad sidestepped the question, saying, "I sure hope salvation is real because I need it."

We tried imagining what our lives would look like without our father. Instead of talking about how much physically and emotionally safer we would be, we absurdly wondered who would care for Dad at some hermit-like location, and how he would direct our careers from a distance.

"Why can't you just be good? Do you not love us enough?" we asked him.

We circled back, saying something needed to be done, questioning when we would find the time. Months of bus-living stretched out before us, the cameras following what seemed like our every move. Concert after concert, we had to keep smiling, doing our song and dance like nothing was wrong. Was there a way we could get help without everything falling apart?

We could not tell Jair because he might tell Maria. We could never hope to talk to her now.

AT SOME POINT, MIDNIGHT CAME AND WENT. I WAS TWENTY-THREE. I went to my bed in a daze. Everyone else was already sleeping. How had almost twenty years gone by without me figuring out how to tell someone—anyone? I retrieved my iPad and sent a message to Sean, seeing if he was still awake. If he was asleep, I would take it as a sign.

But he was up, ready to listen to whatever I wanted to say. I asked him to go back to the night he'd confided in me about his past relationships. He had been afraid that if he confessed his past, I might not want to speak to him again.

I typed,

Every time you've seen hesitation, or doubt, or non-happy tears from me, it's because I feel guilty for not telling you. It's not something I did . . .

I stalled until he gently reminded me of his investment in our relationship.

I continued,

It's something that was done to me . . . when I was very young. Something that would land someone at the place you work, frankly.

My finger was on the trigger. Alas, I found I couldn't bring myself to detonate us all.

I began sobbing as I wrote,

It's so very far away. I've healed and moved on.

I was using the words I'd heard Sean say.
He responded,

I see where you're headed. Hey, let's stop there. Thank you so very much for telling me. I am so proud of you right now. And although I have no clue what you must have gone through, just know, I'm with you. And I love you so very much. I know that was so very hard to tell me.

I wondered whether I had doomed us all.

Me: I have a request.
Sean: Anything.
Me: Please don't talk to anyone else about this. My family already knows. But please don't talk to them about it either.
Sean: It'll stay here, sweetheart.
Me: I'll understand if you need to know more someday. I barely told you anything except there was something to know. And that was the part that was killing me slowly.
Sean: Hey, you're still standing. Breathe.
Me: I love you, Sean Fisher.
Sean: To the ends of the earth, I'm with you.

WE WOKE UP IN THE MIDDLE OF NOWHERE, SOUTH DAKOTA. I couldn't remember getting on the bus after messaging Sean in a thoroughly exhausted state. We were supposed to be visiting friends who ran a buffalo ranch and maybe have a little celebration for my birthday, then continue through to the West Coast.

Without explanation, Dad refused to go inside to greet our hosts. Since neither parent gave instructions to us kids on how to spend our time, most of us headed across the huge ranch to go fishing and tag along on four-wheelers with the other family. It felt good to be outside in the chilly, windswept sunshine with little to no cell service.

Dad finally made an appearance for dinner. Sean had shipped a surprise birthday gift to the ranch. He'd named a star after us and made a wooden plaque with its coordinates. I was dazzled at the gesture, which would let us look at the night sky and find our star even when we were apart.

MARIA CAME TO VISIT JAIR AGAIN, AND I SENSED DRAMA. THEY were in the process of recording a song together, and I suspected the emerging issues went beyond differences of creative opinion. I even heard there was growing disagreement about the plans for their housing and future life together. I hoped they had not picked up on the recent revelations about Dad. I purposely avoided talking to them as much as possible.

Over the next three weeks, we performed at radio stations and theaters in California, Colorado, and Oregon. We visited Yosemite, hiked down and back up the Grand Canyon in one day, filmed self-defense classes with champion wrestlers, attended a West Coast Swing dance party, and tried surfing for the first time.

Dad's silent treatment lasted a day or two before he was back at the helm, with just as much power as before. He boldly injected himself into the building conflict between Jair and Maria, holding lengthy conversations in the back of the bus with Mom and Jair while we drove from gig to gig. It seemed Dad was vying to get Maria on board and in line with the plans he had for Jair.

We stopped in Las Vegas on Dad's birthday. He said he wanted to take Mom for a "wild date," so she dressed in her highest heels and shortest skirt. The next morning, I jolted in shock when I first saw my mother's embarrassed face. One of her eyes was encircled with a large purple splotch. She looked for all the world like she'd been punched straight in the eye socket.

She immediately explained, "I fell."

I whispered, "Mom, tell me the truth. Did he do that?"

"No, I swear. I fell. He didn't do anything. It was my heels—I tripped on the curb . . ."

I wasn't sure I believed her. Either way, he'd made her wear those shoes. She did her best to hide the bruising with makeup, and we didn't bring it up again.

My belief in potential change was fading. We said this time would be different. But how? I'd said I would leave, but when? I began to think my family was stuck on an unstoppable runaway train.

My entries in the journal Sean and I shared showed a tentative effort toward truth culminating in a confession penned in red ink, spilling out the truth that Dad was sexually abusive and there seemed no hope of making him stop.

Once I saw the words on the page, I knew I couldn't let Sean see them. I ripped out the page and left a note of explanation,

This page had to be removed. Not the right time. Not the right place. I'm not yet free to say everything I wrote. Please, please, please bear with me. Some things are unspeakable.

18

TUG-OF-WAR

RETURNING FROM A MONTH ON THE ROAD, JAIR WENT TO VISIT THE
Martin home and returned distraught: Maria had given back the
ring. Their engagement was all over the TV show, and it was too late
to erase her from the early episodes, the first of which had already
aired. Soon her family would leave our church group and move out
of state. Best-case scenario, she'd drop her suspicions and the danger
of her "knowing" would go away.

I was now portraying my feelings and actions differently based
on who I was speaking to. From what I said to Dad and the family, Sean and I were not physical, we spent our time progressing
through a worldview checklist, and our connection was not a threat
to the family or the band. When I interacted with Sean, I presented
myself as emotionally committed to a future together and blamed
the family's intense schedule for keeping us from being able to date

normally or spend more time with his family and friends. The gap in the narratives grew dangerously wide, requiring constant care not to say the wrong thing at the wrong time to the wrong person.

Sean and his family attended the release party for our newest CD. We hadn't been cleared to call each other boyfriend and girl-friend, so we held hands with our arms hidden behind our backs.

When the TV producers saw our obviously growing repartee, they were interested in acknowledging Sean as a potential suitor of mine. When a teaser to that effect aired at the end an episode, Dad flipped out, and any further reference to Sean disappeared from the show.

We continued to rendezvous during the small windows I was home and was unable to arrange an approved visit. He would message what time he would get off work and I would "go for a run" to meet him.

The band flew to Ireland, traveling for another month straight. We journaled, sent letters, talked on the phone, instant messaged, and video called on the iPad.

Some part of me felt the doom approaching despite the outwardly happy clamor of touring. I had always genuinely enjoyed myself in Ireland, yet halfway through the trip, I suddenly could barely manage a smile. I saw fear on the faces of family members as they questioned what was wrong with me. Dad radiated a dark energy, and I couldn't be around him without feeling intense anxiety. His presence was constant—an adjacent room at a hotel, three seats up on the bus, behind the soundboard, in front of the camera. When I displeased him at a rehearsal, I was slow to seek his pardon and he iced me out for a weekend.

I was constantly tired, so I claimed jetlag. I wasn't hungry either. *Here I am*, I thought, *in my favorite place, doing what I love, and I can't be happy.* Mom counseled me to pray and find the good. I tried to edit my thoughts with a positive outlook when writing in the shared journal. I listed every piece of good news I could think of, trying to trick my body as easily as I tricked my mind.

WHEN WE RETURNED FROM IRELAND, SEAN WAS WAITING AT THE airport, flowers in hand, flanked by a few members of our home church. We rarely saw them anymore, but this time we were home long enough to squeeze in a Sunday gathering. Sean and I were able to switch journals. The band had two more busy months before touring began to slow down for fall.

Mom came to me as I was repacking my bags, saying she had some hard news. She told me she'd been confronted by the church mothers, who thought Sean and I were setting a bad example for young people in the community. She said they were confused why Sean was allowed to pursue me when he didn't have the same religious education.

I wondered if we had been careless—if someone had seen us getting handsy. Mom said they even questioned whether Sean was a true Christian. I was angry they doubted Sean's salvation yet not Dad's or mine.

God seemed a million miles away from me. I felt like an impostor when I tried to pray, and I was doing my part to cover up the family secrets.

I called Sean with my tablet and broke the news. The criticism was abrupt, unforeseen; the width of my narration gap was revealed. I assured Sean I had no intention of pulling away from him. I swiftly did what I could to reframe the scenario. Fellow Christians were supposed to criticize us if they loved us, I told him.

My subsequent journal entries to him sounded as if two different people were constantly fighting for the pen.

My siblings must have sensed the tension converging around me as rehearsals became more turbulent. Dad no longer blamed my mistakes on deficiency of skill; any weakness in performance was a weakness of character, an act of rebellion, deliberate sabotage of the family.

He decided to film a live concert based on our latest album, though we hadn't yet figured out how to bring the newest songs to the stage. He also planned to add major production at great expense—over $30,000 for the lights alone, he said. The number shocked me. How much money was the band pulling in to justify such a price tag for a single night's production?

Between concerts, we rehearsed in hotel conference rooms. During one marathon practice session, he reached for a child's shoe lying nearby and hurled it at someone's head. The target ducked and the shoe missed, punching a jagged dent into the wall beyond. Something about the awkward silence made me want to laugh. His actions were like a toddler's petty tantrum. No one would dare condemn him for ruining items he owned, but the wall didn't belong to him.

"Clean this place up!" he barked and returned to his place at the soundboard.

In another nameless rehearsal room, Dad lectured me until his temper boiled over. When he lunged forward, Jack and Jedi put their bodies between us. Throwing his hands in the air, Dad stalked out of the room without a word, effectively suspending practice.

Later, he gave me a strict ultimatum. Mom must have finally told him what the church ladies said. He declared I was being led astray by an unbeliever, letting myself be tempted into sin, fighting God's will and authority. I was forbidden to talk to Sean again until I had finished my systematic theology study according to my father's standards. He refused to go back to rehearsal until I gave my word I would obey. My protests moved him not an inch.

I wandered through the next few days emotionally shut down, pouring my misery into the journal whenever I could safely retreat into my bunk, writing to Sean in the only way available to me:

August 1, 2015. My life, my beliefs, my decisions are falling all around me. My mind is a torrent, and my heart is a mess. There are two sides of me: one side thinks I should just get out and go away as far as I can, and the other side thinks the only way to fix myself is to stay and figure it out. I just don't know. I feel like I don't know how to protect you from the damage going on over here. If I defied my parents, I would have no way to live. I feel like they've forced me to go against my heart. I feel trapped, discouraged, and alone. I feel like no one understands—including me.

God, please forgive me for my anger, for my hypocrisy, frustration, and despair. Please help me depend on you for your joy, peace, love, hope, faith, kindness, endurance. I don't know what's right and wrong. Please help me love and honor my father though I feel I am incapable of it.

August 2, 2015. I am not being heard. I want to grow. I want to get married. I want to head into the next chapters of my life. I want to explore, speak, feel, and connect. This is not a priority for anyone in my family it seems. God, show me how I'm wrong; don't make me hard-hearted. Sean, I love you. I miss you. I miss myself too. It's so strange.

SURFACING AFTER TWO FITFUL DAYS OF SPEWING WORDS ONTO THE page, I finally realized how I could persuade Mom to let me talk to

Sean. He was considering coming to see our live concert filming, and if I didn't communicate anything different to him, he was likely to show up regardless. She spoke to Dad and came back with a softened stance. She explained their request was not that I refrain from talking to Sean but rather to stop acting as girlfriend and boyfriend until we addressed the concerns of the loving authorities in my life.

I called Sean the first chance I got. There was a shift in his vocabulary and a guarded wariness in his voice as he asked questions about recent events. Within days, we were back to communicating as often as before. He said the way my parents were treating us was wrong. He was all for us working through whatever issues we deemed were important, yet emphasized it was our right to decide what those were.

When I hesitantly asked Dad if I could get his opinion on some recent systematic theology study, he declared the topic wasn't a priority now. I could have screamed.

He singled me out over lunch the next day. "Jess, I think of you as a . . . well, not as a child, more like a teenager, not quite an adult," he said. "In some ways, I want to give you the room to grow, but there are lots of things you don't understand about life, things you don't understand about me."

"Dad, I think there are things about me you don't understand either," I countered.

He shook his head in disagreement and insisted, "No, I do understand you—so much more than you think. It's *you* who doesn't understand me."

I ignored him and he repeated himself to make sure his assertion was the last one standing. "Jess, *you* don't understand."

READY OR NOT, IT WAS TIME TO FILM OUR FIRST LIVE CONCERT. This festival was usually the peak of our jam-packed summer; however, the toll of immense emotional stress again rose to overshadow any enjoyment of the things I loved best.

The day before the big shoot, I saw an attachment show up in my messages from Sean. Clicking through, I found a lengthy document of immensely personal disclosure. After scanning it hurriedly, I deleted our conversation. My parents could never see what Sean had just told me. In a breathtaking move of vulnerability, he had decided to share his complicated experience with early-childhood abuse involving a neighbor kid. I felt a powerful involuntary response as sure as if I'd rammed two fingers down my throat and couldn't help but vomit up an account of my own experience in return—though I didn't. I realized he must be sharing this because he now *knew*. My thoughts were still whirling when another message arrived.

Sean: I think I've figured out what happened in your past.

I don't know how long I deliberated before responding with the inevitable answer.

Me: I think you have.
Sean: I just have to ask one thing right now. Are you safe?

I replied yes, needing to close the door on any further questions. Yet my mind continued to turn the question over and over, wondering whether my life had been one endless stretch of danger—never safe, ever. His confession made me realize I still had never once been brave enough to do as he had. I felt compelled to heave it up at once, a lifetime's worth of unmarked boxes holding pain, anger, and fear.

First, I had to sing onstage.

I played my fiddle and danced under the lights. As soon as I was done, I began to type. Behind my drawn bunk curtain, I wrote through the night with heat streaking down my armpits. Then a chill rattled my bones and chattered my teeth. I stared at each uncensored word hovering in the open. I wrote down my earliest memories, significant times my father had touched me inappropriately. I sobbed as I realized there was no possible way to relate their totality. The instances were innumerable.

I began writing with the idea of showing Sean, but seeing the potency of my account emerge, I knew I couldn't show him. I could not commit this level of telling. This was the bomb; this was the trigger. Ten pages, twelve. Still, it came pouring out. Eventually, it came to me: *I was writing to my mother.* I was writing everything I hadn't said to her back when it might have mattered, back when it might have changed things.

I thought of my most recent conversations with her and felt a flicker of old hope. She was only asking me to obey my father's rules and punishments because she didn't know what he'd done to me. Once she knew, she would help me; she would finally act.

On the morning of August 19, I handed my mother a fourteen-page letter typed on the iPad. Utterly spent by the fit of revelation, I could not stay awake. I wrapped myself in Sean's quilt and shut out the light. I woke when my mother wrenched back my curtain, the tablet clutched against her rib cage.

"Jess," she said, her lip quivering. "Is this true? It's true, isn't it?"

She said she was going to confront Dad, a few yards away, in the back of the bus. I refused to accompany her, afraid to leave the fragile safety of my cocoon. She asked me a few clarifying questions, nearly choking on the words.

"Mom," I whispered, "that's not even all of it. It's only what I could think of right now. Most of it blends together."

She came back, saying he'd refused to read it and sworn I was lying. She went to him again and even when I heard his voice rising above the hum of the highway, he didn't come out to face me. Eventually, I followed Mom to him.

The conversation was the strangest of my life. I had not expected Dad to confess; there was no reason for him to. He defended and denied. He blamed and complained. His wife had gotten fat and ugly. He had been unhappy. Society and religion raised children incorrectly, not preparing them for the real world of adulthood. He had messed up, he wasn't perfect, but he had tried to fix some of the important problems and his effort had to count for something. There were stories he would never tell us, aspects of his life beyond our understanding. He had been hurt too; he had been let down. He had suffered, and he had done his best regardless.

Mom accepted the blame of not being a good wife. She said she was likewise imperfect, a bad mother, a bad lover. She wished she could go back and have the chance to do better. There was no way to change the past.

I fell into a daze, unable to distinguish what I was feeling. I went back to my bunk and tried to sleep. I panicked when Sean came to mind. What must he be thinking? It was of utmost importance my family not become aware of Sean's realization or my vague confirmation. When Jair had told us about Maria's initial awareness, we'd reacted with self-preservation, denial, and fear. Within two months, she had been cut off. I could not let the same happen with Sean.

Soon we would be back in Nashville for a few days, and I expected to see him at a home church gathering. I hoped he wouldn't immediately question me. If he did, what would I say?

I NEEDN'T HAVE WORRIED. THE NIGHT WE ARRIVED HOME, THERE seemed no time to waste on words. I snuck out of the basement after the rest of the family was asleep and ran down the driveway to Sean's waiting car. Maybe we meant to address his confession and his guess; more than likely we wanted nothing more than to get lost in physical release.

This type of bond was new to me, intimate and powerful. I knew I should think it was evil, I just didn't understand why. I had not chosen to be a part of the other lies of my life. Being with Sean was something I wanted. We held only the furthest of physical lines due to my fear of having intercourse without the authorization of marriage. Since there could hardly be any hope of my father ever allowing me to marry or be free of his control, I felt justified in my disobedience. Dad was the last person in the world who had a right to tell me what to do sexually.

We were correct in assuming we would have to steal our chances to be together. My family kept a careful watch over me at Sunday church. As we lacked opportunities for more in-person discussion, Sean began sending me links, videos, and articles with topics ranging from narcissism and sociopathy to family enmeshment, attributes of high-control groups, and the long-term toxic effects of unaddressed childhood abuse. These terms and their definitions were totally unfamiliar to me, and most of the information went over my head.

I was afraid to be caught listening, as if this type of information was blasphemy or contraband. I cannot remember my family discussing the practice of secular therapy and psychology with anything other than dismissal. When people refused to live according to God's rules, of course they felt bad and lacked purpose. God was the answer everyone needed, not easy excuses for sin and selfishness. So, even as I resonated with certain information Sean was sending,

I feared being led astray; I feared being tempted to follow my own feelings instead of Scripture.

While Sean was neither a professional psychologist nor a qualified pastor, some of his coworkers were both. He was trying to make sense of what he had stumbled into. I was not yet able to appreciate or comprehend the level of support and information he had access to. I was taught that the only people allowed to claim truth on moral issues spoke with the authority of God backed by meticulously interpreted scriptural evidence. Though Dad was not a pastor, he was a man, husband, and father, all biblical qualifications for being in charge over me, his daughter.

MOM AND I SPOKE NO FURTHER OF WHAT I HAD WRITTEN OR DAD'S reaction to it.

Once, I stumbled upon her having a secret phone call. She told me it was a counselor, and later lamented the person was no help. I doubted she had been forthcoming enough to get any accurate or applicable advice.

Another time, she admitted she was praying for God to free us, even if this meant supernaturally removing Dad from the picture. "God could take him away in a second, if he wanted. He could have a heart attack."

While I was disappointed yet again by my mother's lack of follow-through, I had done nothing to back up my own statements from earlier in the year. In the five months since I declared I was going to find a way to leave, I'd barely considered any real action. Now I found myself wondering why I couldn't simply move out. I felt embarrassed at my lack of autonomy—likely due to the articles I'd been reading, since I hadn't used the word *autonomy* before.

I would have to persuade Dad to begin giving me my share of the band's income. If he could be convinced, I might be able to create some foothold of independence. I could get my own phone or save up for a car. Having my own vehicle would radically change my level of freedom when we were at home. I recalled Dad talking about how Jair would begin to receive his band money when he got married and began a household of his own. Granted, the wedding hadn't panned out. Yet it was still Dad's sole indication of our individual claim to the family's earnings.

I tried to test the idea in band meetings, also floating the suggestions of less touring, more time at home, and diversification of our roles within the band. I could write songs for a while—work on a solo project of my own. Unfortunately, these sentiments only played into my father's narrative that I was selfishly turning against the family, trying to hurt my siblings, and undermining God's will. Dad denied he was in control, saying he was only trying to help us with our business.

I was so frustrated by the word games, the manipulation, the way we normalized his crude manner and absolute authority while ignoring the inexcusable damage he had done. I wished I could trap him in his own hypocrisy, catch him in the act of being so unreasonable that everyone else couldn't help but see.

One night, he got on a rant claiming he was the smartest person in the room, smartest person in the business, lamenting no matter where he went in life, others couldn't keep up with him.

I interrupted to ask, "Do you think there's anything you could learn from someone else?"

The wind was strong in his sails, and he kept on boldly, insisting he had never encountered anyone who knew as much about "the important things" as he did.

"What about the other men of the church?" I asked. "The other fathers—do you think they know anything you don't? Could they teach you anything important?"

He paused awkwardly before declaring, "No," then tipped a hand back and forth. "Well, I mean, I could learn details of house building or animal care from them, but on the big things? No."

In the following weeks, I kept returning to my proposal of moving out, until Dad eventually confronted me.

"Where, Jess?" he demanded, "Where would you live? How would that work?"

"I . . . I could find an apartment," I stuttered. "I could attend rehearsals and still travel on the bus."

"You know what?" He crossed his arms. "I don't think it's ever right for an unmarried woman to live on her own."

My fleeting sense of clarity dissolved, hopelessness settling back in place. I wavered, worrying that I was indeed trying to justify my wrong desires by focusing on his faults, avoiding the beam in my own eye.

During our next band meeting, I zoned out, watching the windows rattling in the rain. We, the four oldest kids, and Dad were circled up in the back of the bus. Someone referenced me in passing, and Dad snorted in amusement, his mind going straight to a suggestive interpretation. The word *bear* had been used in the reference, and he made a quip about me being "bare," saying he would enjoy seeing me in such a state, sans clothes. My whole life I had accepted Dad's assertion of ownership over me and my body. Any inner reaction of discomfort or disagreement was pushed down and suspended so I could get through the moment without being angry, sad, or scared. I needed to be disconnected so I couldn't be shocked.

But this time, the offhand comment took my breath away. For a split second I saw the situation separate from me and my father, struck by how wrong it was for any man to make such a comment to a young woman who was not his romantic partner.

Heat found its way into my voice as I spoke up sharply, "I would appreciate if you didn't make suggestive remarks about me."

The contagious wave of chuckling stopped short.

Dad was incredulous. "What? Are you upset over a joke?"

"It's not okay for you to say you would enjoy seeing me naked," I said, doubling down.

Turning to the other kids, Dad raised his thick eyebrows and let his jaw hang open. His audience immediately followed his lead.

"Jess, don't be so easily offended," someone said.

Another voice chimed in, "You wouldn't be complaining if Sean said it. You'd take it as a compliment."

I knew why they had to say such things. Countless times I had done the same, jumping in to follow the cues given by our father. And yet, these chiding comments shocked me too. Clearer than ever before, I saw the mob-like response we'd been conditioned to act out on whomever he was punishing. Eat or be eaten. Shame or be shamed. How could I object to the technique simply because it was leveled at me in this moment? To blame them for their complicity would require acknowledging twenty years of my own similar actions. Even as I was ridiculed by the group, I inwardly judged myself. How could I protest without making myself a hypocrite?

For the millionth time, I apologized and went silent, putting the system back in balance. I didn't have the strength to fight against them all.

19

DETONATION

It was a blustery day in mid-September. The crash of applause was spirited enough to penetrate through the sound isolation of my in-ear monitors. I waved goodbye and strode off the stage with my fiddle tucked under my arm. The audience began to mill about the patchwork of picnic blankets and folding chairs.

We'd begun the month at a state fair, playing twenty-three outdoor shows over the course of twelve oppressively hot days. Though an approaching storm might thin the crowds, it would bring a welcome drop in temperature.

After doing my part to clear the stage, I realized I was late in remembering to get my iPad back from a younger sister, who used the device to flip through harp charts during performances. She must have taken it back to the bus with her. When I approached and saw her face, cold dread jabbed a finger into my gut. She was pale and visibly trembling as she let me take the tablet from her hands.

"Jessie . . . ," she whispered in a tiny, haunted voice. "Why would you do that?"

"What?" I asked. "Do what?"

One tremulous word illuminated the riddle of her reaction: *pictures*. My mind instantly made the leap, and I knew what had happened.

I groaned. "Why did you . . . ?"

I disabled the passcode during concerts so she could have unhindered access to her chord charts. In the time since we had left the stage, she must have found what I thought I had deleted. During the month-long stretches apart, I had started sending Sean pictures, blowing a kiss or sharing a beautiful location I wished he could see. With each subsequent separation, I looked for an opportunity to send a suggestive candid, following the progression of our physicality, and regularly wiped my messages and photos. Obviously, I'd missed something.

I thought I might go to hell for saying it, but I asked my little sister not to tell anyone. Though I knew we were all told to report on each other, I hoped to buy some time.

"Please give me the chance to tell Mom and Dad about this myself. It would be better if I talked to them directly." I put what I hoped was a comforting hand on her shoulder. "You shouldn't have to ever see anything like that. I'm so sorry."

I doubted there was any viable way to spin this that wouldn't end in disaster once my parents found out.

As soon as I was alone, I reactivated the password and searched through my photos. I couldn't find anything compromising. I went to my messages and tapped Sean's name. Dragging down multiple times, I scrolled back through our thread from recent weeks. A wave of nausea took hold of my stomach when I saw portions of my naked body. I thought I'd looked beautiful and sexy. Despite my father's urgings throughout my childhood and teenage years, this was the first time I'd taken this type of photo. I deleted the pictures, cursing myself under my breath.

I knew it was confusing for my family to watch me anger my father so frequently lately. These pictures would only confirm his accusations. My conflicting allegiances bound me like a straitjacket, my desire for Sean and my obligation to family pulling my heart in opposing directions. I'd lied myself into a corner with no moves left to play.

DEFERRING MY DEMISE AT THE EXPENSE OF MY YOUNGER SISTER, I let her keep my secret without any legitimate effort to alleviate her burden of knowledge. I had sincerely meant to take action when I made my promise to her, but the act of turning myself in was too much to contemplate. I eventually warned Sean there could be trouble on the horizon. Suspecting there was plenty I wasn't telling him, he encouraged me to make serious plans to speak to a counselor, a professional who could assess and advise on my situation.

The Fishers invited the oldest four kids to attend Sean's birthday party, and Dad allowed us to go. In the nine months since Sean and I had met, this was the first time I had ever been to his family's home. Everyone was delightful and welcoming, saying they'd heard so much about Sean's "special friend" and they were happy to finally meet me. Some of my siblings gave an incriminating report when we got home, telling our parents I was obvious with my affections.

Next, Miss Hope reached out to see if I would be interested in being her plus-one at a dazzling fundraiser concert in New York City. Legendary songwriters would be singing, and Hope claimed she didn't want to go on the two-day trip without a companion. Dad gave permission once he was satisfied Sean wouldn't be a part of the itinerary. This would only be the third or fourth time I had ever been away from the family for more than a full day.

Hope and I got talking so quickly and deeply in the airport, we almost missed our flight out of town. I was surprised to learn that, although she had been born to Tennessee parents, she had spent most of her childhood in Honduras; she regaled me with anecdotes of pet monkeys and armadillos. The way she and Pete had met and began their life together was directly opposed to the instructions of my upbringing. As a couple, they had disparate backgrounds and hadn't debated core philosophical theories before starting a family and getting married, yet their family culture seemed genuinely happy, healthy, and open to welcoming me into their space. My favorite part of the trip was having an enthusiastic audience in Miss Hope when it came to expressing my feelings about Sean. Who was this girl, popping out and instantly thriving at the slightest chance of freedom? I admired this version of me.

When I returned from New York, Dad asked me for a summary of the trip, making it obvious he was only interested in information related to the concert. He was disappointed to find I hadn't made any strategic connections.

"If Mom went, she would have gotten fifteen business cards!" he complained.

I apologized, tears coming as I admitted I'd simply been myself.

"Well, I've been working this whole time while you went and goofed off." He asked whether I was going to pay him for his work. I had no answer.

A MONTH AFTER MY YOUNGER SISTER FOUND THE PICTURES, I WAS offered a seat at the Fishers' table at a songwriter awards night. Their efforts at including me were obviously increasing, and they were smart to realize their open door at industry events appealed to both my true interests and my father's business ambitions.

On October 11, Sean came to pick me up, much like our first and only other date all the way back in March. I savored the night, afire down to my toes at witnessing the lifetime accomplishments and career success of people who lived, loved, and breathed words and melodies out of their souls. A small, defiant voice from within wanted to jump up and declare, *I will be one of you. We are the same!*

Mr. Pete leaned over and whispered, "I truly believe that could be you up there one day. You have what it takes."

On the way home, Sean was tense. He was trying to convey to me the likely severity of my father's issues. If what he suspected was correct, the continuation of chronic patterns would have serious consequences. I knew he spoke truth; I saw the growing danger every day. But I kept straddling the gap, pretending the storm would hold off forever.

I SLIPPED INSIDE THE HOUSE TO THE SOUND OF SEAN'S TIRES retreating down the gravel drive. The house was dark, and the bedroom I shared with my sisterly buddy was empty. The enchantment of lyrical inspiration still lingered in my ears when my sister Jet came to my door.

Yes, Sean was gone, I told her.

Yes, I had enjoyed the night.

Her questions continued, each query sharpening in intensity.

Another sibling appeared, and the air shifted around them. I felt like someone had forgotten to bring me my script in a scene they were playing. There was no time to catch my breath before they were asking me, "Jess, have you had sex with Sean?"

"No."

"You're lying to us, Jess," a sibling said. "I'm going to ask you again, have you been physically inappropriate with Sean?"

I was silent for a moment. "That's none of your business," I tried to say in an even tone.

There were now three of the oldest siblings with me in my room, which began spinning on an uncertain axis.

Suddenly, the Bible was being read aloud: "If your brother sins against you, go and tell him his fault. . . . If he does not listen, take one or two others along with you."[1]

"If your brother sins, rebuke him, and if he repents, forgive him."[2]

"Jess, we are only doing what Scripture tells us to do. You need to confess the truth."

"As for those who persist in sin, rebuke them in the presence of all, so that the rest may stand in fear."[3]

"Did you send dirty photos to Sean?"

Finally. The waiting was over.

My inquisitors reached their climax. "You need to tell Mom and Dad," they commanded.

"No," I said.

Yes, right now, they insisted, or they would do it instead.

Fear arrived, blinding, seizing, maddening. Eventually—kicking and screaming if necessary—I would be made to go. I had invited and constructed the inevitability of it all, somehow longing for a forced end to my duplicities.

Flanked by my siblings, I was marched up to my parents' room. They were awake and I recognized a rehearsed quality in their expectant silence. Attempting to intuit my script's lines from their faces, I followed their guidance through the excruciating exchange. I had taken vulgar pictures and sent them to Sean. I had been physically inappropriate with him. My confession successfully obtained, the judgment could begin. The fullness of Dad's power had been compromised for months. His clashes with me had thrown his authority into question. My transgressions now restored his strength, demonstrating a need for centralized leadership in the family. He'd warned everyone about my rebellion, and I had proven him right.

Over the next few hours, I was told my secret-bearing sister had suffered anxiety-induced vomiting fits that gave her burden away. Mom screamed at me for hurting her child. After the tortured revelation, my parents had gathered the oldest kids to discuss what should be done with me. Together they prayed God would use them to convict my heart and lead me to repentance. My immortal soul hung in the balance.

How dare I take half-naked photos. No self-respecting woman would do such a thing. How dare I be sexually inappropriate. What would Hope and Pete think of me? I had ruined any future chance of a relationship with them or their son. Dad declared Sean was no longer welcome at our home. If he showed his face again, he would be greeted with guns.

I tried to keep track of the blame. It was my fault; it was Sean's fault. At one point, it even seemed my parents' fault for trusting me too much, giving me too much freedom, too much reign. Never again, they vowed. I was forbidden to communicate with Sean in any way. Since we had never been "dating," my parents assumed there was no need for a formal breakup. I knew this was not accurate.

"I can't just never talk to him ever again," I insisted. I couldn't ghost him, cease all communication without explanation. Who knows what he would do?

Why would he assume something bad, they asked? They pushed and interrogated, their worst fears activated, trying to see how much Sean had figured out.

I said I would have to see him in order to end things.

"You have proven yourself to be irresponsible and can't be trusted with him," they said. "You cannot be alone with him again."

Could he not come over to the house, and he and I step out onto the front porch for a short, private conversation?

No, I had lost such privileges. He could come over, but I would have to say what I had to say in front of the family.

They let me send a message asking him to come over for a talk. Though it was the middle of the night, he responded, saying he could stop by the next evening. Exhausted from my inquisition, I was finally allowed to sleep.

WHEN I WOKE, I TRIED WRITING OUT A SPEECH, ATTEMPTING TO bridge the gap between my two realities, but nothing made sense. They existed separate from each other and could not be combined in any sensible way. With all parties in the room tonight, I would not be able to adjust for both what Sean and my family would expect to hear. So I chose to write that Sean had made me uncomfortable, pushing me past my physical boundaries, writing nothing of how I kissed him first and genuinely hungered for his touch. He would not recognize the relationship I described as ours. I planned to ask for space while hoping he would refuse to believe the words I'd be forced to say.

When the dreaded hour finally came, I welcomed Sean into the living room as calmly as I could manage. While no one was obviously gathered, kids milled purposely around the doors and hallways. I walked Sean to the couch and began reading from my written statement. For a moment, he was stunned into silence, as if waiting for me to laugh and admit I was only pulling a strange prank. When he heard my voice starting to catch, he knew this was no joke.

"Jess, what are you saying?" he asked after I fell quiet. "Let's go talk about this."

"I can't," I whispered unhappily. Tension throbbed through the house.

His eyes widened as he looked uneasily around. "What do you mean, you can't?"

Mom was suddenly at my elbow, summoned by my wordlessness. "Sean," she spoke as sympathetically as possible, "sometimes these things just don't work out." She reached out and gently touched Sean's knee. Dad did not appear.

Sean's chest expanded sharply as he sucked a huge gulp of air into his lungs. "Do I need to say what's really going on here?" He raised an arm above my shoulders, pointing vaguely out into the middle of the room. He was gambling hard. I had confirmed so few of his guesses. How could I have let him come here? He couldn't know how dangerous this was.

Kids stared.

Mom's eyes flashed. "What's going *on*? My child was having vomiting fits, Sean."

Sean shook his head in disbelief. His eyes searched mine for a clue, a sign. Met with nothing but my mother's continued accusations, he moved to rise.

I dove across his lap, wrapping my arms around his waist, burying my head against his torso, clinging like a rag doll. His pulse was pounding—I could feel it.

A few seconds later, he struggled to his feet and broke my hold.

"I'm leaving," he said over my head to my mother. His face shifted down so our eyes would connect. "I love you," he said with clarity and force, each word emphasized.

Are you coming with me? He didn't have to say it out loud; I heard it.

My reply was equally plain.

Deep hurt flared in his face, and he turned away.

I tore down the center of me, my head, my heart, pulled apart by two opposing ropes, both too strong to break. *I* broke instead, tearing, fraying, bursting, weeping.

He left, and I collapsed.

Mom chastised me for crying and making a scene. This was supposed to be a clean break with quick closure, not a messy drama. Headlights swung around the yard and away. My iPad and laptop were confiscated. Upstairs, Dad must have heard everything, but he never appeared.

Nothing made sense to me. Like mismatched halves of a ripped picture, my seams couldn't match up. I fell into the fracture, vanishing into the gap.

20

THE DARK AGES

M<small>Y MOTHER WAS WAITING ON ME, BUT</small> I <small>WAS STILL IN THE BATH</small>-room getting ready. I stood before the mirror and watched my body disappear into the wall behind me, black clothes camouflaging my rapidly thinning frame among the shadows, leaving a lonely face suspended in midair. Cold hummed in the core of my limbs as I gathered the hair at the nape of my neck. I twisted the strands mechanically and felt the roots strain beneath my scalp, ignoring the resulting flicker of warning in the corner of my mind. *This is my hair*, I assured myself and pulled tighter and tighter for proof, until my ears and jawline were fully exposed by a severe ballerina bun.

Though we barely had time, Mom and I were going to attend a play, just the two of us. It felt like a desperate effort to bring me back from whatever edge I was walking. I was supposed to be delighted.

Grabbing my purse and coat like a sword and shield, I edged down the hall and out the door. Mom drove. My chest began to loosen as we approached the city.

The performance was a cleverly adapted two-man production of *The Screwtape Letters* by C. S. Lewis. It used to be one of my favorite books. Fiery red backdrops and devilish wit portrayed a realm of inverted theology in which a high-ranking demon mentors his nephew in the art of leading a human soul away from God. Ah, yes, such temptations of the flesh, such pride of the heart. Was I getting the message?

The ride home was an eerie continuation of satirical theater, my mother playing the concerned parent, me the wayward child. If we kept driving, I wondered, would we break through to some other story? If I had more time alone with her, could we find a way back to each other? I missed Sean. I longed to say his name.

Then the cold night air was whipping my skin and we walked toward the quiet, low-lit house.

As my eyes adjusted inside, I was startled to notice Dad in the dining room. Rising, he maneuvered around the table. I passed in a mirrored path on his right, heading for a glass of water. I drank hurriedly, tensing under my coat, glad for its layer of protection around my body.

Dad confronted me as I turned, his words hitting a panic-inducing intensity.

"Don't you know you're not allowed to wear your hair like that?" he demanded. "You look awful."

Out of my mouth flew the words building in my mind, "It's *my* hair."

Now I understood what the floating face in the mirror had done. On one hand, I knew I was not allowed to wear my hair in unapproved styles. Simultaneously, in some alternate world, I knew it was wrong of my father to claim ownership of my head. My very person had become a battleground. Split, drawn in opposite directions, which would I choose? I let the pain in my temples anchor me to my quaking body as I pictured the demons and flames in the theater. Was this ridiculous, or was I risking my soul?

My mother entreated me to conform during the standoff, proving her sympathy was only available if my father was not there demanding her support. When I pulled her one way and Dad the other, Dad's string always won. She loved me, but she loved me after him, and he demanded everything. Before I was allowed to sleep, I was made to apologize for my symbolic, semiconscious rebellion, recanting any defiance.

I KEPT WRITING TO SEAN EVEN THOUGH I DESPAIRED OF HIM EVER seeing the journal again:

October. As seas go, this is rough. Sean, I don't know what I think. It changes almost hourly. It hurts so bad to be apart. I don't know why I haven't grabbed my backpack and shown up on your doorstep. I hesitate because of the good here, despite all the frustrations and confusion. This really, really hurts. This is not the end. This is not the end . . . Reality has been hard to define . . . We have another gig tonight in less than half an hour. This is so hard. I want to figure out what I think, how I should feel, but I keep putting that all aside so that I can simply get through a concert without being the absolute wreck I am on the inside.

INTO THE LIGHTS I SMILED. THE AUDIENCE SAT SHROUDED IN THE sea of darkness, laughing in echoing waves at our cheery sibling banter.

"This next song is one I really love," I said in my bright, assertive stage voice. "You may have seen us back when we were part of *The Sound of Music* family competition." A few hoots came from the back. "Our beautiful mother will join us for our rendition of another favorite song from that movie. Make her welcome!"

Dad triggered the backing tracks from his post at the soundboard. I sang until it was time for Jair's pipes solo, then stepped back from the spotlight. My smile evaporated. The instruments held a long note, and the little kids stepped up to sing.

I shouldn't have turned to look. Back when our family had first started rehearsing this song, I was unable to get through the lyrics without bursting into tears. Now, here was Jada, not yet five, in her white dress and curls, singing, "Edelweiss, Edelweiss, every morning you greet me." I pictured the family in the movie escaping over the mountains together. I saw a tiny white flower, standing against all odds, innocent and trusting, brave and resilient, a symbol of hope in the face of evil. Youthful voices pronounced together, "Small and white, clean and bright, you look happy to meet me." My eyes went blurry, and a hard, hot lump materialized in my throat. I missed the high note. Music, one of my dearest, earliest loves, was betraying me.

After the concert, the meet-and-greet clogged the lobby.

"I wish I was in your family," gushed a girl in a long denim skirt at the front of the line.

I'm losing my mind, I realized, shaking dozens of hands with my recovered smile back firmly on my face. I couldn't keep doing this much longer.

MUCH WAS MADE OF THE DECEPTIVE NATURE OF MY ERRATIC EMO-
tions and the depravity of my flesh. My parents told me I was being
led away by a seductive cocktail of brain chemicals and addictive
obsession because I had gotten physically involved with Sean.

"You think this is love?" they asked. "Look what it's done to
you. If Sean really loved you, he wouldn't be trying to pull you away
from your family, away from your God-given calling."

While a significant part of me couldn't accept that what I had
done with Sean was wrong, I felt guilt and shame. I was the worst
of all things: willfully unrepentant. I read scriptures about the war
of the flesh, including, "The heart is deceitful above all things, and
desperately wicked,"[1] and "The mind governed by the flesh is hostile
to God; it does not submit to God's law,"[2] and "The spirit is willing,
but the flesh is weak."[3]

When I tried to draw attention to Dad's abuse, control, or hypocrisy, the family would change the topic back to me and my problems.
It was unchristian of me to withhold forgiveness, they said, pointing
to Matthew 6:14–15: "If you forgive other people when they sin
against you, your heavenly Father will also forgive you. But if you
do not forgive others their sins, your Father will not forgive your
sins" (NIV). The strength of this command was so total I felt unable
to continue any case against Dad.

UNWILLING TO LET OUR LAST PARTING STAND AS THE FINAL CHAP-
ter in our story, I worked on a letter intended for Sean. We could

not continue our relationship unless we brought our thoughts and actions under God's leading and conducted our relationship through the permission and regulation of my parents. We played the Opry and neither Pete nor Sean was present.

After weeks of being edited to my father's specifications, my letter was finally approved, and I was given permission to send it in an email to Sean and his parents—better to get the truth of the situation out in the open with everyone involved. I confessed my wrongs and outlined the only path to reconciliation: obeying my father's conditions for our interactions. My devices were still otherwise off-limits to me.

Having finished the original journal from Sean, I began a new one, bright green with a matching twin I hoped to get to Sean one day. I couldn't know if he was still writing to me, or if he even still wanted to be with me. I filled the new journal to the halfway point in eighteen days otherwise crammed with tour dates, TV shooting, and travel.

When I figured out how to log on to my email on a desktop computer, I saw a message from Miss Hope. She was worried for me and for her son. One direct plea burned itself into my conscience—that if I had stopped loving Sean, I should let him go.

I began to lose time. I played gigs I don't remember, visited cities I never saw. I sat for interviews without being able to recall what I had said after I left the chair. I needed to feel and care as little as possible, otherwise I would collapse into sobs and shaking fits. Black mold was discovered growing in our rental house, forcing us to move out immediately. This hideous infection seemed to mirror my inner experience.

My devices were returned to me on strict probation. There was another exchange of approved letters with Sean around Thanksgiving and then around Christmas. Each time, I reiterated Sean's need to conform to my family's beliefs before we could be together. He countered with increasing confidence saying my father was dangerous and we should be allowed to conduct our relationship as adults on our own terms. His invitation toward a better, freer life awaited me. He would hold his ground.

Dad sent Sean an email of his own, which I later saw in part, including the statement,

> You have forced me to become involved where I had no desire to be involved.

Unable to stop there, he continued,

> You have brought out the worst in Jessica, and if you really care for her, you will either leave her alone and move on, or rewind and start doing things right. We have serious reservations that you are a Christian and put God's will first in your life. If that is not in place, then there is no foundation for a successful marriage. In today's society, people are seeking to redefine marriage, and it is important to know not only what somebody truly believes, but why. If you cannot answer these foundational questions, seeking a relationship with Jess is putting the cart before the horse.
>
> You cannot dodge life itself. Even today there is no good reason to not get it all right. You do not get to make the rules of life. Neither do I. You either fight the one who makes the rules or join his side.
>
> Nobody is perfect. Christians are just the ones who admit they fall short and commit to change directions. If you put God first, you get the girl. But if you try to shortcut God, you will not get the girl.

Don't be afraid to ask, and be honest. After twenty-five years of marriage, I am used to talking through hard things with Brenda. It is never easy. But it is the only way to build good relationships.

Sean responded with a single line I wouldn't see until much later:

I'm confident Jess and I can discuss and determine what is best for both of us at this time.

Dad escalated with a scathing reply of multiple pages, including these highlights:

We will not hesitate to stop you by any means necessary,

and

Given all cultures through history, I think we are well within the normal range in our actions.

FOR CHRISTMAS, EACH OF US OLDEST SIX KIDS RECEIVED THE GIFT of a cell phone, my first. I would only be allowed to use it for a few days before it was included in another device ban, leaving me with no way to converse with the outside world though I was twenty-three years old.

Later that same Christmas day, we had plans to visit relatives. Though I didn't want to go, I dressed and joined the family preparing to get in the car. Dad stopped me, commanding me to fix my downcast expression. I was so miserable that my face was apparently unpresentable. Taking off his belt, he spanked me for my disobedience. Dull, half-muted thoughts flickered off to the side of my disembodied brain as he beat me: *I'm ruining Christmas for my little sisters and brothers.*

We were slated to play the Opry the next evening and arrived with only a few minutes to spare before our call time. As I rounded the corner of the backstage area, I was shocked to see Sean and his roommate standing by the side door. I hadn't seen him since October. I gave what smile I could manage and went into a panic trying to guess if I would get in trouble for acknowledging him.

Once inside the dressing room, Dad stood guard by the door until it was our turn to play. There was a package of Christmas gifts from the Fishers for me. By the time we took the stage, Sean was gone. Physical pain racked my body knowing he was no longer nearby.

Though I brought the package home, I was instructed to return it. I only did so after sneaking out one of the items inside: a book called *Rising Strong* by someone named Brené Brown. I hid it under my bed until I could find an opportunity to read it. I hoped it could somehow give me actual, much-needed strength. I was doubtful.

Everyone seemed willing to continue ignoring the danger of growing awareness. With Maria, likely other members of her family, and now Sean, the cat was inevitably escaping the bag. I was starting to wonder whether a SWAT team was going to come busting into the house at any moment. If so, would my father and brothers pull out their matching assault rifles in a supersize version of Ruby Ridge? I hoped I had successfully erased the contraband links, articles, and research Sean had sent me. I was certain my iPad had been searched with a fine-tooth comb.

Surely Dad could feel the temperature rising. What was his

plan? How was he still in charge? If the rest of us all rose together against him, wouldn't he crumble? That must be why he was setting everyone against me, why it was necessary for him to whip me for my rebellion and bad attitude in front of everyone. *See?* he seemed to be saying. *This is what happens when you disobey, when you step out of line.*

I wished I could stop being down, stop being problematic. If I continued to hold on to my feelings for Sean, it was going to kill me.

In a final surrender, I agreed to write a definitive breakup letter, no further theological requests, no more asking him to find his way to me. I said we should stop pursuing each other. When I wanted to include the line, "I believe you are a good man," Dad berated me and made me start the letter over, shouting, "You cannot say that! Sean is *not* a good man." Reversing feelings, facts, realities, I was caught in the riptide, tumbling without a chance to come up for air. I knew my breakup letter would arrive by New Year's Eve and it would all be over.

21

WHO'S YOUR MASTER?

At my lowest point, I reached below my mattress and pulled out *Rising Strong*. The author, Brené Brown, began with a dedication to "the brave and brokenhearted who have taught us how to rise after a fall."[1] Nearly everything about the book challenged me and took me inward. All else faded away and I was forced to deal with the contradiction of myself.

I was brokenhearted. Could I be brave? The book boldly asserted that we must face the truth of our lives and rumble with our most terrifying emotions. Asking for help is a sign of courage, not weakness, and vulnerability is what leads to connection. I viewed that last word like a starving child, craving connection as one needs food and air.

Many of the author's conclusions were too much for me at that point. Where was her scriptural evidence? Where did she get her authority? Her words unleashed were like a firehose in the face, and I gasped through the gushing torrent, holding on to what I could.

Next, I read a novel called *The Shack*. It bypassed my indoctrinated mind and cut straight to my heart. Its almost fairy-tale portrayal of God as something other than what I had been told, as a woman, as a collective, as a joy-filled belonging, rang truer than the interpretation of Scripture I'd been shown. My soul yearned for a greater being or knowing I couldn't currently see in the Bible. This blasphemy terrified me, but I tried to be open to this spirit.

I lost the ability to write songs and stopped journaling. I felt I'd said and written too many words without action, too many thoughts without clarity. Instead, I tried to be quiet, to transform by drawing myself up and together again. It seemed essential to conserve my energy wherever possible. I lost fifteen pounds, and sleep was fleeting, plagued with nightmares.

We moved into a new lodge-style rental house and continued filming for our TLC show, now in its second season. Though I was beaten down, sometimes literally, hope had been rekindled. It came to me without preamble, suddenly present and undeniable: I still loved Sean. I wanted to be with someone who thought I was worth standing up for, someone who wanted me to be free. If it wasn't him, *I* was still worth fighting for, and I would fight on my own.

I wrote a new letter to Sean, explaining my realizations and recent readings, declaring my intentions to stand up for myself and one day accept his invitation, then kept watch for the opportunity to send it. Solo trips up the long driveway were off-limits, and my devices were sporadically policed. Since I was not allowed to go anywhere on my own, my restrictions amounted to a type of unofficial house arrest.

One January day, I made the impulsive decision to ask one of the television production assistants if he would be willing to mail the letter for me. He had always been kind, and something in my gut told me I could trust him. I saw his eyes drop to the name on the envelope and register recognition. He looked back to me with concern but agreed. When it became clear he wouldn't be informing my parents, I asked him if my correspondent could use his (the production assistant's) address to reach me. Again, it was agreed without question, and I was grateful. Had I been asked to explain, I would have lost the courage.

With our secret courier, Sean and I revived our communication. He urged me to read another book, and when I struggled to get my hands on a copy, he sent one. It was titled: *The Object of My Affection Is in My Reflection: Coping with Narcissists.*[2] He also sent a cell phone stocked with prepaid minutes. Under my mattress they both went.

WHEN DAD SUSPECTED I WAS AGAIN THINKING OF GAINING INDEpendence and financial freedom, he went back on the attack against my barely rising spirits. The whole family was sucked into long standoffs where my rebellion had to be squashed, and everyone was forced to show they were on Dad's side.

My mother privately confided she wanted to help me without Dad's knowledge. It was a head-spin. Which sentiment was true— that she believed I deserved freedom, or that I needed to submit to Dad? She told me I had close to five thousand dollars in a bank account where my Opry checks had been accumulating the last few years. It was one of the few gigs that paid each performer individually. She also arranged for me to cowrite a song with a business acquaintance, securing my first chance in months to be without family supervision for a few hours. I immediately got word to Sean when and where I would be. By fudging the times, I was able to leave an hour before my scheduled appointment. We met in a community park and had a few minutes together. He urged me to begin the book he had sent.

The next day, I gave my family my six-month notice. My parents had refused to seriously consider what my leaving the band and business would entail, continuing to book appearances and schedule gigs. I insisted I would no longer participate past my deadline. Dad said I was not allowed to leave until I had a foolproof plan for setting up my new life, which included successfully preparing my sister Jasmine to take my place—a forced transition both Jasmine and I had resisted for a while.

Dad escalated the conversation into an all-inclusive inquisition. The room took on the air of a courtroom. Side by side, Mom and Dad were opposite me, with a rotating selection of other siblings flanking them like a jury. I sat on the floor with my head in my hands as I bore up under a stream of lecture. I was an apostate, a Judas, a viper in their midst.

Hours into the ordeal, Dad accused me of having given myself over to the devil. I had no response to this level of condemnation. He fixated on the point, demanding I admit my allegiance. My refusal only poured fuel onto his agitation, making it impossible for him to back down. He instructed someone to start filming on a phone, for documentation purposes.

"Say it, Jess, whose side are you on?" he continued to demand, louder, more aggressive. "Say it! God or Satan's?"

"You won't let me say I'm on God's side," I protested.

Mom had been crying. Her voice was tremulous and timid. "We want you to say: 'I'm on God's side. I'm just messed up right now and I've made bad decisions, but I want to get to the right place.'

And that's not going to happen overnight. But say you're willing," she pleaded. "Say you want to. Say you have to change some things."

A hint of anger brought an attempt at truth.

"You know what? I want to," I admitted. "But I'm not willing— and I don't understand the difference." I wished I could be the smiling, compliant daughter dancing on a string like before, but it was too exhausting. I couldn't keep up the act anymore.

Dad stuttered, incredulous, "That—that—that's what the core of Christianity is about! Welcome to *real* Christianity, sweetheart!" He gestured sarcastically. "Welcome to being an adult."

I kneaded my forehead. How much longer was this going to go on?

Mom tried to bring the intensity level back down. "Jess, I went through the same thing you're going through. I understand your pain, your anger, your frustration, your bitterness. I closed myself off from him for a long time."

Was she referring to God or Dad?

"I *am* closed off," I agreed. "It started about a year ago and the more you guys try and push, the more I shut down . . . I just . . . I don't want to listen to these people and I just—"

Mom was horrified. "These people . . . ? Am I your mother?"

Dad brought his main case back to the foreground: "You won't listen to God, Jess. That's the truth." He waited for a moment, striking a thoughtful pose for the room. "What would it take, Jess?" he wondered. "I want to know if a guy came along who was really, really good, what would Jess be saying then?"

Dad launched into a lecture on how he couldn't identify with us because he had always tried to do better and didn't understand why we didn't do the same. He had the vision to see someone's true potential, like a master carver sees a block of wood. He didn't understand why we girls hadn't helped our unsatisfactory suitors become better versions of themselves, why we weren't driven to strive for excellence in ourselves. Only when people's attentions began wavering did he leave his ramblings and return to the issue at hand.

"No one can serve two masters, Jess," he warned. "Who's your master? Say it!"

"No!" I said. "I'm not going to."

"Say it." He intensified his voice menacingly.

"I know what you want me to say, and I don't want to say it," I said, anxiety building sharply in my chest.

Mom whimpered, "Just say: 'I want God to be my master.'"

"That's what salvation is!" Dad exclaimed. "You confess in your heart that Jesus is Lord, is *Master*." He leaned closer. "You need to be honest with yourself. Who's your master? Just because you won't say it doesn't mean it's not true."

Mom tried one more time. "What benefit is there for you holding out like this? Remember when you were little and I used to ask, 'Has the devil been giving you candy?'"

I nodded.

"What benefit are you getting for continuing this behavior? For choosing to dishonor your parents' request, which is to not have an inappropriate physical relationship and to talk about the important issues. I mean, is it just like eating candy? Does it taste good?"

"Who's your master?" Dad goaded.

Mom whispered, "Jessie, there's only two."

Dad urged, carried away, "Say it, be honest with yourself."

Mom said, with a flicker of hope, "And the thing is, you can come back from the dark side. You can!"

Dad agreed sagely. "We all started there."

"The dark side seduces." Mom nodded. "It does."

A few weeks ago, we had gone to see the newest *Star Wars* movie in which a rebellious son turns to the dark side of the Force and murders his father. I had been compared to the villain multiple times since then. To them, I was already a father killer.

"Jess, the lie is there's a third way or a fourth way," Dad said. "There's only two. Jesus said you're either for me or against me . . ."

"Fine," I spat out, the sarcasm unable to be heard above the weariness. "Satan is my master. Can I go now?"

Silence fell.

"What?" Dad couldn't believe his luck. I had confessed on video, in front of the family.

I was crawling with shame at my capitulation. "Whatever you want me to say." My voice cracked and I began to sob. "Satan is my master. Can I go now?"

I rose, sucking a few heavy breaths.

How could a simple desire to be independent turn into a rejection of God, family, and everything wholesome? I had become the black sheep, the scapegoat. Blame was thrown upon my shoulders, giving others the chance to purify themselves with the fire of their zealous condemnation. By refusing to smile, be patient and long-suffering, I was stepping into uncharted territory, away from my family and our religion. My mother and siblings couldn't possibly think any worse of me now. If choosing physical and emotional safety was rejecting God, I was indeed damned.

Leaving to go to my room, I called behind me, "Sorry, guys, I love you all."

Multiple accusing voices chorused, "Liar!" as I left the room in disgrace.

22

BLUE LIGHTS

REALITY WAS FRAGILE AND SHIFTING. WHENEVER I GAVE DAD AN
update on my exit plan, he tore it to shreds, saying I didn't understand the world and I could never survive on my own. I learned our
cousin Audrey—the sister of Christian, who used to record with
us—didn't have a roommate and quietly filed the information away
in the back of my brain.

I began to believe Dad would never give me permission to go; I
would have to escape. I tried to think of what I would need to take
with me, realizing I would struggle to part with my creative works.
When the old house had burned down, the loss I had mourned
the hardest was my writings and compositions. If Dad objected
to my assertion of ownership over my own body, mind, and soul,
he would likely do the same with my creations. The band needed
them as much as it needed me—maybe more. I had either written

or cowritten thirty-one of the thirty-six songs we had recorded on our CDs and performed at our live concerts. The next time we pit-stopped on the road, I took cash from the merchandise case and bought a tiny flash drive. I began filling it with copies of my writings, dragging folders and files from the computers whenever I found the chance. I added a few childhood photos, mourning the family I saw pictured there.

I gathered what physical items I could claim as my own. Hard copies of writings, a few sentimental dance awards, my Irish Music World Championship medal, stacks of letters and journals—all went into a set of small plastic containers I took from the basement. I wrapped them in bags and arranged for the production assistant to sneak them out to Sean, leaving them around the corner of the porch when no one was looking.

WE WERE BACK IN MINNESOTA FOR A FEW DAYS, STAYING AT THE same hotel where less than a year ago I had first told Dad I would figure out how to leave. The band was preparing to shoot a performance of the last cover song required by our TV show. Dad was unsatisfied with the arrangement and lay back on the hotel bed, doling out insults as we rehearsed.

When the appointed time arrived, we asked if we should head to the set. Dad was silent. It was unclear whether he was faking sleep or had genuinely nodded off. The band members debated whether we would be disobeying if we went ahead with the filming.

"Look, people are expecting us," I said. "We're professionals. I'm not going to leave them hanging. I'm going."

A few of the other kids followed me. Jair and the rest stayed. The crew was ready with lights and equipment already set up. We waited for a few awkward minutes before the producer asked after everyone else. I was tired of covering for Dad, sick of being embarrassed when he changed plans last minute or threw a fit.

"Last I saw, he was lying asleep on the bed upstairs." I shrugged. "I don't know if he's coming down. I would ask him."

Someone's device pinged. "That's Dad," they said. "He says to come back upstairs."

"Sorry, guys," I apologized to the crew.

By the time I got back to the hotel room, a report had been made: I had bad-mouthed Dad. Jair took the lead in rebuking me. He was tense with anger, sharply gesticulating within my personal space. The rebellion of my soul was one thing, but sabotaging the family business or undercutting Dad's strategic moves was another.

Whatever window of closeness Jair and I had shared during his relationship with Maria had slammed shut. As I looked into his hard face, I couldn't glimpse my brother. In my eyes, he had become Dad's strong right hand, the clear second-in-command, echoing our father's wrathful presence, all against the wishes of his younger self.

As the room's pressure rose, Dad let the scene play out. I imagined he was happy to get his wish—he no longer had to be the bad guy. The system had become self-regulating.

When Jair seemed to decide my reaction wasn't penitent enough, he accused me of leading the other kids astray. He slapped me full across the face.

I reeled with the shock and physical momentum of it, my cheek stinging immediately hot. I sensed a body coming at me and wheeled blindly. Jair caught my wrists and held viselike until I succeeded in momentarily jerking free.

The aisle between the beds was small, the hotel chair blocking the path. I heard a shuffling at my back and pushed straight through the chair, stumbling out into the hallway. The door slammed on rising voices behind me.

A startled cameraman stood before me. Turning quickly away, I plunged two doors down and darted into another room. As I lay panting on the bed, my pulse racing, I realized my shin was bleeding from forcing my way past the chair leg.

I was informed via phone call that the sisters with whom I had been rooming would stay elsewhere for the rest of the trip. I was now too corrupting an influence to be around children.

THE WINTER LANDSCAPE WAS THICK WITH SNOW AS WE PLOWED down the Wisconsin highways. Dad was at the wheel since we were traveling without our regular driver. I was on edge whenever there wasn't someone else around, a crew member, an onlooker, an audience whose presence might curb the worst of Dad's rages. He got especially angry when he drove, shouting for people to come to him with status reports or to give him back rubs and entertain him with conversation.

I was sitting on the bench, deeply absorbed in the book Sean had given me about narcissism, when Mom approached Dad with a lengthy to-do list. She asked permission to speak, and he let her begin only to stop her abruptly moments later.

"Bren! *Bren!* What are you doing? This is horrible communication, terrible organization," he complained. "How many times have I corrected you on this? There should be a summary, an outline, a time estimate of how long you need my attention."

My mother withered, physically retreating into herself. He banished her to the back, instructing her to return when she had a better presentation. I had been reading about the long-term effects of living with an extreme narcissist, how the endless bending to their demands creates or capitalizes on a lack of personhood in their victims, how someone can be broken in their psyche. I saw that my mother's current anguish was the same pain I'd seen the day I first wondered how a mommy could get in trouble.

Haunted by my enduring inability to fix the situation, I followed her. The foldout bed my parents shared was open with pillows and backpacks scattered across its cushions. I tried to be practical, offering to volunteer for things, even if it had to be behind Dad's back. Before we could make significant progress, Dad's shouting voice reached us.

"Jessica!" he called.

Dad yelling my name from the front of the bus meant he was commencing an impromptu quiz of everyone's activities and goals, and I was up first. According to his habit, he would go down the line after me until he had set a fire under each sibling. For occasions such as this, I kept a few perpetual to-do lists of my own, one of which I was able to give a ten-second brushup as I walked to the front.

Dad was staring ahead at the frosty road. I lowered myself into the folding seat above the exit stairs. Through the glass door to my right, I could see the cold ground rushing by.

He asked, "What have you been working on?"

I wished he could get a taste of his own medicine, that he could be knocked from his seat of power where he was godlike, all-powerful and absolute. It was wrong for him to face no consequences. Even so, I began reciting my list.

"Jess!" He stopped me in the same manner. "How old are you?"

After a testy pause, I answered, "Twenty-three."

"And you still don't know this?" he snorted. "First of all, if I have to ask you a question, you're already wrong. Give me an overview, or a summary and an outline." He went on for a bit, and I was quiet, mentally discounting his tirade even as I waited for him to finish. "Now," he said eventually, chopping the air with each word, "stop, apologize, and start over."

You idiot, I thought, still thinking of Mom. *She loves you and you've broken her.*

I reread the first item on my list.

Without warning, he struck out with his right arm, his hand leaving the steering wheel and balling into a loose fist. It was so unexpected there was no time for me to flinch or jerk away. The back of his hand slammed hard into my partially open mouth, knuckles connecting with lips and teeth. My jaw tingled. I saw stars. I gasped for a breath and lurched to my feet.

I felt my way back toward Mom, one hand reaching out to steady my steps, the other cradling around the lower half of my face. When I reached the hallway between the bunks, I felt the bus begin to rapidly decelerate, sending the vehicle into a lurching sway.

I was seized by animal panic. The bus was pulling over. He was coming after me.

Mom looked up as I crashed into the bed at the end of the hall, and I saw her expression change. "What happened?" she cried.

The bus reached its careening halt and my vision tunneled. Reverting to a toddler, I blubbered sloppily, "Don't let him hurt me, Mom."

Up on the bed I sprung and cowered down behind her, trying to hide myself, ready to deny what was happening even as it took place. In the last second of suspense, I caught sight of my reflection in the mirror and saw my bottom lip was lopsided.

Then Dad was filling the doorway.

"*Brenda!*" he roared. "She directly disobeyed me." He pointed at me, and I willed myself to disappear. "She refused to apologize."

Had he asked me to apologize? My brain rushed, then stalled, trying unsuccessfully to process the previous twenty seconds. Everything started to blur. I shrank in size, sinking back into the furthest corner of myself, trying to escape the scene unfolding around me. My body was in shock, useless, registering its position in odd, fragmented ways. We were in the back of the bus, then we were in the front. Voices came to a crescendo as my ears turned against me; what they heard made no sense.

Dad said my rebellion was complete. I must give in, or he wouldn't go back to driving. We were a cargo of madness on the side of the road. I sobbed among my mother's shrieks. This fight had to be won, Dad said.

Gibberish came out of my mouth. I didn't know how to apologize for the entirety of my being or how to make him stop. I was standing. I was sitting. Sequence abandoned me.

Dad had a fistful of my hair, twisting the roots against my scalp. He forced my cheek into the cushion of the bench, bending me in an unnatural way. I could have sworn I was watching from the ceiling. I was so incredibly sad, longing for everything to be over. Maybe we would evaporate into the air, bursting like snowflakes, and there would be no more violence, no more rage.

Then I was struggling on my back with a forest of fingers jabbing into my face. Nails raked down and I felt a sting followed by the slipperiness of blood.

If I didn't give in, Dad said he would kick me out of the bus. At first this didn't register, then I felt a whisper of relief. *Yes, let me go.* No, Mom begged, not in the snow.

Then I was seeing blue lights reflecting from somewhere. A cop had pulled up behind us, perhaps seeing the aggressive pullover. The frenzy of action ceased for a moment, followed by a frantic scattering. Hushed commands were given to the little ones. As the collective attention focused on the cop car, I was left dazed and numb. Heaving myself forward, I staggered to my bunk, rolled my battered body inside, closed the curtain, and lay still.

I was ashamed I couldn't smile and sell the lie. Blood and bruises would betray me. I had to be hidden. I heard the cop arrive, asking if everyone was okay. I waited for anyone to say anything that was true. The cluster of voices, straining mere moments before, were impossibly cheery and light. Yes, everything was fine.

No! I screamed inwardly. *I am not fine. I am not okay. I'm still in here.* My cries never found their way to my swollen, senseless lips. I wanted to escape. I wanted to be rescued. I wanted to believe I could rip back the curtain and be seen, be saved. Instead, I kept quiet until the bus began to roll again.

I wept, going hysterical as I came shaking out of the shock, the engine noise rising to cover most of my sounds. Why could I not reach for help when it literally came to my doorstep? Despair poured out of the black hole within me, saying, *No one stopped him.* My father had hurt me in secret for years. Now, he could hurt me out in the open and no one would do anything about it, not even me.

After all these years, I was somehow still waiting for permission to accept my reality, permission to believe I wasn't the liar or the crazy one. I needed permission to not be eternally okay. I needed protection and support from the other people who witnessed what was happening to me. But those things looked like they were never going to come. It was up to me to save myself, and I was unsure whether I could do what would be required.

I let myself escape in sleep. When we arrived at our destination, the family continued with our itinerary as if nothing was out of the ordinary. They toured a high-end guitar factory, returning with gifts and stories.

Mom said, "Wow. I wish you could have been there, Jess."

They told me about the many beautiful instruments they'd seen until I felt embarrassed that they had to witness the ugliness of my swollen face. I didn't want to be alive anymore.

23

THROUGH THE LOOKING GLASS

A SINGLE DAY FELT LIKE AN ENDLESS STRETCH OF ETERNITY, YET I lost track of weeks, the months changing faster than I could follow. I sensed my time was dwindling. The intangible countdown seemed now to signify my last chances at getting out. I was tearing away the mask I'd built to protect myself from the reality of my father, and I saw him as he was and had long been—the dark presence from which I had no reprieve.

On a bitterly cold day near the end of March, I tried to leave. There was no preparation or strategy. I found myself once again crying and shouting, parrying against theological and philosophical attacks. I ran downstairs, heading for the secret phone under my bed, only to be cut off. The mindless instinct to flee pushed through to the surface and I made for the closest exterior door. More bodies moved to block me, and I was told, for my own safety, I couldn't be allowed to pass. Flailing weakly, I beat at the wall of arms maneuvering me into a corner.

Seeing a raised cell phone, I cried, "Why are you filming me? Please just let me go!"

I nearly tripped over my youngest sister who wrapped herself around my legs and feet. "Why do you want to leave us, Jessie?" she sobbed. "Why?"

Further and further the inner destruction went as I tried to sever myself from the oldest ties that bound me, thread by painful thread. I strained against the longings I didn't know I still carried: that my mother and father would love me well, that I could still fix what was wrong. I had to steel myself against the nostalgic memories of the tickle song, of boxing with purple gloves, of dancing, of music, of shared mountaintop moments when we laughed until our sides hurt and I felt loved, wanted, and seen. I could not let it be enough to make me stay.

Reoccurring nightmares came with frightening vividness. I was trapped in a labyrinthine burning house, flames shooting to the beams and the light fixtures, sparks cracking and hissing in the floorboards. My family went about their routines without a care, smiling and asking me why I seemed upset. "We have to get out!" I screamed until I was hoarse, while they laughed and carried on until the blaze engulfed them. I would sit bolt upright in a sweat, heart racing, the dread following me into my waking hours.

My paranoia was fed by once finding a sibling sitting watch over me while I slept.

LATE ON THE MORNING OF APRIL 7, 2016, I WOKE IN MY ROOM alone. My chest radiated deep, annihilating exhaustion, undiminished by a night without rest. An endless tunnel of depression hung behind my eyes.

Eventually, I rose, dressed for exercise, and headed to the gym set up in the garage. I lay on the bench and raised rust-flecked fifteen-pound dumbbells that had become too heavy for me. I squatted, leaped, and stretched while staring at my pale, blank face moving in the mirror.

My iPad's ringtone chimed. Jair was asking where I was, saying I was supposed to be in the studio.

I found him at the music computer, editing the audio of my vocal from the live concert we had filmed last year.

"That's too far," I objected when Jair overcorrected a wobbly pitch. He kept working wordlessly and grabbed another note further on, manipulating my captured voice. "That one doesn't need anything. Jair, you're touching it too much."

He pushed the chair back from the desk sharply. "You do it, then!" he barked, stalking out of the room. "You have five minutes."

When he was gone, I sat down and skimmed through the malleable, brightly colored blobs representing each note. Within ten minutes or so, I went to the stairs and called up to Jair, saying I was done. Hearing no reply, I went to make myself breakfast.

The activities of late morning sans schedule were taking place throughout the house. Mom wasn't there; she'd had a meeting and it must have gone late. Jair sent me a message a few minutes later. *Check your email.*

A quick check of my inbox revealed a bizarre surprise: Jair had sent me an invoice. The current home address we both shared was proclaimed across the info section. He'd tallied up dozens of hours, given himself a generous rate, and sent me the bill for more than $6,000. He listed his video and audio editing work for the DVD. At the bottom in a section marked "Comments" he wrote, "Don't know why I work for someone so ungrateful and hard to work with."

When I tried to speak to him in person about the email, Jair refused to acknowledge me. I did my best to remain cordial as I framed an email of my own, pointing out he did not work for me, nor I for him. I sent the message and put the argument out of my mind.

The youngest kids were hanging around the kitchen as I opened the fridge to see what we had. I pulled out ingredients for a salad, telling them they could have some of what I was making. There was a bowl or two, multiple containers of food, and a stack of paper plates on the counter when Dad made an untimely entrance. I picked up my plate and took a bite of my prepared salad, stepping away from the island. The little kids scattered.

"What are you doing in the kitchen?" Dad asked, displeased. "Jess, do you know what you are supposed to be doing?"

I was supposed to stay away from household chores, focus on music. There was the chance this wouldn't escalate if I placated him. Until the words came out, I didn't know I'd chosen to say what he didn't want to hear.

"You know what, Dad?" I set my plate down. "No, I *don't* know what I'm supposed to be doing."

He erupted. Yes, I did, he insisted. I was rebelling. I knew my place.

Dad declared the Bible told him to discipline his disobedient children. Reaching for his waist, he began to unbuckle his belt. It seemed to happen in slow motion. As my gut tightened with the premonition of physical pain, a strange calmness took hold in my mind. There was a sense of ritualistic purpose guiding the scene. His blows would fall on me and then I would be set free. My hands braced against the counter next to my dropped plate. I focused intently on the scattered taco meat and lettuce as the belt hissed through the air.

Today is the day, said the inner calm. *Now is the time. By tonight, I will be gone.*

It was not a decision; it was a knowing.

On one of the strikes, the loop of the belt wrapped around past my butt and thighs to hit halfway down the outer side of my right leg. I patiently waited until he was done.

After he finished beating me, Dad seemed unnerved. There was an awkward pause, then he began to serve himself food, shouting for the general population of the house to clean up before anyone else could eat. Taking out his phone, he sat at one of the tables and motioned for me to sit in front of him. I heard the start of a video being recorded, and he began to interrogate me.

I didn't speak.

He scoffed, "You keep saying we don't listen to you. Well, here's video evidence that I'm listening and you're refusing to talk."

Every time I'd let him win, I had been terrified of the punishment, the beatings, the insults, the silent treatments. I had feared the rejection, the judgment of my soul, the shame, the banishment, the loss of family and belonging. He had done his worst and I was still here.

"Did you have oral sex with Sean Fisher?" he pressed, trying to compel me to engage with him. "Are you doing what God wants, Jess?"

When he gave up trying to record me, I stood and tried something completely new, the words unpracticed in my mouth: "I'm not sure if I'm even allowed to say this . . ." I took a tentative step backward. "But I'm going to leave this conversation."

I turned slowly and left him at the table. As I walked away, I was waiting for the lightning, the retribution, the damnation.

I SHUT MYSELF IN MY ROOM. THE CAMEL'S BACK WAS BROKEN, SUD-denly and without warning. I hadn't decided that today would be the day I would leave; yet there was no choice left but to accept that I had reached the point of no return. I didn't know how it had happened. With nervous hands, I dug out the phone from my mattress and turned it on. I sent Sean a short text:

I'm coming out tonight.

Then I stuffed it back under.

I wondered how I would leave. *They can't keep me under constant guard forever,* I reasoned. And it wasn't as if I lived in a barren wilderness without other phones, humans, or roads. It's not like I was chained in a basement in the woods. How strange that I was picturing the prospect of flagging down a car or knocking on some stranger's front door. In this day and age? How absurd. But I would do whatever I needed to do, absurd or not.

The image of my family's world shrank, taking on the properties of a bubble, small, confining, fragile. If I could break through to the outside, the rest of the universe seemed like it would help me rather than hurt me worse than this. The balance tipped; the gravity reversed.

Dad came to my room. He said he couldn't let me stay in his house. "You should make a list of the things you want to take with you." He had obviously sensed the same change.

I got a piece of paper and made the shortest list I could think of:

1. birth certificate
2. passport
3. Social Security card
4. the clothes and shoes I'm wearing

I wanted it to hit him, how little I needed. And then all I could think about was my family, my sisters and brothers, my mother. Could I really leave them?

The corner of my bedroom seemed to loom large, that spot where I had been surrounded only a few days before, crying, flailing my hands in front of me as they hemmed me in. I was not who they saw when they looked at me. They saw a saboteur, a Judas, a traitor trying to destroy their life. Someone who wanted those selfish pursuits called freedom and independence and didn't care who she hurt along the way.

Tears came to my eyes. They, too, were not as I saw them. They were not the obstacles. They were not the wall keeping me in. I wished I could tuck them into my jeans pocket with my flash drive and bring us all to safety when I ran. How had our hearts survived this?

Staying helps no one.

I quaked at the memory of tiny arms wrapped around my shins, a face smothered with a voice breaking, asking me why.

I cannot save them here.

In their eyes, I was the problem, and I could not show them otherwise as long as I continued to stay.

I dashed my tears away, wiped my hand on my leg, and winced. The outside of my right hip was excruciatingly tender. Curious, I went to the mirror and bared my side. Halfway down my thigh, a plum-colored splotch was growing amid an angry red arc, showing where the bend of the belt had reached the farthest and hit the hardest. I zipped up my pants and went to show Dad my list.

When I did, he backtracked, as I thought he would. He told me I couldn't leave, but his weapons were dwindling. If he beat me again, I would still be standing. First, I had to leave, then minutes later I

217

couldn't. Obviously, both threats were empty and therefore lost their power. Didn't he see the inevitability yet?

Not long afterward, he returned to my room radiating a totally different energy. He pointed his finger and jabbed it close to my nose with a wild half smile. "I'm going to sue you," he whispered menacingly.

I almost couldn't take in his words; I was so completely mesmerized by his eyes. I don't know if I had ever seen such an ugly look there before, but if I had, it had been from on top of a tiled counter when I was nine.

"I will sue you for the concert DVD," he snarled. He alleged my leaving would keep him from being able to release it and the potential revenue would be lost. "I know things you don't. I will sue you," he repeated.

My mind went to a passage from *The Object of My Affection Is in My Reflection* about how narcissists project their motivations and feelings onto others. Because they cannot truly empathize with another human being, they see only their distorted reflection in others, and assume everyone is motivated by the same inner forces. I experienced a moment of bell-sounding clarity.

He is projecting his fears onto me. He's trying to scare me with what scares him. He's afraid of me leaving and afraid of me staying. He's afraid I'll sue him.

This was the last part then, waiting him out through his last grasps at control over me, this seesaw of shifting threats he hoped would command me.

He can't even see me, I realized. *All he can see is himself.*

By the time Mom returned, the house was hours deep into the standoff. While she'd been gone, everything had somehow lurched forward well beyond her reach. Now, the best of her appeasement would not be able to restore the old order of things.

Almost immediately, Mom, Dad, and I were gathered in my parents' bedroom, sitting in the same positions as when I had been pressured to claim a master. The studio disagreement and invoice were explained. Dad's account of my subsequent defiance and beating seemed to imply my reaction was puzzling, as if there was no long-term issue that might explain my unwillingness to capitulate after this particular round of discipline.

"What do I do, Bren?" Dad put the problem to Mom with resignation in his voice.

I mentioned Dad's threats to sue me.

When he said I was lying, Mom didn't know whom to believe.

I braced myself, clenching my gut to stave off the nausea threatening to rise. They seemed confused about why there wasn't any coming back from this.

I knew if I tried to argue my way out, I would get nowhere. What was the simplest way to say this?

"I just don't want to be here anymore, Mom," I said. I knew asserting any "wanting" would be judged but would also avoid philosophical battle.

"Where would you go?" Mom and Dad demanded.

I said I needed to make a phone call. They brought me a cell phone and I dialed Christian's sister, Audrey. A warm, sweet voice sounded after a moment. "Hello, this is Audrey."

"Hi, Audrey." My heart thumped in my ears. "Could I come over?"

There was a tiny pause. "Of course!"

My parents stared at me.

"Can I . . . ," I started, ". . . bring a bag?" I finally finished.

I heard a slightly longer pause, then decidedly, "Of course. Stay as long as you need."

I thanked her and said I would see her soon. She texted the address of her apartment. My confidence doubled now that people were expecting me on the outside. If I didn't show up at Audrey's, questions would be asked.

Dad said I couldn't leave until we had a band meeting, and some of the other kids weren't home, so I would have to stay until evening.

"WE NEED TO TALK ABOUT JESS LEAVING," DAD ANNOUNCED. IT was astonishing to hear him say the words. The sun was setting, and the entire family had gathered in the dining room around the table.

"Jess can't stay. She's ruining everything we've been working for. The ramifications of her actions will reflect badly on us." He propped his hands on his hips. "We need to decide what her fair share is."

Was this a trap? I wondered.

"What do you think that would be, Jess?" He motioned around the room. "Guys? What do you think? How much should we pay her for the stuff she's done with the family?"

"I just want my writings," I said, knowing the flash drive had only a small portion.

Dad immediately frowned and the older kids shifted uncomfortably. "No, those belong to the band," he asserted.

"I want my writings," I repeated. "They are mine."

Dad cut me off, saying, "Everything you wrote was on company computers, on company time."

Anger flushed high in my chest. "That's not true! This is a *family*!" I stuttered, throwing my arm to point at Jair. "So—so, when Jair plays video games at night after everyone goes to bed, and I stay up to make something of my own, it's *company* time?"

"We have to pay her," Dad said to the rest of the room. And then to me, "We don't want you to be able to say we treated you badly."

This short, nonsensical discussion was the closest thing we ever had to a negotiation about band finances. None of us kids knew the amount of money the band made or where it went and when. Dad eventually suggested a monthly payment that could be sent to me in the form of a check. I wonder if the number surprised any of the kids. I wonder if it occurred to them to ask what they were owed.

I said I wanted to wait and negotiate after I had sought counsel.

"No," Dad said. "Whatever you don't take today, you leave."

I shook my head. "I'm leaving, but I don't agree to that."

While I insisted this topic would be revisited, I was unsure I would ever be able to come back and claim what was mine. Clearly, the train I was jumping from would continue to travel without me. I wouldn't be able to derail it without jeopardizing the rest of the family. Besides, who was going to believe me and take my side when my own family didn't? They would tell their version of this story to each other and to the world.

"Jess," Dad said finally, part warning, part delusional benediction, "when you ruin your life, get pregnant, and finally realize what you've done, you'll come crawling back. And you know what? We'll forgive you."

AT MY MOTHER'S URGING, I STUFFED A CARRY-ON SUITCASE WITH a few changes of clothes and shoes. I tucked in a few more personal items, the file with my identifications, and grabbed the prepaid phone and contraband books from under the mattress. It was decided I could take the iPhone I had received at Christmas but would mail it back to them as soon as I bought another. Dad did not allow me to take my laptop or iPad, claiming they were company property. At the last minute, I asked if I could take my fiddle. I was surprised Dad said yes.

Jack, now seventeen years old, volunteered to drive me to Audrey's place. Jet insisted on coming along as well, unreachable behind her rigidity. Jasmine's face is forever burned in my memory, her words severe and haunting. We stood inside our shared bedroom, knowing it was time to say goodbye.

"How dare you!" she whispered, glaring at me. "How dare you leave me here."

I grabbed her shoulders, trying to speak evenly. "Jasmine, listen to me. You do not have to do what they tell you. You don't have to do anything you don't want to."

We were both acutely aware of what would be forced onto her when I left. The mantle I had worn in the band had been marked for her, and she would be made to take it whether or not she wanted it.

"I'm not doing this to you," I insisted, but for all practical purposes, I was.

A few of the younger kids gave me confused hugs. They truly thought they might never see me again. Mom began wailing hysterically, stomping in place, and I saw her scratching wildly at the dresser in the hall before I turned away, in danger of beginning to cave. I felt her sanity being thrown onto my shoulders, and I prayed it would slide back to her as I moved away.

Dad did not come to see me go.

I had to slip into total numbness in order to walk out the door. The suitcase and fiddle went into the trunk, and I climbed into the car's front seat. Jack, Jet, and I pulled away from the latest rental home. As the drive stretched out like an eternity, I wondered if I had left my sense of time behind. I could have vomited at any moment, so brutally was my stomach churning. I remember no conversation in the car. I texted Sean, giving him Audrey's address and the time I would likely be arriving. I pressed my fingertips to my temples where I felt my skull would split open with every excruciating throb.

Then we were at my destination, and no one seemed to know what was supposed to happen. Jack typed in the gate code I'd given him, and we pulled through slowly, rounding the parking lot lined with manicured shrubs and cleanly marked curbs. Jack carried my few things as we climbed the stairs winding up the outside of the building. I held my breath during the knock. This was it. I was crossing over the threshold to whatever waited beyond.

Let it be love. Let it be freedom, I thought.

Audrey opened the door. Jack and Jet hung awkwardly outside as I stepped in. I did my best to smile until they left.

I felt I could tell Audrey nothing, but my anguish was unmistakable, and I saw it bring tears to her eyes.

Less than an hour later, I ran full force into the warm and solid form of Sean Fisher in the parking lot. I collapsed into his open arms and sobbed.

Part 3

24

SQUARE PEG IN A ROUND HOLE

I WAS IN A NEW WORLD. EACH MORNING WHEN I OPENED MY EYES, I wondered if I was leaving a dream and stepping into reality, or the other way around. While the relief was immense and immediate, I felt every emotion suppressed or denied over the previous twenty years fighting to be released at once. I slept odd hours. If I woke and was still tired, I would bundle back into the blow-up mattress in Audrey's living room until dark. Sometimes vivid nightmares derailed the first few hours of my day. When I became hungry enough, I would scrounge for something to eat, only to cry over a plate of food I eventually abandoned on the counter.

The Fishers, Sean, Audrey, and her family all made me feel welcome despite my disoriented state. They belonged to this world and knew their place in it. They went to work and navigated normal daily tasks, and I watched in awe and confusion, wondering how I would learn to do the same. I was cut adrift from everything I had known. There was almost an element of withdrawal at play; I had become accustomed to nonstop action and forced busyness to the point of chemical dependency. It was a struggle to keep from defaulting to the other extreme—complete apathy. Who was I apart from my persona as a performer, the oldest of twelve, the black sheep?

Being with Sean was surreal. He was now working at a hotel in downtown Nashville, beginning to pursue photography as his creative passion and future career. We spent nearly every moment of his free time together. One moment I would feel guilty for my abandonment and rejection of my family. Then my perspective would flip and I would feel the pain of their abandonment and rejection of me. I felt close and in tune with Sean, then panicked as if he was a stranger who would never understand what I had gone through. I refused to tell him any details of my history yet, worried if anyone ever came to see the fullness of my tangled background, they would rightly flee from me. To his credit, Sean did not push me to talk or immediately explain the roller coaster of our past communication. He assured me there was nothing I could do or say to scare him off.

From my first day on the outside, Hope and Pete assured me their support did not depend upon my continued relationship with their son. Hope took me to lunch, bought me a new phone, and was determined for me not to feel alone. The Fishers invited me to join their circle of friends and slowly introduced me to dozens of warmhearted people, ready to cheer me on without explanation or expectation. Sean and his parents were also gently persistent in urging me to consider professional help, even offering to pay for therapy or counseling. They revealed they had consulted with a recommended trauma expert while trying to make sense of their concerns over the recent months, and I was welcome to meet with her if ever I wanted.

ONE WEEK AFTER LEAVING MY FAMILY'S HOME, I TURNED TWENTY-four years old. I received a package that included a note from my mother, handwritten cards from my younger siblings, and a check for four thousand dollars. Mom explained I could expect to receive a matching check at the beginning of each month from now on. I knew I'd earned this amount and more over my years of work in the band, but I felt the checks would help my father keep my siblings turned against me. It was important that I become financially independent as soon as possible, so I could make a way for myself without burdening my new community or staying beholden to whatever expectations my parents might reveal in the future. If I saved the majority of each installment, I could buy a car by the summer. Once I had a car, I could find a job.

EARLY ONE MORNING DURING THE SECOND WEEK AFTER MY DEPARTURE, I was roused by a string of missed calls and the chime of a voicemail. I experienced a rush of alarm when I recognized my mother's number, and I quickly played back the recorded message. Her frantic voice said Dad was being rushed to the emergency room in an ambulance. She gave their location and little else. I tried calling back while dressing hurriedly. She didn't answer. Audrey let me borrow her car and I sped toward the address, taking a moment to text Sean where I was heading.

Disturbing images flashed through my head as I tried to guess at my father's possible injuries and their origin. Had he attempted to take his own life? Had an altercation with Mom or Jair escalated, and if so, was anyone else hurt?

Sean called, worried I was being rash and unsafe. What if this was a trap, or a stunt to get me back? I had not considered this, but I'd come too far to not see for myself what was happening. *I would rather know*, I decided.

When I arrived in the hospital room, I found Dad propped up in bed with Mom by his side, both lucid and without visible wounds. I waited awkwardly for the story. Apparently, Dad was having difficulty passing a series of massive kidney stones. Assured of the lack of medical emergency, I felt silly for coming—used.

"The problem is," Mom explained, "his recovery could take one or two weeks. We're supposed to leave for Ireland the day after tomorrow, and we can't make this trip without both you and Dad. We wouldn't be able to pull off that many last-minute changes."

The plans had been in place for months—plans I had committed to before leaving. If I didn't agree to go with them, I would be deserting my family in an hour of need. Besides, Dad wouldn't be there, and it was just one week. It was difficult for me to identify any specific risk beyond the unavoidable tension sure to run throughout the ordeal. I was not yet able to state my discomfort or emotional stress as a valid reason to say no.

Everyone other than my family strongly advised me not to go. When I told him I was going to say yes, Sean thought I might be crazy.

"It's Ireland—my favorite place," I said, trying to prove the argument to myself. "And I won't be alone; I've seen the schedule. I can't leave them high and dry."

I insisted I would be safe with Dad gone, but Sean protested. I felt weirdly defensive, as if Sean was the crazy one for making my family out to be the bad guys.

The trip was fast and strange. I joined my mother and siblings at the airport, fiddle in hand, looking for all the world as if nothing had changed. The littlest kids were obviously confused to see me so soon. Whenever we were greeting people or posing for pictures, I was included. The minute the spotlight clicked off, I was given a wide berth. I had become "other." On the last night of the trip, I told Mom I had arranged a ride from the airport.

Her face fell. "So, you're really not coming back, then?" she asked.

"Back with you guys?" I could hardly believe she had been hoping for this. How could she ask me to willingly return? "No." I shook my head miserably.

"I understand," she bristled. "You have a new family now."

ONE THING WAS CLEAR: IT WAS TIME FOR PROFESSIONAL HELP. I couldn't hope to make forward progress if I didn't first learn how to avoid getting pulled into my family's disorienting orbit. The Fishers put me in contact with their recommended expert and I scheduled to meet her in the beginning of May.

Sean gingerly asked whether I would yet be willing to tell the authorities what had happened to me. Imagining such a scenario brought on a jaw-rattling episode of the shakes, leaving me mute and crying in his arms. He stroked my hair and assured me he wouldn't force me into doing or saying anything. He cradled my tearstained cheeks in his hands.

"My priority is you," he said. "Keeping your heart safe is the one thing I will always fight for. It will all be okay. I promise."

How could he be sure? I still hadn't told him anything more.

I had no idea what to expect from therapy or a therapist. The notion of seeking help was anathema in our family, and this felt like a rebellion against the Bible as the ultimate guidebook and source of authority. That the therapist was a woman only compounded the matter.

Dr. Lee Norton was a renowned trauma specialist in her fifties. As she peered almost owl-like through her glasses, I found her to be cerebral yet grounded and utterly unfazed by my troubles. We talked for almost three hours at our first meeting and, instead of exploring my feelings, she focused me on the task of creating a chronological timeline of my life, illuminating hallmark events. I found it almost impossible, my words halting, my scattered emotions threatening to veer off a cliff in starts and stops, my thoughts jumping in bursts of memories that ranged from vivid to vague. Over time I learned why this was the case.

The previous summer, after I'd first told Sean about the concerns of the church members and my parents' growing criticism, he had gathered with Maria Martin, her brother Jonathan, and another musician friend of ours, all people with whom my family had once been close before pulling away. A conversation about my family's strange culture evolved, with each of them guessing at what went on behind the curtain. Sexual abuse was brought up and Sean heard Maria's view of the canceled engagement with Jair. The following week Sean had messaged me about his own past, saying he had guessed what had happened in my childhood.

After Sean and I had been cut off from each other, during the period we now called "the Dark Ages," he'd struggled to make sense of the situation and ended up getting into two different car accidents in a short span of time. Concerned for their son, the Fishers had sought advice from friends in the mental health field who advised them to see Lee due to her extensive work with victims of complex trauma. She also had years of forensic experience working with dangerous criminal offenders and was familiar with assessing threats.

I learned that Lee had explained to them the dynamics of insulated, abusive family systems and warned of potentially serious risks if the system was threatened. The fact that I was well beyond the age of majority and still completely subservient to my father's dictates indicated how much he dominated my perceptions, judgment, and behavior. The more someone's natural autonomy and self-reliance were thwarted, she explained, the less likely they were to try to extricate themselves from an abusive environment. Some people would never leave, even under conditions of extreme abuse. Not much could happen unless I first found it within myself to leave and claim a new life.

Lee urged utmost caution. Sean was eager to swoop in SWAT-style, but he had nothing that would substantiate a search warrant or prove anything criminal was going on. Both Sean and Maria had been threatened by my father and were wary of protecting themselves and their families. There was a very real concern that everyone in my family would deny any wrongdoing if questioned, undermining any investigation and giving Dad the chance to escape, retaliate, or manipulate the situation. At the time, I was incapable of summoning the needed courage. Instead, Lee helped Sean set and articulate clear boundaries for him to hold while encouraging me to come forward into safety through his letters.

Just sitting in the chair at Lee's office, I felt I was beating some sort of odds. If I threw myself full force into this work, I had a shot at being healthy.

THANKS TO THE LATEST SEASON OF THE TV SHOW, I WAS RECOGnized in public, at the thrift store, at Panera Bread, and found myself at a loss whenever excited strangers approached me to ask about my family or the band. Once I dyed my hair darker to match my grownout roots, I was relieved to no longer see "Jessica of the Willis Clan" when I looked in the mirror, and I stopped being spotted by fans.

In the shelter of anonymity, I applied for a library card, joined Sean on road trips, and learned to watch TV like a pro, binging whole seasons of shows I'd never heard of. Some evenings Audrey would be free, and we would sit on her couch eating snacks and giggling at old classic movies. A nasty inner critic shook its head; I was going off the deep end, wasting my life away.

When my suppressed creativity built into waves of anxiety and restlessness, I collected a few leatherworking tools and began making bracelets and other small items. The Fishers let me set up a workstation in an empty corner of their basement. Far from the extroverted needs of the stage or the articulation of songwriting, carving leather required an almost trancelike repetition of tiny, decisive movements. It was calming to craft something with my hands, to see a physical, tangible result emerge from a few hours of work. I could listen to audiobooks or more TV shows while I tooled, and this combination of activities became my go-to coping mechanism after long, overwhelming therapy sessions.

When I struggled to offer Lee a solid chronology of events, I offered to share with her the fourteen-page document I had shown my mother almost a year earlier. After reading it, Lee followed up the next day, texting me,

I better understand your experiences,

and

We need to talk about the safety of the rest of your family.

She scheduled me for her next available appointment.

I was nervous to see her—this person who had glimpsed my worst secrets. Would she find me unfixable, unworthy of her time and effort? I searched her bespectacled eyes as she laid her hand on the thin sheaf of stapled papers. She seemed sympathetic yet determined.

"Now we can truly begin," she said softly.

Lee accepted what I had written impassively, confident she could help me through the process of addressing my past experiences. She believed I could learn new and healthier habits and acquire tools to make a better life for myself. Her reaction threw into contrast how differently the same fourteen pages had been received last year when Dad denied and Mom panicked. Why had the conversation ever shifted away from Dad and the danger he posed? My experience had been completely ignored as I sat there in the bus, listening to him elaborate on life's disappointments, his multitude of frustrations and injustices. He had gone on to label me the biggest problem in the family, and no one had batted an eye. I absorbed this sequence for the first time.

Liar. The label echoed down through my life, a reputation crafted to discount my reality. For my accusations to be overlooked, my father needed to make me the bigger villain, switching the narrative away from him and his faults, activating the group against a common enemy. During the onslaught, my truth had been swept away.

Here, I was receiving a different, life-giving response.

I was believed. I was not crazy. I was *not* the liar.

25

WHIPLASH

UNDER LEE'S TUTELAGE, I BEGAN TO BETTER UNDERSTAND TRAUMA. She became my spirited professor, giving me as much homework as I could handle as we dove headfirst into my oldest memories. Writing and reading came the easiest for me, so she recommended books about the complicated nature of abuse and we would meet to discuss and reflect on a weekly basis.

Holding a whiteboard on her lap one afternoon, she sketched a cartoon brain and drew a vertical dividing line through its center with a fat, squeaky marker.

"Roughly speaking," she said, pointing to the left half, "this side deals in facts, order, sequence, language, thinking, logic."

I nodded.

"Over here"—she shifted to the right—"Are your feelings,

emotions, imagination, and creativity. Ideally, both sides work together to process your experiences and store memories."

She added an almond-shaped dot in the middle, saying, "This is called your amygdala. Among other things, it is responsible for activating your fight-or-flight response."

I envisioned it as the big red button my brain pushed during a freak-out.

Following along with her illustrations, I learned that overwhelming experiences send the amygdala into overdrive, shutting down communication to the analytical brain in favor of gut instincts more likely to help us survive. Memories recorded in this state are intensely emotional, physical, or visual, lacking the essential context of sequence and articulation of language. The brain then struggles to categorize and store them in their proper place. Like a loop of snagged thread in the fabric of a sweater, these distorted recollections are loose ends that catch on our surroundings and convince our brains we are back in that surreal moment, suspended in time, fighting for survival.

My work with Lee was meant in part to reintegrate fragmented memories so they could be properly synthesized into my story, repairing the damage, making order from the chaos.

As I stared hard at the whiteboard, something about the pattern seemed familiar. If psychological healing was sometimes facilitated by the process of figuring out how to put overwhelming experiences into words, I realized I'd long dabbled with the cure. That's what music and writing had done for me all those years. I took this as another sign I could be good at this; I had as good a chance as anyone to be healthy.

Lee urged me to remember that the road of recovery wasn't a straight line to a set destination but an ongoing, lifelong journey. With her help, I resolved to acquire as many other tools as could be added to my mental health toolbox. Dr. Bessel van der Kolk's classic *The Body Keeps the Score*, a genuine tome of a book, was instrumental in helping me plunge deeper into the science of trauma and served as an introduction to countless other methods of recovery besides talk therapy. Even though I found the accounts of other survivors too triggering at first, I kept seeking out their stories, determined to become strong enough to witness what they had gone through. Their truth helped me admit what had happened to me, supporting my ability to believe and assert my own experience. My empathic reaction toward other victims allowed me to be kinder to my past self. It was staggering to realize how many of us had felt alone in our unique encounters with confusion and fear.

A scene long buried in mental cobwebs came back to me: I was perhaps ten years old, riding in the back seat of our van when I caught a glimpse of a scarlet billboard towering over the interstate. A young, wide-eyed girl stared down with a single statement hanging beside her: "One in four girls will be sexually abused." I remember a tiny bell sounding in the back of my head. What did the phrase mean? Did that number apply to me? To my sisters?

Now, in my adult study, I was seeing updated statistics in context. I recognized myself in widespread patterns, which lessened the sting of loneliness and shame. I learned the names for my coping mechanisms, which helped me begin to unlearn maladaptive habits. *Dissociation* was the term that described my splitting and inward escape during moments of shock and distress, the mind's alterative when pain or fear is not escapable and flight or fight are not valid options. *Compartmentalization* was how I carried contradictory messages and dealt with constant anxieties. *Hypervigilance* was what made me jump out of my skin whenever I was startled.

Pete and Lee helped me apply for financial assistance from MusiCares, a charitable organization that supports music-industry professionals in need. The aid of MusiCares enabled me to continue receiving high-quality therapy while I worked to gain my social and financial footing.

IN JUNE, I WAS CAUGHT OFF GUARD WHEN I RECEIVED A TEXT MESsage from Jet. The band was getting pestered with questions about me, asking where I had gone and what I was doing. She asked me to come over and film a video to help lay the online questions to rest.

With hardly a thought of refusing, I obliged.

We filmed small clips in which I smiled and joked in the vein of our old stage banter—but apart from those moments, I suffered the same invisibility I had felt in Ireland, my family pretending I didn't exist despite my physical presence. The visit sent my confidence spiraling all over again. Either they were crazy, or I was, and it was infinitely easier to accept the insanity of one person over the many.

Back in Lee's office, I unleashed incoherent emotions onto her before regaining my equilibrium. Why did I feel the need to go when they called me? Why did I keep doing this to myself? Lee said it was normal to experience cycles of regression and progress. Two steps forward, one step back, repeat.

As a result of my study, my vocabulary exploded, giving me the ability to articulate banished pieces of my history. I would quake and stutter, but the words were finally coming. Lee even took me to meet a lawyer who walked me through the legal names and definitions of various criminal acts. I was astounded to learn I was a victim of child rape, which in Tennessee was defined as "the unlawful sexual penetration of a victim by the defendant . . . if the victim is more than three (3) years of age but less than thirteen (13) years of age."[1] Sexual penetration was defined as oral sex "or any other intrusion, however slight, of any part of a person's body . . . into the genital . . . opening of the victim's . . . body."[2] According to the current laws of the state, Dad could still be prosecuted for these actions, even though they had happened over a decade ago.

ON THE FOURTH OF JULY, SEAN AND I DECIDED TO VISIT A LOCAL park to see a fireworks display. The day was slipping into golden hour, sending sun flares through the tree branches. When Sean needed to use the restroom, I hopped on the swings at the playground. I had always enjoyed sweeping through the air with my eyes closed, wind in my hair, the ground rushing below. I heard a joyous shriek and instinctively turned to look for its source. A tiny girl with braided pigtails was frolicking in the jungle gym. She bent to dig her hands in the ruddy mulch and her ruffled bloomers landed in the dirt. A short-haired man sprang in from my peripheral vision, hooking his large hands under the girl's armpits to set her back on her feet. He leaned down as he brushed her dress clean. She beamed up at him, wrinkling her nose to match his silly expression.

Suddenly I was counting the kids on the playground—ten, fifteen, almost two dozen, all playing in the summer sunset. *One in four*, I heard the billboard and the books say, *maybe less, maybe more. Studies show. No one really knows.* The childish bodies transformed into numbers. Number three was on the monkey bars. Number seven was zipping down the slide. Statistics said there were multiple victims within twenty yards of me. I dragged my feet in the mulch and stopped swinging.

Who?

Another piece of information snapped into focus. *Studies show 93 percent of victims know the perpetrator.*[3] There were three other men and a woman standing around the edges of the play area. I looked closely at the silly-faced father, the fanny-pack-wearing mother. For a moment I was convinced the endangered child and abusive parent would be revealed by my scrutiny, as if I could spot them by some sign. There, in the red skirt. There, in the striped shorts. Then the curve of the swing seat pressing the underside of my thighs became the cold rim of a sink. I shrank within my skin until I was the size of the other bodies on the playground.

Me.

It was too sad, the bottomless well of sorrow I was slipping into. I had to stumble away quickly, turning my back on the laughing children and their loving parents. Before me, the hill dipped toward an outdoor band shell where a star-spangled banner was spread across the back of the stage. A sea of people applauded the musicians while everyone waited for the main event. My compulsive head count reached one hundred and fifty-eight before Sean found me.

"What's wrong, hun?" he asked with concern. "Are you okay?"

My eyes grew hot and flooded. "I think I want to go home," I whispered. But I wanted to go away to another world where daddies were safe and mommies had someone to love them, where there weren't hundreds of the invisible wounded among us. It was too much to carry, too much to witness. Better to hide and disappear. I would take Sean with me, make him understand. We should escape with our own imperfect lives to build a tiny, insulated existence while we had the chance, because the problem was bigger and deeper than we could ever hope to fix.

As the severity of my past came into sharper focus, my worries about my mother and siblings grew. My father's behavior fit into the broader pattern of abusers, narcissists, and sociopaths with chilling accuracy. Without exception, the pieces of research I encountered indicated that serial adult sexual predators of my father's nature never stopped abusing if a supply of victims remained accessible; they would continue to be repeat offenders until reported and apprehended.

COMBINING THE CHECKS FROM MAY TO JULY, I WAS ABLE TO BUY a used car—a blue Nissan Rogue, which seemed aptly named. With a set of new-to-me wheels, I had no excuse for not finding a way to earn my own money. Even though I'd reassigned any future song-writer royalties of my songs to my new bank account, I was loath to pursue my own career in music or performing, feeling the need to stay clear of anything my family might see as competition for their act or infringement into their sphere of connections.

Maybe I should move across the planet and go to school, I mused. *No one would think to look for me there.* A part of me had always dreamed of being free to learn, study, and read to my heart's content. There was no longer anyone around to dismiss my longings for higher education as pointless. Studious, serious—I could imagine a new version of myself, born from academia.

No matter my plan, I would need money. Unfortunately, as far as a résumé could tell, I was a twenty-four-year-old who had received no education and worked no jobs. I had no high school diploma, degree, or work experience in any nonperformance fields. I decided to try selling my leather bracelets before applying for a hospitality or retail job and began teaching myself how to create a website. I thought I was doing well, making progress.

THE SUFFOCATING HEAT OF SUMMER HAD REACHED ITS FULL FORCE when Mom called to say they'd decided to put everything into storage and live on the tour bus for the rest of the year. "I don't know how we're going to do it," she admitted. "I don't know when we'll see you again."

I felt pulled, activated, like a sleeper spy who had no ability to override the programmed response within. I told her I would come help them pack and move. Keenly aware of the compromising incongruity within my mind, I drove north in my new car. I was both curious about and appalled by the two cymbals crashing in my head.

The house was in a whirl of commotion when I arrived, kids scattered across different rooms, packing boxes and carrying bundled items out to the trailer backed up the driveway. Mom hadn't known exactly when I was arriving and came bursting onto the scene in distress. When she caught sight of me, she flashed her best smile, then excused herself with the recollection of a task. I went about gathering things of mine, filling up my car's back seat without challenge.

When Mom didn't reappear, I went and found her upstairs. She launched into a stream of random news until she was forced to pause for breath. I asked if I could help with anything.

"I'm just so glad you got out," she sighed. "And I'm so glad I was able to help you. I just want to help all you kids."

I blinked. *I'm not crazy*, I reminded myself as I remembered her stomping and wailing.

Mom shook her head. "I feel like the end is coming."

I had a mental vision of a train launching off the rails, pitching over a cliff into oblivion, smashing into rocks, flaming pieces of wreckage tumbling out of sight. Impulsively, I asked her whether Dad might give me my laptop with the rest of my writings. She said I would have to ask him. She accompanied me to the master bedroom, where other kids were conversing with our father. I waited to make my request, wondering if he would acknowledge me at all.

"Dad," I finally spoke up. "Could I have my laptop?"

He scoffed and shook his head. "Jess," he said, his expression pained, "you're not even close." The room stayed still as he repeated himself, each echo fading in sequential resignation, "You're not even close, Jess. Not even close." He had nothing else to say.

I said goodbye to the others in the room, hugging Mom. When I expected to turn to go, I found myself rooted to the spot. I was somehow crying.

My voice was reedy as I asked Dad, "Can I have a hug?"

"What?"

"Can I have a hug?" I whispered, feeling exposed and unprotected.

He considered for a long moment. "No," he finally said, "maybe someday in the future, but not now."

26

POINT OF NO RETURN

"WE NEED TO WORK ON YOUR INTERNAL LOCUS OF CONTROL," LEE said, reaching for the now-familiar whiteboard. She sketched two stick figures. The person on the right had arrows radiating outward in all directions while the one on the left was surrounded by an inward-facing volley.

"Do you believe the events of your life are out of your control?" she asked.

I hesitated. A flash of words and phrases shot through my head: *preordained*; *God's will*; *sin of the flesh*; *obedience*; *rebellion*; Dad clucking in disappointment, "*Not even close.*"

She pointed to the person about to be stuck full of barbs: "This individual believes they can't do anything about their life." She explained this person blamed others, saw themselves as a victim, was unable to know what they wanted and how to get it, and could feel depressed and helpless.

Her finger swept to the other side of the board. "This individual believes their actions can affect the outcome of their life." They had a developed sense of self, autonomy, and a healthy ego-strength. This person could take responsibility for their decisions and was resilient, hopeful.

My eyes traveled back and forth, adding imaginary details to the stick figures. The one on the left had blonde hair she was not allowed to put in a bun, a lifetime of secrets she was obligated to protect. She wouldn't be forgiven unless she forgave, she would go to hell if she didn't submit. The other figure had brown hair, wore sneakers because she liked them, could talk a blue streak about the things that made her happy, and suspected her body was mysterious, good, and wise. I was somewhere between them.

"Isn't having an ego a bad thing?" I asked, thinking of my father's boastfulness.

Her head shook no. She meant ego as a sense of self and personal identity.

Apparently I had it backward. Healthy egos were balanced, able to recognize the real world and function in it. Weak egos were needy and fearful, overreacting from emotionally inflated beliefs. I thought of the narcissist, how he seemed so dominating, so full of arrogance on the outside, with his appetite always too large and his supply never enough, when inside there lay a wounded, shame-filled core, a void of personhood.

I didn't want to be stuck in unhealthy patterns or perpetuate cycles into future generations. If I continued to run from the truth, I would remain complicit in my own ruin. The choice for health required that I plant my feet and look pain in the face. Know it. Name it. If I was going to beat the odds, I had to become strong enough to do the right thing when the moment of fear and grief was upon me.

I began to see the uncanny similarities my father shared with the profiles of cult leaders and psychopathic murderers. With my own eyes and ears, I had witnessed his paranoia range from claims about the government to the end of the world, at times using the exact phrasing and wordings of other infamous figures. His ideological interpretation of violent standoffs made me wonder if there ever would be a way to successfully save the rest of my family members without a similarly major incident. I told Lee of my father's remarks, like "The government can't take away a kid who's carrying an assault rifle."

It deeply disturbed me to see stories of killers who evaded arrest, rapists who were set free, wife beaters who were released on bond only to find their victims and make them pay. If I told the police about my father's crimes, no one could guarantee he wouldn't find a way to hunt me down and stop me "by any means necessary," as he had threatened Sean.

Despite my fears, guilt about my persisting silence began to grow.

When Sean next brought up speaking to law enforcement, I had an irrational fit of hysterics, saying, "Don't make me go back there. Please. I can't do it. Don't make me go there."

As if my brain was seeking a balancing point, skeptical voices rose within me, questioning whether the information or research was wrong, or whether I was exaggerating, misremembering, fabricating, and therefore couldn't trust myself. For twenty years I had publicly proclaimed my father to be a loving genius. Which story, told by my own mouth, was true? He couldn't be both a wonderful father and a dangerous criminal.

Lee introduced me to the concept of "cognitive dissonance," the state of simultaneously holding two mutually exclusive beliefs and being stuck between their inherent opposition. Sometimes the contradictions stayed hidden inside the subconscious. Mine had grown too massive to be ignored and were causing huge crises of conscience, freezing me in indecision and anxiety.

There's the name for my crashing cymbals, I mused.

Lee encouraged me to try to listen to the warring voices, to write down the messages they told me to believe. I had her assurance that I could disprove false stories about myself and my world. I could take steps toward a congruent life by aligning my actions with my core beliefs. This mind was mine, she reminded me; I could reclaim it as I had reclaimed my hair, my body, my future.

I TOOK OUT MY BIBLE, WHICH I HAD FORGOTTEN I HAD BROUGHT with me when I left. It sat next to my bed for a few days, and then I opened it to see if I would see something different, to see what the passages I had read since I was ten years old would look like in a new context.

As I flipped and felt my way through whole chunks of tiny text, I could tell I was searching. Once again, I read about the plank in my eye, how I would not receive forgiveness if I did not forgive others, how obedience was required of children and submission and silence required of women. I realized one part of me was looking for biblical excuses to not have to report my father. Even as I found them—"The LORD will fight for you, and you have only to be silent"[1]—I felt the twisted interpretations slipping and cracking apart.

The so-called rebellious part of me was almost ready to stand in a new level of opposition.

THE WILLIS CLAN WAS TRAVELING IN IRELAND WHEN SEAN TOLD me Jonathan Martin, Maria's brother, was back in town. He had been on the road playing in bluegrass bands over the summer. In my view, Maria and her family were on the long list of people I thought we'd treated unfairly. They'd been struck from our lives without hesitation. We had almost been family, and yet they were given no closure or explanations.

Sean said Jonathan was interested in talking to me. Would I be willing to get together?

"Yes," I said. "It's probably time we talked."

After confirming a place and time to meet, I grew nervous. Though a part of me longed to have the truth out in the open, I still feared what my unguarded words might unleash. The bomb was back on my chest, the trigger in hand. I had a vague sense of what I should do yet felt I lacked the ability to set it into motion.

When I saw Jonathan's lanky form approaching the sun-dappled patio, I had the distinct impression I was betraying my family. He was polite, and we started speaking easily enough. Perhaps he understood how precarious I felt. Perhaps he felt the same. Our talk stepped carefully around the elephant.

He told me that since reconnecting with members of our old home church community, his conscience had been weighing heavily on him. He felt there were things he needed to tell them. I was clearly meant to read between the lines. It seemed he had put together signs and rumors from Maria, Sean, and his own observations.

I wanted to pour out excuses, to say telling was too dangerous, an effective response uncertain, the chance of justice unlikely. *You haven't seen the way this could go,* I thought silently. *You don't know what you're up against.*

He said he was praying for guidance and shared scriptures he believed declared God's desire for us to live in healing and freedom.

I could see no biblical God other than the one who stood condemning me over the shoulder of my father. I said I wouldn't tell him what to do; I couldn't ask him to speak or refrain from speaking. I purposefully didn't ask him to specify what he knew.

EARLY ON THE MORNING OF AUGUST 24, 2016, MY PHONE RANG. I stared at the screen, watching a name illuminate in the dark until the call went to voice mail. I had not spoken to anyone from the original home church group in over four months. Minutes later, another name flashed bright. Why were the wives calling me?

This time, I picked up with an unsteady hand. The voice in my ear was careful. After a delicate exchange of greetings, I heard a short exhale before the flood came tumbling out.

Jonathan Martin had met with the church fathers last night, she said, and he'd had some very disturbing things to say about my father.

Her words hit like a dropkick to the stomach. I willed myself to breathe, consciously telling my lungs to expand and contract. It felt like the night the iPad pictures were discovered.

Finally.

The woman apologized but asked if there was anything I could tell her.

What had Jonathan said to them? For all my years dreading this moment, why had I never planned what I might say? Though it was always going to be a shock, it had been a long time coming too. My newly expanded vocabulary caught in my throat. I cared about this community, but they were not my therapist, and they weren't bound by confidentiality or professionally educated on such matters. I hadn't yet learned how to tell my story to normal people, to open my mouth and say "child rape," "assault," "molestation." I remembered sitting in a circle as the church group agreed women were to be silent in the gatherings. Scriptural instructions for interventions came to mind:

"My brothers, if anyone among you wanders from the truth and someone brings him back, let him know that whoever brings back a sinner from his wandering will save his soul from death and will cover a multitude of sins."[2]

"Do not admit a charge against an elder except on the evidence of two or three witnesses."[3]

I stammered that there were things to know, but I couldn't say them right then. And that if they had anything to ask Dad, they would have to speak to him themselves.

The voice on the other end of the line pitched upward, saying that, although it was awful to say so, this was both unbelievable and yet not completely surprising.

I had no more words. My brain raced as the line went dead. My family was out of the country. Was that better or worse? I pictured the church men arranging a well-meaning intervention set on confronting my father, only to see the imaginary scenario devolve into a fatal, door-blocking, gun-shooting standoff. Would they be able to grasp this wasn't fixable with an accountability system or prayer? How would the rest of my family respond? Who would they heed? I thought of my mother's late words: "I want to help all you kids. I just don't know how."

The cymbals were back, causing a frenzy in my mind, frustrating my ability to act. Nothing felt like the right thing to do.

I began to dial. *You know better than this*, I told myself, but I was waiting for the ring, already counting forward six hours. It was afternoon in Ireland. I had to do this before someone stopped me, bad idea or not.

Click. "Hello, Jessie." Mom was warm, upbeat, surprised.

"Mom," I wailed, "you need to know. You and the kids have to be safe, be warned. I'm so sorry. The men of the church know. They know."

"What . . . I don't understand . . . Who . . . ?"

"It wasn't me, but please, Mom, be safe. Be ready. I'm so sorry."

I hung up, praying that if there was a God, he would help her do the right thing.

27

FOR THE RECORD

THE NEXT DAYS WERE FILLED WITH THE FRENZIED CACOPHONY OF mental cymbals other than my own. We learned Jonathan Martin had shared with the home church fathers his suspicions that my father was sexually abusing my younger siblings.

With the aim of talking them out of making any ill-advised intercessions, Sean met with them to say I had confirmed to him that my father had been both abusive and violent toward me. He stressed both the scope and seriousness of the potential crimes along with our existing fears of my dad's reactions.

A cop from the community was called for advice, and his direction was unequivocally forceful: according to Tennessee's mandatory reporting statute, every passing minute abuse against minors went unreported, people were breaking the law.

I didn't feel ready. Living through my father's actions was not enough; I would also have to survive the telling, the blast of the bomb he had planted inside of me. There was no escape from examination, no passing into anonymity, no right to my privacy without the perpetual moral offense of not protecting others. For my entire childhood, the thought of speaking was the ultimate betrayal, the unforgivable act that would make me responsible for the undoing of my family. Now, silence was my sin.

"Someone else can report it," Sean told me. "But the cops are going to need firsthand testimony to be able to do their job right. Either way, it's got to happen. It's past time."

I would never feel ready, but there was no one else who could do my part.

Forgoing anonymity, Jonathan Martin called the sexual abuse hotline at the Department of Children's Services (DCS) on August 29, 2016, naming my father for suspicion of sexual and physical abuse against minors. We would later learn the District Attorney's office received the DCS report the next day and immediately asked the Tennessee Bureau of Investigation (TBI) to begin an investigation with utmost speed and caution in order to limit any unwanted media attention or interference due to my family's celebrity.

Jonathan was the first to be called for an interview. Sean followed a few hours later. He phoned me before leaving the sheriff's office.

"They want to know if you can come in tonight," Sean said.

"Now?" I had counted on one more day to mentally prepare. "Can't I come in tomorrow?"

I heard him ask a question and realized he was still with the investigators.

"We're almost done here. They want to see you as soon as possible," he said. "I can be here for moral support now, but I'm working tomorrow. Do you want me to be there?"

"Of course I *want* you to be there . . . but I just think I have to do this by myself. I can't be worrying about your reaction to the things I'm going to have to say. I'm sorry," I apologized, "that came out wrong."

"No, that's okay. That makes sense," Sean said.

"Maybe I'll see if Lee's lawyer friend could come with me. I don't know . . . I don't want to mess this up. Would that be allowed?"

Sean said that would be fine and they would expect me tomorrow afternoon.

When we told Lee the TBI was involved, she received it as the best of all possible news. She quickly coordinated for her friend to meet me at the interview, and the friend promised she would stay in the background and only say something if requested.

I had been discussing the possibility of moving in with the Fishers sometime toward the end of the year. Now that I would be on the record giving testimony against my father, their gated community seemed like the safest place for me to be.

With the details for my meeting set, I tried to rest. As I slipped into anxious sleep, I realized it was August 31—my parents' twenty-fifth wedding anniversary.

IN THE MORNING, I FORCED MYSELF TO EAT. I LAYERED ON INCREAS-ingly heavier clothes until I admitted I was not shivering from a lack of warmth. Staring at my face in the mirror, I half-wished I could slip back into my dissociative, compartmentalized state of five months ago. Instead, I had to trust my lips to move when I commanded.

I must give them what they need, I told myself. *Don't panic. Don't overthink. Just say anything that's true.*

I drove to the TBI office as steadily as I could manage and still arrived early. The lawyer met me in the parking lot. She was practically a stranger and just what I needed—a human security blanket.

Upon entering the long brick building, we were led to a rectangular boardroom with midnight blue walls and a large pill-shaped table in the center. An oversize sculpture of the Tennessee State seal hung centered on the narrow wall. We were offered bottled water and black high-backed chairs with leather padding. The lawyer introduced herself to the two serious-looking men in short-sleeved button-down shirts. I could tell they knew each other, and their small interaction was an unsettling reminder I was now surrounded by people whose daily job included the handling of crimes and witnesses.

The men sat. Farther to their left, a calm African American woman smiled gently. The short-haired man directly square with me introduced himself as Special Agent Holt and said the smiling woman was a victim services coordinator. Speaking softly, she said she would remain present for the interview and be my point of contact for any help I might require throughout the duration of the case. I thanked her, and the room grew still.

I felt Holt's keen eyes lock onto me, steely under the fluorescent lights. I noticed his brawny shoulders set firm. He thanked me for coming in and asked me to verify I was there of my own free will. After outlining the hotline call as the initial reason for their investigation, he eased into a few preliminary questions such as my full name, date of birth, place of residence.

I didn't want to make any mistakes and sheepishly explained that since leaving my family home, I'd been sleeping in my cousin's living room, and was now in the process of moving in with my boyfriend's family. I gave them both addresses.

"Where did you last live with your family?"

I gave them the address of the last rental house and couldn't remember the zip code. We'd been on the road too much over those last few months for me to fully memorize it. I explained we'd lived in a succession of rentals after our house burned down in 2004. At least, I thought it was 2004, the day after Christmas. I was flustered, berating myself for not taking time to recall or organize such details of the timeline beforehand. Would my story be discredited if I got basic facts wrong?

I said we had moved from Chicago when I was nine. Or at least, we'd moved right around my ninth birthday. Holt assured me I was doing fine; he would ask me for more detail when needed. He requested the names of my siblings, and I did my best to sound confident on their ages. When I used to introduce everyone onstage, it seemed as if I couldn't get down the line without making a mistake.

In one long and laborious discharge, I vomited out my hidden history, sometimes disordered, frequently awkward. When I recounted instances of sexual abuse, cold sweat poured down my sides while my teeth rattled in my head. I promised them I was okay, I just needed to keep going. If I lost my train of thought, Holt would ask another question to get me going again.

"This is with his fingers?"

"Yes, with his fingers, he would touch me there."

"Over your clothes or under?"

"Both."

"How often would you say this happened?"

"I don't know, I . . ."

"Five times, ten times?"

"No, more like a hundred . . ."

"A hundred times?"

"It was night after night, over years . . . not all the time. He would stop doing it for a while. They blend together. But if I had to guess, at least a hundred for sure, yes."

"Which house was this in? The one that burned down?"

"Yes, well, all the early houses. Because of what the room looked like, I know the first time I can remember was around four years old, in Chicago. It could have been earlier. It's just my first memory of him doing that."

I told them about Mom coming out of the shower and not knowing what to tell her. I told them what happened on the sink counter with the southwestern tiles. I could tell this part was important, because of how Holt slowed me down and double-checked things I mentioned.

I spoke of the back rubs, the French kissing, being "Daddy's secretary." I mentioned the requests for naked pictures, how my mother asked me if "Daddy had been touching me weird" and I nodded in reply.

I described being held down on the floor when he would "wrestle" me after I complained about being groped, how he humped me to a song I wrote and beat my mom with a belt. I had difficulty referring to him as "Dad" and increasingly used "Toby" throughout the interview.

We talked about the family's relationship rules, the origins of our home church, and Jair telling us, "Maria knows."

The second agent came and went, possibly being replaced by another man, I don't know; I lost track. As long as I didn't lose my primary listener, I could maintain my momentum. The telling took on a power of its own and I detached to a certain extent, feeling as if I could float up into the air and look down at the bodies flanking the table, compelled to unburden myself while staving off the reality of what would happen afterward. There was nothing beyond this suspended instant in time, this room gripped with Agent Holt's distilled focus and steady push forward into the crux.

When his eyes glistened with tears, I wanted to thank him. It was different telling a man. Like Lee, he was a trained professional and did not let himself be overwhelmed or overtaken. Simply seeing my hurt move him, despite his masculine strength, was intensely reparative. I felt a fresh measure of courage. The good guys had been here the whole time, waiting for me to do my part.

My shame was the deepest when I admitted to knowing my younger sisters had continued to suffer abuse, yet I did nothing about it.

"And you said this was which time again?"

"The first time we were in Minnesota."

In 2015, my twenty-third birthday.

"And you knew something had happened how?"

"Mainly just the look on their faces, Mom and my sister. I didn't even ask what happened. It sounds stupid, that I didn't ask, and they didn't tell me . . . but I knew."

AT SOME POINT, WE STOPPED FOR A BREAK. I WENT TO THE BATH-room and was offered some food. I can't recall if I ate or not. Firmly immortalized in my memory, however, was the moment I thought I saw the second agent doze off. He'd been given the job of taking notes and, for a moment, I panicked. Maybe my account was less than shocking to him. Maybe he heard stuff like this every day. For me, this was the most terrifying and difficult thing I had ever done, and it mattered to me I do it well. It had to count. Holt was the one in whom I'd put my trust, and he had to know what he was doing.

I knew, unequivocally, the goal needed to be putting my father in prison.

The victim services coordinator gave me her card and double-checked I had a safe place to stay. She also asked if I needed help getting connected with a therapist. I told her I already had someone. Regardless, she took my phone number, saying she would reach out to make sure I had continued support.

After the break, the questions resumed. I told them about meeting and liking Sean and how my family found out about our private pictures. I stumbled through Jair's slap in the face and described the scene with Toby on the bus.

"This started how?"

"He told me to give him a summary and an outline. And to apologize. I didn't apologize and he punched me in the face."

I admitted I hid from the cop who'd shown up, struggling to make them understand why. I described the beatings, the bruises on our legs, the restriction of food, the objects thrown and swung at people's heads. I told them how Dad claimed the molestation was a function of teaching me, and how he micromanaged outside influences. His wrestler background, his end-times theories, his Ruby Ridge fascination. They wrote down the number of guns we owned along with the location of the ammunition and disaster food rations.

I tried to minimize my call to Mom after the church ladies started asking questions. I didn't want them to think I was trying to undermine the case. They told me I was not to talk to anyone else in my family until further notice.

I began to lose track of what I had already mentioned, worried I was going to leave out the crucial detail without which they would fail to accomplish their objective.

Eventually, they must have stopped me. Or maybe I ran out of steam. When I stood, my knees were wooden and strained, my head pounding as if a hatchet was lodged in my hairline. Agent Holt seemed inwardly coiled, bits of forceful energy guiding his motions. Looking at him, one could not help but be certain decisive action was coming. Though my count could have been off, I estimated I had been interviewed for over four hours.

A few days later, I would return to TBI offices to sign the written version of my "statement." I don't remember when it was first shown to me, but I was shocked to see it didn't read like my oral testimony. Multiple hours of questioning were distilled down to a few pages of foreign-sounding paragraphs, not reflecting the living, breathing version of my experience I had tried to share. *This is what they heard?* I panicked. *This is what they took away?* My life up until that point was being turned into an abbreviated report. There was no way a handful of paper pages was ever going to convey everything I had felt, seen, and survived. I'd stupidly assumed there must have been a camera somewhere, documenting my every word, but Agent Holt was gone, and I was supposed to sign this paper. It felt like everything was at stake.

I had mentioned my fourteen-page letter in the interview and now I asked if I could have it submitted to the case alongside this shorter summary statement. The suggestion was approved.

I also decided I would show the letter to Sean, which would mark the first time I had shared any details of my sexual abuse with him. His jaw clenched as he read while sitting at the kitchen island, forcing his gaze to continue from page to jarring page. He held me a long time after he finished.

When I delivered a stapled copy to the TBI, I hoped they would really read it, and it wouldn't just disappear into someone's file cabinet or office wastebasket. I hoped it would be enough.

28

CORROBORATION

THE SILENCE WAS MADDENING. I KNEW THE AGENTS HAD TO BE working hard, yet my brain couldn't help obsessively speculating on their progress. Mom began calling on repeat and I worried what she might do if I continued to ignore her.

At one point she called multiple times in a row and, despite the investigators' directive, I picked up, saying I was busy and only had a second to talk. She made light chatter, saying they were back from Ireland and on the road to their next gig. With a casual air, she asked if I had heard anything lately, because she didn't know why I had been so upset last time we talked. I said no, hanging up with an abrupt goodbye.

When I informed the investigators, they urged me to disregard any further communication attempts. According to rumors from the church group, my father hadn't been present for their latest meeting, and my family claimed he was away on business. Not knowing my father's whereabouts was alarming, so I went over to stay with the Fishers immediately.

On Sunday evening, three days after giving my testimony, Mom left me a breezy voice mail saying they were all set up to play their concert for the night.

Less than forty-eight anxious hours later, another message appeared. This time the recorded voice was fragile, breaking with emotion at the end:

> Hey, Jessie, it's Mom. I know everything that's going on now. I don't know if you've been instructed not to speak to me—you may have been, in which case, I understand. But if you haven't, then I'd love to talk to you . . .
>
> I just want you to know the rest of this family is in favor of everything going on and is cooperative, every single one of them. As crazy as it sounds, I think it's all gonna work out for the better. That's hard to believe, but I'm starting to see a light at the end of the tunnel, Jess. I love you.

I tried to get an update, asking the TBI if my father had been located or arrested. I was told that, though agents had indeed made contact with the rest of my family, my father was still at large.

SINCE GLIMPSES INTO MY OLD LIFE HAD BECOME TRIGGERING TO me, I had avoided my family's social media posts and public updates for months. Now I scoured the web for bits of news, a conspicuous blackout, or any indications of what might be happening on their end. The latest post on Instagram was a few hours old, a sunny picture of Jasmine with the caption, "Help us wish happy birthday to our beautiful, budding lead singer, Jasmine!" Scrolling backward, I saw five posts from the last two days. There had to be a mistake; this didn't look like a family currently under investigation, showing thumbs-up, cheesing in huddles, dancing onstage.

I fell down the rabbit hole of Google searches and Facebook livestreams, eventually watching myself reappear back on the stage next to the rest of them. There I was, picking and grinning, hitting my marks, the week after I was assaulted, the day after I told my father I'd leave the first chance I could find. How had no one seen what was really going on? I realized it was the rest of us smiling and laughing so persuasively, standing by so casually, cooperating so openly that discredited any suspicions.

Even though I could recall my memories of distress, I felt totally undermined by the girl I saw in the pictures and video. Her primary method of coping with the trauma had been to deny and deflect, participating in the delusion preserved forever in the time capsule of the internet. She'd learned to do her job so well that she could make me doubt myself. I was either lying then or lying now. Who would believe me over her?

IN THE AFTERNOON, A CALL FROM A TBI AGENT YANKED ME BACK to the present. He asked if I would I be willing to attempt monitored communication with my father at their direction. I said yes, despite instant dread.

He explained more of the situation when they arrived at the

Fishers' house to meet with me: they had reason to believe Dad was turning off his phone to evade law enforcement but planned to make himself reachable over the following hour. At the agent's instructions, I sent a message both to Dad's cell number and email saying I'd heard he wanted to speak to me, and he could me call if he wished. The goal would be for me to get him to admit to any of the criminal abuse.

We waited an hour, and when there was no response, they left, saying I should, of course, contact them immediately if he reached out at any later point.

The next day they were back, again thinking my father might tip his hand. It was obvious there had been developments of some kind. An agent stayed close until nightfall. I slept with my phone in reach, wondering when the suspense would end and how. In my nightmares, a black mass of tangled wires grew in my chest, throbbing with terror, crowding out my oxygen.

ON SEPTEMBER 9, 2016, AGENT HOLT CALLED TO SAY, "YOUR father was taken into police custody just a few hours ago in Greenville, Kentucky."

He told me the warrant had already been filed, had been made from my testimony, based on one count of rape of a child, a class-A felony. The press would catch word of it soon, so I should prepare myself.

Local news broke the story with breathtaking speed, and when his mug shot hit the internet hours later, I physically recoiled from the screen. Already wearing an orange jumpsuit, he glowered directly into the camera with dark circles hanging under his eyes,

a furrowed black brow tipping his head forward, a full beard surrounding a mouth pressed straight and short. *His eyes! His eyes!
Could everyone see now?*

My stay with the Fishers became indefinite. While we
didn't always know what to say to one another, I could feel their
tenderness and unwavering care. I was grateful to have a stable
sanctuary. When my family arrived back in Tennessee, they were
essentially homeless, and they parked their bus in the driveway of
one of the church families. I checked with TBI to see if I could
visit them and got the okay. I was encouraged to hear they had cooperated with authorities and hoped this action meant I wouldn't be
viewed as an outcast and betrayer.

Mom materialized on the doorstep of the church family's house
and gave both Sean and me an emotional hug. Before we could even
enter the house, she began talking in her networking voice. On one
hand, her composure and positive energy was a relief, since a part
of me had been concerned I might find her shattered and unable to
function.

"We are going to help people," she said emphatically, saying
God's plan was at work this whole time and now the family would
raise awareness and speak out against sexual abuse.

Her words displaced the air from my lungs. As we ate and visited
with the church family, my mind cycled in fits and starts, calculating
and recalculating. *I'm not crazy*, I reminded myself, as had become
my habit whenever I felt a crisis of reality. *It's because Sean is here*,
I thought. *She's in performance mode.*

THE PRESS STARTED SCOPING OUT THE OLD FAMILY PROPERTY AND Mom decided to accept a relative's offer to stay at their out-of-state farm until things calmed down. Most of the family would remain in town just one more day to cooperate with more DCS and TBI interviews. Sean had to work, so I went to the property on my own, determined to see my other siblings and try to leave things in a good place before they were again gone indefinitely. I also wanted to hear what had happened from their point of view over the last few weeks.

When I arrived everyone was spread out, some in the bus by the barn giving testimony, others at the old gun range where the TBI was executing a search warrant for my family's plethora of computers and electronic devices. When Mom next had a free moment, I was able to sit down with her and start piecing together her point of view.

Led by Agent Holt, a group of agents had taken them directly from the stage after their Ohio show, separated Mom and each of the oldest kids, and questioned them until daylight. They made it clear that she would not see the kids again unless she cooperated. Over the following days, the agents had directed her in communicating with my father, trying to catch him admitting to criminal abuse.

I asked where he had gone, still not understanding why he hadn't been with them and when they had separated. She said she'd kicked him off the bus in Kentucky, but I felt this wasn't the whole story. Everyone was in self-protection mode, and I might never know what had truly happened in the flurry of action that led to my father's arrest. He had indeed been turning his phone on and off, and eventually the agents had told Mom to agree to meet him at the venue of the band's next concert. A warrant had been made just in time for agents to apprehend him at the appointed time and location.

One of my younger sisters was currently speaking to a female agent on the bus, trying to articulate the unimaginable. I gave them wide berth, remembering how I hadn't wanted anyone else to hear what I needed to say during my own interview. I shared with both Mom and Jen some of what I'd told Holt. Jen responded by relating a few of her comparable memories, and we noted similarities and differences. I was stunned as old suspicions were confirmed, and I grieved that we hadn't unburdened ourselves to each other until that moment.

I hung around to see the band's visibly shaken manager and booking agent arrive. I had been unnerved by Mom's promotional comments about the band speaking out against sexual abuse, and I anxiously waited to hear whether they were going to step back from the spotlight or immediately take up a new banner of purpose. The booking agent was adamant: the Willis Clan, as we knew it, was dead. The current band agreed to cancel all appearances, and their website and social accounts were taken down.

Jasmine, Jet, and Jair acknowledged me with wordless embraces, fracturing the icy wall of rejection maintained since the day I'd fled the family home. As they traveled to find a temporary sanctuary of their own, I wondered how we would navigate forward and begin to repair our wounded connections.

I LEANED HEAVILY ON LEE AS I ATTEMPTED TO UNDERSTAND HOW the ongoing legal process would unfold. She did much to both temper my anxieties and set realistic expectations. She warned the investigation would reveal new levels of my father's perversion. It was unrealistic to think he would confess or cooperate with the authorities, and it could be difficult to bring him to justice without much in the way of evidence. To some degree, it was a he-said, she-said situation. I had no way of proving the specific incident used in the warrant—no DNA, no record, no corroboration. But the greater the number of other family members coming forward, the weightier my accusations would grow. Lee believed, as the agents obviously did, there would be evidence on the computers. I prayed this was not true, as it seemed too horrible to imagine the existence of such things—even though they would aid and expedite the investigation.

She urged me to be patient with the rest of my family, emphasizing the need to safeguard my personal progress amid what would surely be a messy fallout. The case could take years to resolve. She reminded me that each traumatized individual deals with their learned patterns of survival in their own way, and many try to avoid the challenging work of recovery, preferring instead to depend on the coping mechanisms developed under duress. Sadly, the long-term effects of unaddressed trauma almost always reemerge.

Whenever these topics triggered an inner siren call of duty and panic, Lee led me to root out the tendrils of acute codependency in my relationships. Why did I feel my mother's safety and happiness were my responsibility? The concept of boundaries was still a hazy one for me; however, Lee framed them as a necessary counterpoint to *enmeshment*, the blurring of one's personhood within a dysfunctional group until individual autonomy is lost and members fuse into an overly dependent unit. The description hit a chord, especially when my further reading showed that dissenters often became scapegoats at the urging of a narcissistic or abusive leader.

MY FATHER WAS EXTRADITED FROM KENTUCKY, WAIVED HIS RIGHT to a preliminary hearing, and was held in our local jail without bond. Though I knew people who went to see him, I stayed clear and gathered tidbits through the grapevine. I heard he was insisting I was a liar who admitted she wanted to follow Satan. He maintained he hadn't committed the crimes he was being accused of and apparently even said he should have shot Sean Fisher so all this could have been avoided.

Few people came to my father's defense, yet I still heard eyebrow-raising questions, such as "Have you perhaps exaggerated or misunderstood a confusing scenario?" and "Did he ever apologize?" It was also asked whether my father's actions weren't something that should have been dealt with inside a traditional church setting.

After two more weeks of aggressive investigation, TBI produced a report of their findings. Mom shared the news that criminal evidence had indeed been found on the computers despite my father's best efforts to hide his tracks.

"Photos?" I asked in disbelief.

Video, she said.

"Of me?"

No, she said.

This meant it was no longer he-said, they-said, but I was devastated. I even felt a wave of denial, wanting to pretend it wasn't true. I was nonetheless told my father was still insisting he had not done the things that the video proved.

Lee said if trial could not be avoided, I would need to prepare myself for the nasty business of testifying in court. Authorities would make an effort to keep information as anonymous as possible, minimizing the risk of retraumatization, especially where minors were involved. Unsavory media outlets had already confirmed that one public charge had been made by a family member, though my name had not been mentioned so far.

While I cannot recall the exact date of my initial meeting with the district attorney who would prosecute my father, I will never forget my first impressions of her: cerulean blue eyes, hair cut short and sharp, a voice without a shred of compliance or submission, the stance of a pit bull, and a chest scar partially visible above her neckline.

This is poetry, justice, pure karma, I thought to myself, certain she was the embodiment of everything my father would despise and fear in a woman.

As protocol allowed, she kept me updated on the case and quickly secured my admiration and respect. She had seen the evidence and did not seem to care who my father was, how he felt, or what he claimed. His reign was over, and it was her duty to secure what justice could be had. Whatever she needed from me, I was ready and willing to give.

Her job was to balance the pursuit of justice with reasonable compromise. If she sought too harsh a punishment, my father would have no incentive to take a plea deal and the ensuing trial would invade our efforts at new lives. If she made too weak an offer, he would face lesser consequences and could be free to hunt me or Sean within a decade. Nightmares of the prison-revenge movie plot gave me no peace.

After studying the case with her team, the DA selected four separate events of abuse that translated to four felony charges. Together, their respective sentencing guidelines amounted to a cumulative hundred and thirty years of prison time. I learned each individual sentence could be served simultaneously instead of consecutively, meaning the deal boiled down to forty years without parole. I tried to imagine the year 2056. I would be sixty-three years old. If he lived that long, my father would be eighty-six, but I was told adult sexual abusers of children rarely survived so long on the inside. I abruptly severed my train of thought, not wanting my imagination to continue in such a direction.

Though my father was not allowed to contact any of his victims, I was shown pieces of coded letters he began sending to family members at the property. He made it abundantly clear how he felt about the DA's deal, even telling us girls to speak out against his punishment.

> I hope my kids learn why it is so important to forgive and forget. Trying to get justice just hurts the victim more. Things have to be kept secret, not for other people, but for themselves. I have kept secrets and benefited by my silence.

He went on to talk about how he worked so hard to correct the problems society gets wrong, and how disappointed he had been in his marriage. It was the church's fault, his parents' fault, the government's fault. He gave instructions on business opportunities to pursue and how the family could aid him in his philosophical writings. At the end, he nonchalantly stated he had figured out how to escape from jail using fishing line, a fishing weight, fifty feet of strapping, and wire cutters.

That holiday season, I had the unforeseen opportunity to learn about a few of my father's buried secrets. These childhood clues renewed my study of perpetrators and their backgrounds, and I found that many offenders were once victims themselves.

Lee explained that survivors of trauma have the best chance to beat the cycle when they have the support of a healthy family environment and are encouraged in recovery and professional therapy. At some point, healing always involves discomfort, but refusing to heal is worse for everyone in the long run, especially when more people suffer because of one's unwillingness to face the hard work of recovery.

Though it was improbable that anyone would ever be able to examine my father's full history, I was able to find a measure of compulsory empathy for the confused child he once was.

29

SICKNESS AND HEALTH

SEAN POPPED THE QUESTION ON CHRISTMAS EVE. SURROUNDED BY the Fisher family and friends, the magic of the holidays seemed extra sweet. Sean and I had grown closer as life partners; I was already his lover, friend, and teammate. I genuinely wanted to be his wife and celebrate with a special ceremony, yet I viewed the institution of marriage and duties of motherhood with deep-seated trepidation. According to my old worldview, marriage was a covenant before God and could not be broken. Wives were required to submit and bear as many children as the Lord saw fit to send. Divorce and birth control were both off the table. Besides my father's rules for finding a spouse, the conservative Christian world told me to find a godly man, make the God of the Bible the center of my marriage, and everything would work out. Since I had seen those messages used to harm naive people, trap women, and excuse evil acts, I no longer trusted their promises. Unfortunately, I had not yet found a secure spiritual or philosophical replacement.

Though my new life was full of alternative examples of being, certain terms and topics remained especially triggering. I became obsessed with the countless negative messages buried like land-mines in my past as I tried to find a path of my own amid the ruins. I was determined to never find myself in my mother's situa-tion. I walked myself through why I wouldn't: First, Sean was not toxic, controlling, or utterly unable to apologize. He was working on becoming the healthiest version of himself in his own way and treated me with the respect and care I had come to see as required for any healthy relationship. Second, perhaps more important, it was my responsibility to acquire the tools, standards, and support that would give me the strength to do the right thing if ever I or any future children were being hurt by Sean or anyone else.

The only thing I knew for sure was that I had already chosen Sean. We were committed. In my mind, in my heart, he was already mine and I was already his. It had not happened at one moment of decision or as a result of some carefully implemented plan. I was not waiting to make a deeper, more meaningful promise when we signed a paper or read a vow. He was his own imperfect person and encouraged me in health, freedom, and respect. In all our sickness and health, we showed up for each other. So far, each blow meant to drive us apart only forged us stronger. There was no way to guarantee or prove we would make it. Our relationship was breakable, as everything is. But I was willing to take the risk of loving him in the hope he would continue to love me back, openhanded and true.

WE DIDN'T HAVE TO MAKE WEDDING DECISIONS IMMEDIATELY. Most of my family was still living out of state. I was grateful for the space between us and always had a fresh batch of emotional reactions to work through whenever we crossed paths. Layered revelations continued working their way to the surface, like infected splinters pushing back up through the skin. Just when it seemed no worse information could possibly come to light, more excruciating truth would emerge every time someone shared another trauma that had happened to them. After twenty years of survival, with thirteen stories simultaneously estranged and entangled, our collective healing would never be finished and could not be rushed. It was unrealistic to think Sean's and my relationship could be easily celebrated by the same group who had likened our love to a deal with the devil only six months before.

Maybe we should just elope, I thought.

My father's case seemed to be lagging at every step. In the latest anxiety-inducing twist, my father had refused to cooperate with a competency evaluation that was supposed to confirm he could be held responsible for his actions and was not, in fact, insane. Another evaluation was scheduled, but all indications said he continued to insist the punishment in the current plea deal was too severe and the charges incorrect. He wanted to debate the legal definitions including child rape but couldn't find anyone willing to listen to his complaints. When he'd lost his captives, he'd lost his audience.

The DA planned to present the four charges before a grand jury in March. I wanted to avoid having to make last-minute changes to wedding plans in order to testify at an indictment. Nothing seemed less romantic or celebratory.

ONE WEEK INTO THE NEW YEAR, MOM ARRANGED A FAMILY MEET-ing at the property. I prepared myself for the disclosure of more past abuse or concerning news from jail. Instead, I found myself at the center of a brainstorming session with the aim of getting the band back together.

I was caught off guard, and I felt my tenuous boundary-holding skills evaporate. While I didn't want to condemn their ideas, I didn't want to get dragged in either. I asked whether it wouldn't be wiser to process some important issues before anyone got back onstage. Mom agreed yet was quick to frame musical collaboration as the best way for us to heal and repair our unity with God's help.

Soon, I was being asked which songs I'd be willing to contribute to the new album. The band could use my songs to help victims know they were not alone. Even if I didn't want to join, would I really keep them from helping others?

Later, I privately asked Mom about finances, thinking maybe they felt forced to get back on the road to make money. She said there was considerable debt and legal fees.

Hope and Pete helped schedule our own meeting with clinical professionals and representatives of charitable organizations, all willing to help my family focus on becoming healthy and stable. In a circle with my mother and oldest siblings, these pros took turns offering their resources and insights.

When they finished, my mother addressed the group with a smile. "I'm going to say something that's really going to shock you. I *do* believe in therapy—daily therapy. Every day, when I get up in the morning, I read the Bible."

A few minutes later, she began talking about the relaunch of the band, and I had to leave the room. One of my brothers found me and admitted he, too, had concerns. He even implied that the previous meeting at the property had been set up for the primary purpose of getting me to hand over songs.

I felt stupid for not holding my ground. Two steps forward, one step back.

AS MY FATHER CONTINUED TO DRAG OUT THE LEGAL PROCESS, I was suddenly irate that he could still hijack our lives, that his tantrums could leave us all at a loss for closure and justice. No more would I let my life be planned around him. I told Sean I wanted to get married as soon as was doable for our families. Though there was bound to be awkwardness, I wanted to do my part in giving everyone something positive to celebrate. A date was selected in May, and I started looking for a dress.

Perhaps it was the prospect of walking down the aisle alone; perhaps it was the quiver in Pete's voice when he told people I was his daughter. "We drop the *in-law* part," he liked to say. A dark well of sorrow was opening beneath my feet. At first, it was mysterious and alarming. What was happening? Why was everything suddenly so incredibly sad? I stayed in bed and couldn't make headway on any tasks. Eventually, the simple and world-shattering recognition came after being put off over twenty years: my father had not loved or protected me. Inwardly, I was still reaching out, hoping for the hug that would never come. I needed to let go of my childhood dream, that he would have been good, that he would have loved me well. I finally let myself mourn the father he should have been. Even now he was fighting, insisting I was wrong and he was right. I would not have a father-daughter dance at my wedding. I grieved as if he had died.

An old instinct kicked in and I reached for paper and pen. For the first time since I left my family's home, I set words to a melody and stepped into the flow of unbound feeling. I had feared this part of me was broken, and it came alive slowly, painfully. I followed, letting my subconscious work its way into meter and time.

Twelve months before, I had hidden in my bus bunk, unable to see a way to freedom. It had been the coldest, darkest period of my life. I reflected on how far I'd come in a single year and felt my father's shadow grow smaller in size. I should never again let him define my story. I should never again assume I was the fragile one.

History is written at the hands of those who win
The battle must be over for the writing to begin
Take a piece of paper, open up a vein
The feather and the finger pulls against the grain

I stared at the verse and saw an invitation, a prophecy of what I would one day do.

I BEGAN TO RECONNECT WITH SOME OF THE PEOPLE IN MY PAST. I had so much to learn about building and maintaining healthy community. I never wanted to live in a world of us-versus-them again. Though I had countless wonderful and interesting acquaintances, I had few friends who really knew me or I them. Plus, there was the long list of people I was certain I owed an apology to, especially the many girls and young women who were around my father over the years and were never warned about his predatory habits. As I tried to begin making amends, I found most people were gracious and kind to me.

Maria Martin haunted me the worst. When she and I got coffee, I could finally hear her story. I was impressed by her frankness and strength. I realized Jair had to have faced some similar choices as I had when struggling to figure out how to have a relationship and make a life of his own. Instead of leaving, he'd stayed and become what I saw as our father's right-hand man.

The next time I saw Lee, I was in a crisis of conscience. Feelings of anger, betrayal, and criticism toward my family were taking over my inner life. While Mom and Jair triggered the most pointed reactions, I realized what I was facing was not any one person. It was the thing we had turned into, the image we had sold together, the system that had continued on and perpetuated lies. I thought it would die along with the band, like the booking agent had said. Nevertheless, most of our collective coping mechanisms maintained their pattern even though Dad was removed.

In this therapy session, Jair became the focus of my outburst. He had hit me. I had never truly allowed myself to process that fact. I believed he'd changed for the worse after his relationship with Maria and had actively enforced our father's rules toward the end, adding his voice to my oppressor's.

Lee encouraged me to look back into our shared childhood. With fresh eyes, I went to the beginning. Empathy soon shifted my focus away from my own hurts. I cried for the distressed toddler being held down by a grown man while everyone else stood by. I witnessed the boy being forced to experience tactical defeat over and over. I saw the talent used and the person dismissed. I heard my mother trying to cheer up a kid who sensed something was off. I was ashamed to remember the first scene on the highway, where we all begged Jair to apologize for standing up for himself, for protesting our father's antics.

If anything, he had been the first rebel, born fighting even though he didn't understand the problem. I had not fought with him; I had sided with his oppressor. We were both children, too young to save ourselves or each other.

I was grieved for us both and motivated anew to become someone who could do better in the future. From that day on, I could see another, younger version of Jair, the one who had fought alone.

ON THE FIRST BRIGHT DAY OF SPRING, I WAS DRIVING IN MY CAR when I felt the sudden urge to listen to my family's band albums. I had gone from playing these songs hundreds of times a week to associating them with the worst of my traumatic past. As I turned up the volume and let the sun warm my skin, I could feel a hint of new life in the air. Positive associations came flooding back: youthful inspiration, euphoric moments with the midnight pen, showing a friend a new song, the sense of accomplishment when a work was completed, laughing with my sisters till our bellies ached, playing games in the green room before shows, the littlest kids adorably mispronouncing words, catching a split-second eye signal from across the stage and successfully pulling off a spur-of-the-moment change in perfect sync, the thrill of the win, the energy of the team. I'd previously had to close my eyes to the beautiful things or I never would have left. Now I allowed myself to acknowledge them again, along with a deep personal truth: I loved music and I loved my family. If possible, I wanted to find my way back to both, but separately.

THE DA WAS DETERMINED TO KEEP THE CASE MOVING FORWARD despite my father's perpetual stalling antics. In March, she brought the four charges from the plea offer before a grand jury. They would determine whether there was enough evidence for them to believe a crime had been committed. They indicted him on all four counts.

The following arraignment was covered by the press, and official documents were leaked online with improper redactions. Each of the felony charges was listed with a thin line crossed through the corresponding initials and birth date of each victim. The identities were obvious. Though the redactions were later corrected, the salacious news spread throughout internet forums and comment sections. It felt impossible to tune out the noise.

The trial date was set for July 18, 2017. My father's attorney was quitting, seemingly unwilling to keep working with someone so toxic. Mom subsequently increased her contact with Dad in what I assumed to be a time-sensitive effort to persuade him to take the deal. If he refused to plead guilty before trial, we would all be forced to recount what had been done to us, and the media would have a feeding frenzy.

Around that same time, I learned some of my relatives were unsure whether they could attend my wedding on account of their worries that Sean and I were living in sin. I was tired of people passing moral judgment on our relationship and told Sean I wished we were already married and done with it. He said he was ready to go to the courthouse the next day.

In a burst of inspiration, we contacted Lee. Her husband was a lawyer, and he called in a favor with an old-friend-turned-honorable-judge. We got the necessary license, ordered rings, and were legally married in jeans and a sundress the day before my twenty-fifth birthday. Afterward, we flew on gifted tickets and traveled across Ireland for two weeks, staying in the guest rooms of Irish friends on a semi-secret, budget-friendly honeymoon.

We had a small wedding ceremony two months later. By the time I stood prepared to walk myself down the aisle in front of eighty-some people on that drizzly spring day, there was an anchor of calm underneath the butterflies. No one there would be giving this woman away. When I was halfway to Sean, he abandoned his post to meet me. We walked the last few steps together. We had already won.

As summer approached, I heard my father had a new defense attorney. The deadline for the plea was imminent, and the DA formally threatened to bring a total of a hundred and thirty charges before a grand jury for good measure. Even when I was told my father finally signed the deal and would be sentenced on July 11, I worried he would not be able to go through with it. As with a legal marriage, a signature on paper would not be enough. He would be required to confirm his intentions out loud before an authority and witnesses.

To count on such a public capitulation seemed impossible. I had never in my life heard my father confess a specific wrong and face the consequences.

"I'll believe it when I see it," I told Sean.

30

WHAT NOW?

"Is your decision to plead guilty today voluntary and not the result of force, threats, or promises apart from the plea agreement?"

There was no audible reply to the judge's question. "Anybody forcing you to do this?" he pressed with a hint of steel in his voice. It was July 11, 2017, the moment of truth.

The defense attorney focused intently upon the hidden face of my father, like a coach watching his star player. My father said no.

"All right." The judge shifted in his seat. "Do you understand I can't accept your plea unless I'm satisfied that there's a factual basis for it and that you are in fact guilty of these crimes?"

Silence.

"Are you in fact guilty of these four counts of rape of a child?"

The long-awaited word was only a whisper, barely audible in the hushed courtroom. In all my years, I had never heard my father sound so faint, so fragile. He spent twenty years building a world where he could be the undisputed voice of God and king. When it roared, I had cowered. When it ordered, I had obeyed. When it instructed, I had adapted. My early life was a constant state of listening, forever attuning and preparing for the moment the voice might condemn or command. It told me who I was, what I should do, what I was allowed to think and feel and believe. Now, the tiny sound dropped from his lips and dissipated into nothingness. It was everything he had never said, something impossible, unimaginable. His kingdom had crumbled, unable to survive this one split second of spoken truth.

"Guilty."

His shoulders seemed broken, barely able to resist gravity's pull. For me to leave and begin a new life, I had to stop seeing my father as I wished he would be and face the monster behind the mask. Here, he shed another layer of construction. Underneath was a weak and hollow core, encased within a stiff orange shell with black letters across the back. I did not know this shadow of a man.

Sean squeezed my hand.

The district attorney was ready, reading aloud the accusation from the arrest warrant. Should the case have gone to trial, she'd planned to prove that in January 2002, the defendant performed oral sex on a minor child with the initials *J.J.W.*

Me.

The DA recited the other three counts and finished by saying these acts all happened "against the peace and dignity of the State of Tennessee."

The judge turned back to my father. "And, Mr. Willis, those are the facts that the State would prove if this matter went to trial. Do you still wish to enter this plea of guilty?"

"Yes."

I wondered if he had retreated to the part of his mind that justified and compartmentalized all he had done to me. I knew such a corner had to exist, otherwise he would not have been able to abuse me so. While he was required to say the words, no one could force him to believe them.

"Then, Toby Willis," the judge concluded, "upon your plea of guilty to count one, I find you guilty, and sentence you to twenty-five years as a range-one offender at 100 percent."

Tears leaped to my eyes.

"On count two, I find you guilty and sentence you to twenty-five years as a range-one offender at 100 percent. Count three . . . I find you guilty. Count four . . . guilty."

Though I wished I'd accepted the chance to give a victim-impact statement, what would have been the use? Once the mind has escaped inward, anything can be done with the remaining body, disconnected and abandoned. I know, because I did as much to survive. Under my father's thumb, I had said things I didn't mean and done things I hated. Something told me he was escaping now, signaling to his inner self he was only playing the game, giving the court what they asked while withholding true surrender. He could go on living inside the world he created, alone with himself. He, too, was experiencing the beginning of a second life. If he adapted, he could have another forty years, but not here, not with us. Some things could never be made right. In the long-ago moment when he became my abuser, I lost the father I should have had, and no court of law could right that wrong.

The entire process was over in fifteen minutes. I came, I saw, I heard. Then there was nothing more to do. As far as the law was concerned, justice was done.

LEE INTRODUCED ME TO ANOTHER TYPE OF THERAPY CALLED internal family systems (IFS), or "parts work." After her description piqued my curiosity, she sent me home with a short, whimsically illustrated book on the subject. This therapy model posits that each of us has multiple facets to our natural personality, a plethora of various "parts" within each self.[1] To explore this idea, a therapist may invite an individual to picture and name any distinctive parts that seem to emerge in a time of crisis or repeat a specific message. A strict inner critic might be "the Principal," while an eternally needy character might be "the Invalid." As kooky as this sounded, it was no stretch for me to picture different characters fighting for control inside my head.

According to IFS, trauma can cause an individual part to internalize harmful beliefs or extreme emotions. This part then becomes a wounded "Exile" and can remain locked in its extreme emotional state for years. In the wake of such pain, other parts may step forward to protect an Exile by becoming "Managers," which proactively work to avoid vulnerable states and seek safety through control. Or they might become reactive "Firefighters," which take over during a triggering moment and try to stop pain by any means necessary, be it distraction or addiction. In this way, our most dissociated and hidden parts become the driving forces that dominate and hijack us with their unaddressed pain.

Again, this concept resonated with me in an intuitive way. I had felt hijacked, flooded, conflicted. I had shut off and pushed away harmful memories to the point of telling myself they had happened to someone else, some imagined different person who was not truly me. If I acknowledged it was only a part of me stuck in a crisis mode, the rest of me was free to get curious about healing the issue. *The whole* of my self was not sad; *a part* of me was sad. And instead of forcing that part away, I could invite it closer and ask it what it needed.

Within one hyperemotional session of surreal inner dialogue, Lee had me face-to-face with my Little Invisible Girl. A decade and a half later, she was still up on the tiled sink counter, holding her black boxes, voiceless, bodiless, timeless. After "asking" multiple Managers to step aside, she came to the surface. Her vulnerability had always been too much to handle, so I had exiled her, abandoned her. I had never asked her what she needed. I had never let her put down her burdens. I was finally willing to witness her pain and thank her for the way she had helped me survive. As an adult, I could accept the responsibility of her protection.

When I imagined embracing her, she showed me her natural state. She was the child bouncing wildly in purple boxing gloves, grinning as wide as her chin could bear, shrieking with delight, confident the world was beautiful, convinced life was a great adventure worth celebrating. She was fierce and innocent. She was Little Me.

I shook as I opened my eyes in Lee's office. I would need some time to further process, but I wondered who else might be waiting in the corners of my mind.

SEAN TOOK ME ALONG ON ROAD TRIPS AND PHOTOGRAPHY JOBS. I'd begun earning a small income by nannying for some dear friends, then switched to tooling and selling leather goods over the summer. Inspiration came knocking, and I eased back into writing and composing. Occasionally, I played fiddle for friends or sang backup vocals. When tensions were low I attended family gatherings at my mom's new house. Drawing courage from all I had survived, I focused on gratitude for every day of what I genuinely saw as a second chance at life.

That autumn I learned how to run for exercise without triggering what I had come to realize were intense panic attacks. For years, I had been frustrated by how my physical form would let me down at the most inconvenient times, sparking pain in my chest, making me light-headed, shaky, and out of breath. I had internalized the messages that I was weak, and every unwanted reaction needed to be suppressed, managed, and controlled, so I ignored the dire warnings of chronic stress. Now I believed my body and emotions supplied me with vital information about myself. I tried to speak kindly to myself and pay attention to my physical and emotional needs in order to regain my body's trust. When I ran, I actively formed the words in my mind, *I am okay. This is healthy for me. I am not in danger.* If needed, I would slow and catch my breath. Though the accomplishment was tiny, I was becoming friends with my body while disproving the lie that I was incapable of healthy athleticism. For me, those were no small feats.

Every few months, Sean and I would visit a church, after which the rest of our Sunday would usually derail. I either messily processed a flood of confused, high-intensity feelings, torrents of memories and associations, or went into a multiday struggle to construct coherent arguments against existential dread and instead fell into a pit of numb depression. We would then stay away until I felt guilty enough to go again.

Sean and I celebrated our first Christmas as a married couple and visited Hope and Pete, who were currently living in California. I still struggled with an unsettling déjà vu around my family's plan to relaunch the band. Shortly after my father's sentencing, they were considering appearing on a sensational talk show. In my opinion, no one in our family was ready to be making such plans. I asked Pete and other allies to help persuade them not to go through with it. I was accused of sabotaging the band's opportunities and they stopped keeping me in the loop. Since then, I figured it was best to focus on myself and literally stay out of their business.

I looked into attending Onsite, the experiential therapy retreat where Sean had been working when we met. He was greatly impacted by his time there, and I'd been interested in going since I first got out. I didn't have anywhere close to the funds required, and I had also been advised to wait until after my father's legal case was resolved. Now, I applied to a charitable foundation and received a half scholarship. I secured a spot in Onsite's flagship program at the beginning of February. It was described as "a year of therapy in one week." The attendees left their phones and the distractions of the outside world behind. I looked forward to starting off the new year with another bold step toward mental health and healing.

ON A BLEAK JANUARY DAY, I CALLED ONE OF MY SISTERS WITH A random question. Over the course of our conversation, she mentioned in passing that the band had an interview coming up.

"Oh, with what group?" I wanted to know.

"They're based in the UK," she said, unable to recall their name.

I called Mom. "Hey, I heard an interview is coming up soon," I said.

She explained a news outlet had reached out to them and wanted to help tell the family's story of overcoming and resilience. Plans were already underway to produce an article accompanied by two separate video segments. Filming would begin soon.

Once our call was done, I went to the show's website. It looked like a tasteless tabloid. I regretted not being more vigilant, but the band assured me I would not be mentioned.

The broadcast date of the video was set for the day I was supposed to leave for Onsite. I tried to explain to Sean how panicked I felt, how vulnerable. He assured me the world wouldn't end while I was away, and I would only come back more prepared for whatever I had to face.

AT THE EXACT TIME THE SHOW WAS SUPPOSED TO AIR, I WAS REPEAT-edly refreshing its website on my phone. When the video box finally popped up, I stopped breathing. The video thumbnail was a compilation of my father's disturbing mug shot, an old family promotional photo that included both Dad and me, and a smiling picture of the band's new lineup. I touched play. The image fading in was my face in a group hug, one of twelve. Then came clips from our TV appearances, including a close-up of me singing and fragments from our reality show of Dad with the little kids.

"Toby Willis was arrested . . . charged with child rape . . . the shocking revelation that Toby's victims were his own daughters . . ."

Halfway through the segment, the fast-paced editing of old footage gave way to a grave sit-down with my straight-faced sisters and brothers as the interviewer asked why no one had come forward with the abuse. The responses had clearly been chopped in the editing room.

The male narrator spoke over clips of music practice, "The horrific stories of rape first came to light when their oldest sister, Jessica, told her story to a family counselor who reported the abuse to police."

What? No . . .

My sister shared, "The first time I was able to tell my story was after one of my other sisters told her story, and it was like, wow, oh my gosh, I'm not the only one?"

The narrator interjected, "The boys feel guilt, wishing they'd known . . ."

No, no, no.

"Telling the truth about the abuse," the man's voiceover continued, "led to a creative breakthrough and a new song . . ."

Scrolling down through the article, I stared at the line: "Each daughter thought she was the only one being abused."

I wanted to scream, to run. I felt embarrassed and dirty. What would happen when this video was seen by the people who knew for a fact this story was a lie?

"Jessica reported to a family counselor."

No, Maria Martin. Jonathan Martin. Sean Fisher. The DCS, TBI—they saved you.

"Telling the truth led to their new song."

Those were my teenage lyrics I had felt obligated to let them use.

"The boys wished they'd known."

What happened to "Maria knows"?

I wanted to dash the megaphone out from their hands. I was back in the Dark Ages, voiceless and erased. Blonde Jessica of the Willis Clan was onstage, propping up the never-ending pretty picture, while I was lost behind the scenes. They were using my words of vulnerability, my cry for courage and truth, proclaiming the message, *See? We believe in telling the truth. Good things will happen when you speak up. Smile, be happy, don't be a victim.*

I dialed Mom but thought better of it and hung up before she answered. I was too overwhelmed to have a constructive conversation. I went to Onsite the next day without further contact other than a group text saying I would be out of touch for the week and planned to speak to them all when I returned from my program.

31

TRUTH BE TOLD

A BLEARY FEBRUARY SKY HUNG ABOVE THE INCREASINGLY RURAL
surroundings as Sean and I neared the Onsite campus. Inscrutable
clouds looked as likely to snow as to shower, and the blacktop went
rugged and uneven beneath our tires. This had been Sean's daily
commute back when we met. He was remembering the same thing
and said so. I couldn't help seeing purpose in the shape of it all.
Perhaps I was making too much from mundane coincidence, but it
felt like Onsite had been waiting for me. For a decade, one of the
most innovative centers for recovery had developed right up the road
from my home. It was the place where my husband had once stepped
into a new season of his life, and its relatively close proximity to my
family's home made it easy for him to accept our fateful dinner invitation. I'd even felt the tug that night he'd been our guest, thinking,
That sounds like a place people like me would go.

Although I was sure I wanted to go to this program, no one seemed to be able to fully explain what they did here. What would it be like to experience the equivalent of all my previous therapy in the space of a few days? I believed it was going to be intense, emotional, and deeply healing.

The charming grounds came into view. An elegant nineteenth-century mansion with red shutters and a sweeping veranda porch crowned the top of a soft, green hill. We passed the carriage house and parked by the barn. I could see horses grazing in a verdant field behind the small guest cabins.

"Don't open this until after you settle in," Sean said with a kiss, pressing a sealed envelope into my hands. "It's a letter for your first night."

I tucked the little package into my backpack and stepped out into the damp chill. Sean greeted old friends and made sure I was in good hands before saying goodbye with another kiss and a tight hug.

Once I was on my own, I was led on a tour of the property and shown to my rustic, cozy quarters. Dinner was next on the schedule, then an ice-breaking orientation. I immediately felt I would get a lot out of my time there. More than anything, I was struck by how much Sean had clearly been shaped by his experience in this place. Already, countless things people said and did reminded me of him. By the time I opened his letter in the golden light of a reading lamp, I almost felt as if he were there, tucked into bed beside me.

THE PROGRAM WAS EVERYTHING OTHER PEOPLE HAD STRUGGLED to explain and more. All activities and therapy took place in either a large or small group. The small groups were established at the beginning of the week and stayed the same throughout the program. Each small group was assigned a group leader, an expert therapist trained in Onsite's unique combination of practices.

Morning began with a meditation before breakfast. Then a large group class expounded on topics such as codependency, family of origin, trauma, forgiveness, and the inner child. We broke into our small groups for the rest of the day until dinner. The evenings were filled with various support meetings, educational games, or optional activities. Many people chose to journal or simply rest after the emotionally taxing work of the day.

Though I was willing to try anything, I genuinely thought certain practices weren't going to be "my thing." The staff liked to say, "Attendance is mandatory, participation is optional." As I sampled the wide buffet of experiences, however, it was hard to ignore the immediate results. I had never tried meditation seriously, but by the end of the week I realized it was both one of the most calming and yet energizing things I'd ever tried. While I had never been into "affirmations," I felt them affect me in a very real way. "Breath work" was new to me and quickly unlocked a new level of emotional stamina. Just when I thought I couldn't do or say anything else, my group leader's counsel was to breathe deeply and stay present in my body. Within a few moments, I was able to continue. Mindfully doing such a simple thing made me curious about how many other natural tools I was neglecting to use in my daily life.

Yet these descriptions cannot capture the surreal essence of the experience itself. The program was completely immersive in every sense of the word. The mantra of the place was "Trust the process," and I found the more I trusted and invested, the more I got out of it. People seemed to be visibly aging backward, changing before our eyes as they unburdened years of grief or reached an enlightening breakthrough. In a strange way, the collective element reminded me of being in an opposite version of my family environment. While our culture had also been immersive, it had been stressful and dominating. It devalued interpersonal connection and the beauty of individuality. Our system had put me at odds with all other people who were not us and told me that if I left, there would be no God, relationship, or career that could save me. Onsite saw opportunity for connection at the core of everything and everyone.

The small group sessions made the biggest impact and were the hardest to explain. The process was most similar to the parts work I had begun with Lee. At some point during the week, each person was invited to take a turn working through a particular memory or issue with the support of the group and group leader.

I wanted to wait and think about it for a day or two; I was still unsure what to focus on. Although I knew I would probably always have further work to do in processing my sexual abuse, I felt other forces were pushing up to the surface, needing to be addressed. I zeroed in on my recent inner tumult. The band, the handling of the story, having to face the person I had been before, feeling trapped once again, voiceless, unable to be free—what was it? I had already done the leaving, almost two years ago now. How could I still feel like I was stuck in the same place? My father was gone; there was no house I could physically leave. To go to such vulnerable places with a collection of strangers would have seemed absurd at the beginning, yet each session affected me so deeply. I was stunned by the inevitable bonding process. Each person who took their turn before me inspired me to be braver.

Meanwhile, I learned more about the unhealthy use of "medicators," which could be almost anything one uses to numb or distract from doing one's mental and emotional work, be it alcohol, drugs, relationships, busyness, workaholism, perfectionism, or mindless Facebook scrolling. At first, I wondered whether I had used music this way, but then I realized that, no, I'd used it to speak, process, feel, and connect—not to numb and distract. In a way, then, my small group leader confirmed, music was healthy for me and a type of therapy.

I touched the edge of a vast inner darkness, firmly blocked by a protective wall. Religion and the God of my youth lay beyond. I felt a strong premonition: this was where a large chunk of my future work awaited me. During a counterintuitive forgiveness exercise, I wrote a letter from Dad to me. We were instructed to write from the perspective of a person who had hurt us, saying everything we wished they would say to us. It brought significantly more closure than I'd expected. I gathered tools for my recovery toolbox as fast as I could, knowing my retreat time was limited.

Unexpectedly, the sessions focusing on my other small group members seemed to echo my own struggles. As I was allowed to witness or occasionally participate in someone else's processing, I realized many of their lives held some unique learning that was beneficial for me to incorporate for myself. Each of us carried stories, struggles, and scars.

WHEN MY GROUP LEADER ASKED IF I HAD MADE A DECISION, I SAID yes: I needed to go back to the day I left my family's house. She affirmed my choice and had me step to the center of the room.

According to the method of the session, she guided me in constructing my perception of the scene one character at a time. First, there was me, the me on that day—the Leaving Me, different from the current me standing in a small timbered room at a therapy retreat. The next required character was another previous version of myself, one who felt loved, seen, and powerful in my original identity. That was definitely Little Me, with whom I was only recently reacquainted. Next, I added key family members. Slowly, I eased back into that disjointed, disassociated point in time. I replayed my memory of the belt whipping. I pictured faces, cold and angry.

"What is your brother telling you in this moment?" the group leader asked toward the middle of the exercise.

I tried to articulate what I had felt hanging in the silence, throbbing in the fear.

"You are only in my way," I said as Jair. "I'm ignoring you. I'm going to support Dad in hurting you." Every word came with monumental struggle.

Soon, the group leader moved down the room. "What about this sibling?"

I reached back, shaking in my bones. "I'm going to use the Bible and religion to continue to control you and help Dad control you," I said as Jet.

"And what is your mother telling you?"

"I'm going to ignore what he did wrong to both you and me," I said as Mom. "I'm going to focus on your flaws. I'm going to support him over you."

"What do you need to say back to them?" asked the guide, after I had taken time to process through each of the heavy messages.

"I was right to leave," I sobbed as Leaving Me. "I was barely able to do it. You shouldn't have made it harder for me." It was strange and painful, but I had come too far not to see this through.

The gentle group leader asked if there was anything Little Me, Leaving Me, and Current Me had to say to each other. I found this was the whole point. Little Me had suffered enough and was fighting back against the blame and hurt she had been forced to carry. She deserved to be stood up for, to be seen, to be heard. The tired, broken Leaving Me had all but given up, having internalized every harmful message, becoming unhealthy and self-abusive. The straw that broke the camel's back was when Little Me finally reached a breaking point and said to Leaving Me, *Get me out of here or we will both die.*

I had been told that to be a good daughter, I must obey. That to be a good Christian, I must submit. That to be safe, I had to stay silent. I had given up my voice to survive. It was time I took it back. Every beautiful and broken part of my story was mine.

To end the session, my small group members made a rope of knotted scarves and blocked the way to the door. I had to fight to break past their blockade and my momentum took me out of the room. I burst outside, bawling fiercely, a new version of free.

AFTER I LEFT ONSITE, I WROTE AN ABBREVIATED VERSION OF MY history and told my family I planned to post it on the internet. The band was unhappy with how the tabloid article had turned out but balked at the prospect of having a different version of the narrative released so soon. Though I still didn't feel ready to speak out, the band was determined to press forward, so I felt my continued silence was no longer an option. I decided I needed to break the power of my complicity, course correct my future path, end the secrecy that feeds shame.

I had sent my family an email with what I'd planned to release and took their comments into consideration during an emotional in-person group discussion. The conversation triggered strong reactions and pushed us to talk about how different and complex our pasts had been. Over the years, our individuality was overridden by the apocryphal "we" of our family as an establishment, a product, an entity. While the man behind the curtain was gone, the dismantling of his machine would be a lifelong task.

I also received messages of disapproval and pushback from people beyond my immediate family. They told me that what I was planning to say would taint the testimony of Christianity, undermine the reputation of large homeschooling families, and put my father in life-threatening danger in prison. People asked me if I wanted my father's blood on my conscience. I should use more discretion, not be so graphic, bitter, unforgiving, out for revenge. It was a message proclaimed by voices older than my father, a command passed down through the generations within our larger culture.

But I had promised myself I would no longer make my survivor hold the burdens that were not hers to carry: *Don't tell because you'll wreck the family. Don't tell because you'll ruin a good thing. Don't tell because God will look bad.* I was calling bullshit.

STEPPING INTO MY OWN STORY FREQUENTLY MADE THINGS HARDER before they became easier. Who was I to articulate the immensity of such complicated truth? Was I really willing to face my failings and vulnerabilities? Lee had helped me tackle the original trauma of my sexual abuse and set me on a path to ongoing recovery. Onsite had unlocked a new awareness of just how unhealthy and toxic our larger family system had been.

When I posted my account online, it was viewed tens of thousands of times within a few days. Then fellow survivors began appearing from all corners of my life. I found myself surrounded by people who had been raised in large, controlling families, abused by physical, emotional, and religious means, and who didn't know how to explain it to people who had not experienced it firsthand. We were trying to deconstruct our confusing experiences with faith, relationships, boundaries, and family. I had no idea there were so many of us, young adults kept prisoner in their own homes, children forced to carry the shame of the entire enmeshed system, collectively ignored and unseen. Old acquaintances, mutual friends, strangers from the internet—they all shared their parallel stories and sent me deeper into the patterns that emerged. My father may have been stopped, but the damaging beliefs, closed communities, and corrupt institutions that continue to produce and protect such individuals were alive and well.

I continued to learn more about the effects of sustained trauma, including the relatively new definition of complex PTSD, which describes the additional symptoms unique to victims who are caught in a chronic situation where they cannot get away from their abuser for years or decades. At the invitation of a new friend, I attended a conference on cults and coercive control. Major lights came on as I acquired another sizable chunk of useful vocabulary for describing elements of my upbringing. I also learned our memories can be shockingly unreliable narrators and so sought out ways of determining objective truth of the events, provable evidence of what happened, or signs of where my recollections may have gone wrong.

I BEGAN TO INVESTIGATE THE DETAILS OF MY OWN PAST WITH A new perspective, determined to piece together a more comprehensive account that could break through the barrier of the indescribable world in which these things occur over and over in perpetuity. I started with my old journals and almost quit before I began. The unvarnished look into my past mental state triggered self-loathing and a fresh round of depression. How quickly I had begun to forget all I had survived. The shame was almost unbearable.

Next, I gathered videos, pictures, any miscellaneous content my family had released as the Willis Clan. I researched key moments that predated my family's public life, and I found the truth was frequently far from the narrative Dad disseminated.

I hunted until I found my father's posts on the then-defunct conspiracy forum where he'd vehemently debated end-times prophecies. I found videos recorded during my Dark Ages and was astounded. I had doubted my memories of the worst psychological manipulation; my family's instinct to minimize past events made me wonder if I was indeed letting bitterness or pain exaggerate my recall. But my jaw dropped as I watched the cell phone footage from confrontations in the winter of 2015. My body was screaming, *I remember! And I am not a liar!* as I saw my father command me to claim my master and submit my spirit. Once again, pieces of indisputable evidence gave me the ability to believe my own reality.

My next therapy session broke through a new level of grief as I realized the mental, emotional, and spiritual abuse was worse than I had yet admitted, and leaving had been the hardest part. I was distressed and disheartened to find many extreme and damaging beliefs persistent within me despite my efforts to mentally refute their validity. I still couldn't see Scripture with new eyes. How does one go about exorcising indoctrinated beliefs from the soul and the body?

Gathering all the documentation I could find related to my father's arrest, investigation, and conviction, I read the original arrest warrant and the report from the Department of Child Services hotline. I saw the first round of statements my mother and siblings gave to police before they began cooperating and the contents of my father's pockets when he was taken into custody. I found court transcripts and learned legal terms. When I volunteered to share my experience as a survivor at TBI training programs, I came to appreciate the staggering amount of work and dedication law enforcement and the DA's office had put into my family's case.

Though I had endured plenty of abuse, I could not dismiss that I had also been given every conceivable aid and support in the aftermath. Even during my hardest years, I was fortunate enough to always have a bed, access to food, uncommon niceties, and privileged experiences. So many other invisible girls and boys were not so lucky. Whenever I watched a fellow survivor speak, read a new blog, or heard an impact statement, a fierce motivation flooded through me. Beyond continuing my own recovery, I committed to help the helpers, support survivors, and fight oppressive systems. I wanted to have more than words and empathy to offer going forward.

I KEPT GETTING ADVICE FEATURING THE TERM *HEALTHY ANGER*. Although I nodded my head and readily advocated for its periodic necessity, I privately decided anger was not for me. Nothing good ever came from my father's aggressive outbursts, and I would rather stay clear of something so unpredictable and destructive. Although I'd come to believe in the benefits of integrating my grief and sadness, frustration was still the closest I would let myself venture down the red road of temper. I finally admitted to my new therapist I didn't see the need to go there. She challenged me to articulate my understanding of the word *anger.*

The strongest association was a blending of the concept of the wrath of God and fear of my father. My father's blind fury, petulant fits, and violent attacks all signaled potential physical and emotional harm. I thought of anger as the seemingly all-consuming, irresistible, and dangerous force capable of transforming my father into a monster in the blink of an eye, something that, to me, seemed wrong yet also justified as part of his authority and identity. Biblical accounts of God's anger seemed wrong to me many times, too, but I was raised to believe God's reasons were beyond human understanding and I had no right to question him.

Next, I associated anger with shame. I was taught my human nature was fallen and my flesh would lead me astray. Anger, perhaps more than any other emotion, was unmistakable in my body—hot, tight in the chest, tingling in the hands. Clearly, this was one of the dangerous sins, crouching at my door, desiring to have me, requiring constant vigilance. There was no room for this emotion in a pure, patient, submissive, obedient, Christian daughter. Anger and fear made me feel deep distrust in myself, in my father, and in God.

Setting aside the example and teaching of my childhood, the therapist helped me see anger instead as a valid reaction to hurt, an indicator of violated boundaries and the need for change. When I lost access to my anger, taken away in the name of the Lord, I lost the important ability to advocate for justice and stand up to mistreatment. I thought of the moment in the bus, when I'd let Dad throw me around like a rag doll. I was desperate for someone to stand up and intervene. My anger could have helped me do that for myself. Accepting ownership and responsibility for my life meant learning how to integrate this powerful emotional tool.

ON MOTHER'S DAY, I WORKED UP THE COURAGE TO GIVE MOM A letter. With the help of my therapist, I had finally recognized the endless cycle at the core of our relationship. Every time I had really needed my mother's help, she had let me down by choosing my father. I then told myself I must be the problem; I just needed to learn how to tell her what was happening the right way—then she would do the right thing. The more she let me down, the more I felt I needed to protect her, afraid she might not be able to handle the truth. Even after Dad was gone, I let her tell me she hadn't known, going along with the narrative she needed to believe.

I'd heard the biting and nasty comments from critics: "What kind of mother lets her own children be abused? If I ever suspected something, I would handle it once and for all." But the critics were wrong. I poured myself into the study of domestic-abuse survivors, and according to the data, my mother unfortunately did exactly what many other suspicious, manipulated, and eventually battered women do. Just as my coping mechanisms followed the typical patterns of survivors of childhood sexual abuse, she too carried out the central behaviors of the domestic-abuse survivor and the narcissistically wounded. This helped soften my attitude toward her and put our dynamic into a more realistic perspective for me.

However, as I began to envision how I would make a difference in the world, I knew I would have to stop shielding her. More than anything I had ever known before, I knew I wanted to use my voice to speak the truth. I was writing songs again and had found significant support and opportunity to record a solo album. I had even begun writing down scenes from my childhood. Seeing flashes of my unvarnished life come alive in narrative form highlighted just how much was still hidden under the weight of silence. If I were to ever step back into the spotlight in any significant way, I felt the responsibility to address the past, clear the record, and lean into my own imperfect story no matter how daunting the challenge. My conscience wouldn't allow anything else.

After Mom read my lengthy letter expressing this to her, we met up at a local park, just her and me. Not knowing what her response might be, I saw pain well in her eyes. I told myself I wouldn't ask for her permission to tell my story and, by extension, tell hers to some degree, but when she gave it, a weight lifted from my soul.

I'D HOPED MY FATHER WOULD MAKE SOME EFFORT TO CONFESS, apologize, or at least walk back his accusations and complaints soon after his sentencing was official. This did not happen. My mother eventually divorced him, and he was cut off from communicating with her and the rest of my siblings. I soon realized it would never feel normal to say, "My parents are divorced," or "My father is in prison," or "My abuser still maintains that I am a liar."

At times, I found myself worrying whether there was some further level of closure for which I was responsible, whether I had closed a door too quickly or too finally. I did not want to be the reason any possible reconciliation didn't happen. I looked into visiting prison once but found out my father would have the option to reject my request ahead of time. Giving him even this small bit of control felt wrong, so I honored that instinct and chose not to send an application at that time. I focused on seeing things as they were, not how I had once wished them to be. My father was an unrepentant, repeat offender who had intentionally trained and groomed me since before I could remember for the purpose of abusing me. He was not someone I would now even consider asking for a parental prayer or affectionate hug. I still found little evidence of offenders with his psychological and criminal issues ever making significant progress toward health or rehabilitation. Yet people around me prayed for a miracle. "I'll believe it when I see it," I said, willing to reevaluate based on new information, if it ever became available.

I eventually accepted that choosing to speak my complicated story with my newfound voice was not a judgment equal to the damnation of my father's soul or mine. For years, I had worried that speaking about what happened to me was somehow taking away my father's chance to change and meant that I didn't have enough faith to believe God could redeem him. I was not wrong about the first fear; when I stopped being silent and finally spoke what he had done, the dream was over. Gone was the hope of what could have been, what should have been. The second fear—that ceasing to wait for a rescuer, God or not, meant a failure of faith— was wrong. "Forgive or you shall not be forgiven" had to mean something other than what I understood in my childhood: that I had no right to say my father was wrong or disobey his authority. I could, in fact, both forgive my father and let him face the consequences of his actions. It was right to think I could know and say his actions were wrong; it was wrong to think I could know his soul. Only God could do that.

32

FULL CIRCLE

August 6, 2021

My feet drum an excited rhythm against the rubber floorboard of Sean's new car. I feel as if I'm going to jump out of my skin with anticipation. He is driving the route we both know so well. We soon arrive at a small security checkpoint and give the guard our names. Crossing a line off his list, he waves us into the designated area.

"I can't believe we're here!" I squeal as we park. Our eyes are wide as we look at each other for a loaded moment, grinning, then Sean grabs his camera gear and I swing my fiddle case onto my back. A huge brick building towers in front of us, familiar and dear. Its scarlet arch beckons us up the hill, proclaiming in gold letters, "Grand Ole Opry Artist Entrance." For days I'd been thinking of how this moment would feel. It's every bit as surreal as I imagined it would be. I want to do my very best to be present tonight, so I remind myself to breathe deep and calm.

Inside, the cold air hits our flushed faces. Pete Fisher is waiting for us at the welcome desk. I have finally succeeded in dropping the "mister" from the front of his name. Instead, I now find an occasional "Dad" pops out instead.

"Here, let me take that," he says, scooping up my fiddle case before I can protest.

I experience flashes of memory as we start and stop down the hall. Scores of times I had entered in a raucous group with my siblings, the little ones underfoot and everyone wondering what music star we might encounter at any moment. Other times, my heart had fluttered as I thought of getting to see the handsome Fisher son by the side of the stage. I had worried the bad experiences might push their way into my mind, but no darkness comes, and I realize I am completely happy to be here.

After mostly staying away from performing for more than five years, I am making my solo debut on the Friday-night Opry show. When I finally decided it was time to begin a new artistic life, I had hoped this could be the setting. No other place could mark the moment better.

Dressing room eighteen is mine for the evening. Glamorous portraits of celebrated Opry members hang in black-and-white, like a family tree displayed with pride in the heart of a home. I drop my things and get my fiddle tuned up for rehearsal. When the house band is ready, I go and join them. We play through each of the songs I've selected, then the next artist steps up for their turn to practice. The show and live radio broadcast will start in half an hour.

I think of the people currently filing into the auditorium who don't know my story, who are showing up to have a good time and be entertained. I envision standing at the microphone with the lights blazing down. I am grateful to have this chance, this audience.

After spending the last year surviving a global pandemic, recording an album, and writing the first draft of my memoir, I have so much to say.

I change into a rust-colored gown and add a matching shade to my lips. Friends and family begin to arrive, and I feel myself project my voice and amp up my animation. As my siblings hug my waist, I am determined not to cry before singing. Yet I must stay in the vulnerability and not armor up, knowing my emotions will definitely catch up with me, probably before I leave the stage. But feeling the reality of everything is the whole point tonight.

When it's time to wait side stage, I stare at the round outline on the floor around the main microphone. The circle is used as an iconic motif around the building, alluding to both the famous gospel lyric "Will the circle be unbroken?" and the continued tradition of music in this special place. My heart is in my throat. Legends pat my shoulder and share an encouraging word.

You know how you got here, I tell myself. *You know what you've come to say.*

The announcer begins my segment, "Up next, she is no stranger to the Opry stage . . ."

I wipe my palms against my skirt and begin to walk out in the dark.

"With her family band, she has performed here fifty-nine times . . ."

I turn back to sneak a glance at the band. All is ready.

"This will be her sixtieth appearance, making her solo Grand Ole Opry debut. Will you please welcome Jessica Willis Fisher!"

The guitar and drums begin, and we're off. I'm shaky, feeling the lack of muscle memory, rediscovering how to do this, how to move under the heat of a spotlight.

As the warm applause begins to fade after the first song, it is time to speak. I beam, trying to reflect my gratitude and joy. I tell them it is surreal and wonderful to be back, that it feels like home and a long time coming.

Breathe.

"About five years ago," I say, "I was touring with my family band and was in a really dark place. I stepped away from music and needed to go get help. Ever since then, I've been on this long and sometimes complicated journey of healing. I am so excited to be coming back to music and releasing an album of my own next year."

I play another song, and this performance feels stronger, bolder.

Afterward, I clear my throat in the expectant hush. The room is full of unseen people. More listen over the airwaves. I am remembering just a few years ago, when I had declined the opportunity to speak before a courtroom. I hadn't been ready, thinking it was better for me to be silent.

"I have loved writing ever since I was a little girl," I begin again. "I think it was the first therapy I ever experienced. My father was abusive in every way that a person can be, and for many years, even when I was smiling and singing and performing—even here—I felt like I didn't have a voice. I didn't know how to ask for help. I didn't know how to tell my story."

I knead my hands compulsively, pushing through.

"I am here today to say that I *do* have a voice and I'm going to *use* it."

The audience shows a wave of support, giving me a moment to regain my composure. I pull back tears with all my might because I need to get this out, to state this for the record.

"From now on, I want to use my voice to speak the truth even when it's hard, and to tell my story, and to help other people. Because if you know what I'm talking about, and you've gone through something similar, I just want to tell you that you are loved, you are not alone, and you are worth fighting for; a better, safer life is worth fighting for."

Now I sing the lyrics that were once a prophecy, knowing I am fulfilling the words:

> *History is written at the hands of those who win*
> *The battle must be over for the writing to begin*
> *Take a piece of paper, open up a vein*
> *The feather and the finger pulls against the grain*
>
> *All my story now belongs to me*
> *I will start to build a better life for me*
> *No one else will know what I could see*
> *I am my survivor, and you will be my history*
>
> *Memories are fading even as I speak*
> *I am not the child who turned the other cheek*
> *Power to the people throwing off the chains*
> *Love is all we wanted and only truth remains*
>
> *All my story now belongs to me*
> *I will start to build a better life for me*
> *No one else will know what I could see*
> *I am my survivor, and you will be my history*
>
> *You will be the lesson I wish I never learned*
> *Love will be the reason your reign was overturned*

UNSPEAKABLE

All my story now belongs to me
I will try to build a better life for me
No one else will know what I could see
I am my survivor, and you will be my history
I am my survivor, and you will be my history
I am my survivor, and you are just my history

EPILOGUE

I will never fully understand how I survived what I did. But it seems to me that books and reading have contributed their fair share toward both my survival and recovery so far. I was, and still am, someone who will gleefully lie down on a bed of books just to smell their vanilla-scented, patina-edged pages, and who can go into a spiritual trance simply by brushing my fingertips across the curves of an embossed cover's title and intricate binding.

Writing this book has been immeasurably helpful to me, easily comparable to a year's worth of therapy. I truly believe that just because you "lived it" doesn't mean you automatically *know* it, understand it, or learn from it. I have found it takes effort to be healthy, especially after experiencing such long-term traumas.

These days, I am incredibly happy and hopeful in a way I once thought was impossible. I still have struggles but am determined to keep meeting each new day, as Brené Brown would say, with a strong back, soft front, and wild heart. Art, nature, relationship, and the overwhelming pattern of meaning I see in my life's story keep me believing in a God who is bigger and more wonderful than I can comprehend. Even though I haven't yet found a church where I feel both edified and safe, I wonder if a part of me will always feel guilty for leaving the teachings of my upbringing, even the ones that contributed to my abuse. I frequently remind myself that the opposite of faith is not doubt, but certainty.

If there was a button I could push that would give me a publicly blank slate and hide or erase the dark parts of my history, I think I would probably push it. I would at least be tempted. But this will never be an option for me. I will never be able to avoid all the instances of a stranger walking up and asking me rude questions about my father or my personal life. I came to realize the choice to have a new public career or presence of any kind included the need to address and face my past. My conscience would not let my previous image be the last impression I made on record. Reclaiming my own life's narrative has been deeply empowering and healing.

I've long dreamed of being an author, and since this book makes that dream a reality, I wonder what else I might be able to accomplish in life. (Scholar, detective, and archaeologist were next on the list.) It seems I am only just beginning, and it would be a shame to think too small. I truly believe that to live quietly and contentedly is victory enough. All the same, new visions hover at the edge of my sight, and I am excited to see how they may take shape in my future. I dream of education, of study and research, of contributing to the deeper understanding and prevention of abuse across the world. I dream of coming alongside other survivors and supporting their recovery as so many others did for me. I dream of opposing the environments and mindsets that produce such a bitter fruit.

In the process of regaining my voice, people have asked me both why I didn't say something then and why I'm saying so much now.

All sexual abuse survivors are asked such questions. To the other little invisible girls and boys, I say it is not your responsibility to protect others and keep the peace. Advocating for yourself will most likely make your life and the lives of those around you much harder before your situation gets any better. But it is worth the fight to find safety and know truth.

Statistically speaking, legal justice is rare, and good support can be hard to find. If you are in a position to help, there is so much work to do. Look to your communities, to your organizations, to your local advocates and the experts. Look to your own stories, skills, and strengths. No one is removed from this issue; everyone can always become more aware and engaged.

It surely would have boggled the mind of my book-loving younger self to know I would eventually find my way back and arrive here, that my first contribution to the shelves of humanity would come from the twisted roots of my earliest memories. That my efforts to heal and make sense of what happened would lead me back to story.

This is not the tale I thought I would be telling, but it is mine.

Acknowledgments

To the people who showed up for me, you've saved my life again and again.

To the individuals who saw me in my music and my attempts to connect through the dark, you helped me believe there was something better both out there and within me.

Sean, I would choose you, and us, over and over. Thank you for inviting me to a new and beautiful story. I hope it never ends.

Fisher family, the way you pour out love onto the people I love makes me love you even more. Thank you for being a sanctuary and my chosen family.

John, thank you for doing what had long needed to be done with such courage, humility, and kindness. I want to believe I was on the road to doing what you did.

Ashley, you gave me a soft place to land without question or condition. Thank you.

Lee and Tom, your expertise is unparalleled. I look forward to learning more from you.

Al and Nita, thank you for sharing of yourselves and being keepers of the light.

Miles, you have championed both Sean and me. We are so inspired by you.

Debbie, thank you for lifting up so many artists and caring for the industry we love.

To the many TBI agents and legal prosecutors who worked on my family's case, thank you for working so hard to secure safety for us. You are heroes.

To my literary team at W Publishing: Stephanie, Brooke, Carrie, Damon, Kristina, Grace, Phoebe, Ashley, Madison, Allison, and Mike. You each helped me bring my dream to life with your brilliant skills and dedication. I can't believe we're finally here. Go us!

To my agents Margaret and Sophie. Thank you for being my earliest literary champions. I'm honored and lucky to have you two at my side.

To Taryn, Cindy, and Heather at Monarch Publicity. Thank you for guarding and growing my efforts with such heart and enthusiasm.

To my siblings, we have all been through so much. Let's keep beating the odds and telling each other our truths. Every day is new, and the future is bright. I love each of you.

To my mother, thank you for reading all those countless magical stories aloud to me. Even through our worst times, I always knew you loved me.

To my father, for your own sake, I hope you are one day brave enough to face what you have done and can find the courage to begin your own work. No one else can do it for you.

Notes

Chapter 1: Early Childhood
  1. Psalm 127:3; Genesis 1:28 KJV

Chapter 3: Golden Age
  1. 1 Corinthians 11:9 NLT

Chapter 5: Masked Monsters
  1. Acts 13:22 KJV
  2. 2 Peter 2:7
  3. Hebrews 11:13 NIV

Chapter 6: Sucker Punch
  1. 1 Timothy 2:14–15 NIV
  2. Genesis 4:6–7 NIV
  3. Galatians 5:22–23

Chapter 8: Between
  1. 1 Corinthians 14:34–35

Chapter 19: Detonation
  1. Matthew 18:15–16

2. Luke 17:3
3. 1 Timothy 5:20

Chapter 20: The Dark Ages
1. Jeremiah 17:9 KJV
2. Romans 8:7 NIV
3. Matthew 26:41 NIV

Chapter 21: Who's Your Master
1. Brené Brown, *Rising Strong* (New York: Random House, 2015), vii.
2. Rokelle Lerner, *The Object of My Affection Is in My Reflection: Coping with Narcissists* (Deerfield Beach, FL: Health Communications), 2009.

Chapter 25: Whiplash
1. 2010 Tennessee Code, Title 39: Criminal Offenses; Chapter 13: Offenses Against Person; Part 5: Sexual Offenses; 39–13–522: Rape of a child. Justitia.com, accessed February 15, 2022, https://law.justia.com/codes/tennessee/2010/title-39/chapter-13/part-5/39–13–522/#:~:text=(a)%20Rape%20of%20a%20child,(13)%20years%20of%20age.
2. 2010 Tennessee Code, Title 39: Criminal Offenses; Chapter 13: Offenses Against Person; Part 5: Sexual Offenses; 39–13–501 - Definitions. Justia.com, accessed March 19, 2022, https://law.justia.com/codes/tennessee/2010/title-39/chapter-13/part-5/39–13–501/.
3. "Perpetrators of Sexual Violence: Statistics," RAINN.org, accessed February 15, 2022, https://www.rainn.org/statistics/perpetrators-sexual-violence.

Chapter 26: Point of No Return
1. Exodus 14:14
2. James 5:19–20
3. 1 Timothy 5:19

Chapter 30: What Now?
1. Tom Holmes, *Parts Work: An Illustrated Guide to Your Inner Life* (Kalamazoo, MI: Winged Heart Press), 2007.

About the Author

Jessica Willis Fisher is a singer/songwriter, performing artist, and author who believes that sharing our stories with one another will change the world. Growing up the eldest daughter in a toxic and abusive household, she performed with her family band, The Willis Clan, until her departure in 2016 at the age of 23. Her first book, Unspeakable, narrates her harrowing struggle to both articulate her childhood experience and find her true voice on the other side of emotional, physical, and sexual abuse. A passionate advocate for survivors, Jessica lives in Nashville, TN with her husband, Sean Fisher. Learn more at jessicawillisfisher.com.

THE BRAND NEW DAY FUND

The Brand New Day Fund is Jessica Willis Fisher's charitable fund that supports a variety of organizations and causes close to her heart. She is passionate about the prevention of childhood sexual abuse and domestic violence and facilitating cooperation between advocates, lawmakers, law enforcement, and victims. She also believes strongly in the healing power of music as a therapy and seeks to help women and young adults rise above their past traumatic experiences to build safe, healthy lives for themselves.

Learn more & give at
jessicawillisfisher.com/fund

Signed Brand New Day CD
& Vinyl available at
jessicawillisfisher.com/shop

Use code: READER1
for 10% off any
merchandise purchase

From the Publisher

GREAT BOOKS

ARE EVEN BETTER WHEN THEY'RE SHARED!

Help other readers find this one:

- Post a review at your favorite online bookseller

- Post a picture on a social media account and share why you enjoyed it

- Send a note to a friend who would also love it—or better yet, give them a copy

Thanks for reading!